The Gardens of Adonis

EUROPEAN PHILOSOPHY AND THE HUMAN SCIENCES
General Editor: John Mepham

This is a new series of translations of important and influential
works of European thought in the fields of philosophy and the
human sciences.

The Gardens of Adonis

SPICES IN GREEK MYTHOLOGY

MARCEL DETIENNE

Translated from the French by
JANET LLOYD

With an introduction by
J.-P. VERNANT

THE HARVESTER PRESS

This edition first published 1977 by
The Harvester Press Limited
Publisher: John Spiers
2 Stanford Terrace, Hassocks, Sussex

Copyright © this translation The Harvester Press Limited 1977
First published in France as
Les Jardins d'Adonis
Editions Gallimard © 1972

British Library Cataloguing in Publication Data
Detienne, Marcel
    The gardens of Adonis: Spices in Greek
    mythology.
    Bibl.
    ISBN 0-901759-26-0
    1. Title 2. Lloyd, Janet
    292'.1'3 BL795.S/
    Mythology, Greek
    Food (in religion, folk-lore, etc.)

ISBN 0 901759 26 0

Typeset by Red Lion Setters, London
and printed in Great Britain by
Redwood Burn Limited, Trowbridge, Wiltshire

Introduction

by J.-P. VERNANT

Marcel Detienne's quest for the gardens of Adonis leads him to take us by the long way round that Plato mentions when he advises those seeking the truth to follow patiently along every bend in its winding way. We have to leave the well-trodden paths of mythology and, as we do so, the mirage of the conventional view of the East, transplanted to Greek soil, melts away — the mirage to which we have become accustomed and which the historians of religion at the turn of the century explored exhaustively (as they believed) without ever encountering there any other forms or species than those they had already classified and listed. They found, for instance, a god who disappears in the full flower of youth, vegetation which dies and is revived each year and the spring reawakening of the forces of nature that slumber through the cold winter or are consumed under the burning summer sun. In this book we discover new horizons, a landscape full of perfumes, extraordinary plants and marvellous beasts, an unknown land retaining all the appeal of a fairy-tale country yet whose features are delineated with all the rigourous austerity and sober logic of a scale diagram. There are Herodotus' fabulous stories to fascinate us, telling of the harvesting of spices in the Land of the Sun. Starting with myrrh and ending with lettuce, we see displayed before us the full range of plants in whose context Adonis' story is set. The whole scale of the animal kingdom rises before us, stretching from the beasts that fly to those that grovel: at the top is perched the eagle, then come the vulture, the bat and the winged snake; at the very bottom lurk the snakes of both water and land. But with the rising of the fabled phoenix the two ends of the scale are brought together. The phoenix belongs far above the eagle, close to the sun, yet it is in the form of a larva, a worm born of corruption that it must be reborn from its own ashes and thus, all of a sudden, we behold it placed lower than the snake and even closer to the earth and waters. We see how the sad stories of Adonis and his mother Myrrha are interwoven with those of Mintha or Mint, Phaon the ferryman, Iunx the wryneck bird and sorceress, and Ixion the ungrateful, the father of the Centaurs. We are truly once again in the land of fairy-tales but the pleasure we once felt there as children is now supplemented by the scholarly interpretation of a code or rather of many interlocking codes which offer us the keys to a whole mental universe different from ours, not easy to penetrate, even disconcerting, yet in some ways familiar. It is as if the Greeks had used these fantastic and marvellous tales to transmit as clearly as possible the code to the statements in which they express their own distinctive view of the world. It is this code that Detienne helps us to decipher.

Such is this book which simultaneously affords us both delight and instruction. As for the former, we can do no more than express the pleasure we have experienced in reading — and above all rereading — it. As for the latter, no book can have less need of an introduction. It is self-sufficient and speaks for itself. So rather than write a preface to it, I should prefer to accompany the author on his way to raise and discuss certain questions about some of the guiding themes in his enquiry.

My first question is this: how should we interpret a myth such as that of Adonis? The Frazerian type of classical interpretation saw Adonis as an example of the 'spirit of vegetation'. Detienne rejects this from the outset but he also challenges the over-facile global comparisons which attempt to assimilate one myth to another without taking any account of the particularities of different cultural systems. The attempt to decipher the story of Adonis by tracking down, here and there, gods and heroes that appear analogous to him implies three interdependent assumptions which are bound to affect the entire view of the myth. In the first place it is assumed that every mythical figure can be defined as a separate entity in and by himself and that he possesses some sort of essence; secondly, that this essence corresponds to some reality which, in the last analysis, must be considered to be a part of the natural world since it is found to be represented by one god or another in the most widely differing civilisations. The third assumption is that the relationship between the mythical figure and the reality it represents is a 'symbolical' one, in other words that it rests upon metaphor or analogy: thus, Adonis is born of the myrrh tree, therefore he embodies a spirit of vegetation; he spends a third of his life in the underworld and the remainder with Aphrodite in the light of the sun, therefore he embodies the spirit of wheat in the same way as Persephone does. This threefold hypothesis has already been completely demolished by the work of Georges Dumézil and Claude Lévi-Strauss. A god has no more one particular essence than a single detail of a myth is significant on its own. Every god is defined by the network of relations which links him with and opposes him to the other deities included within a particular pantheon; and similarly, a single detail in a myth is only significant by virtue of its place within the ordered system to which the myth itself belongs. So the Greek scholar must start again from scratch. It is not that he totally rejects the comparative method; on the contrary, he has constant recourse to it, but he applies it from a different standpoint, giving it a different meaning. Now the comparisons are made within the context of the particular civilisation to be studied, by making systematic cross-references between cycles of legends which seem, at first sight, to revolve around figures having nothing to do with each other. The partitions separating the purely mythological tradition from evidence from other areas of the material, social, and spiritual life of the Greeks are done away with. The aim is to define, as one proceeds, as exhaustively as possible, the framework within which the myth must be set so that every detail in its structure and episodes may take on a precise meaning which can, in every case, be confirmed or refuted by reference to other parts of the body of data as a whole. The comparison is only valid in so far as it is carried out within a definite field of enquiry that can adequately ensure on the one hand comprehensiveness and, on the other, internal coherence. With an aim such as this the nature of the work of comparison becomes infinitely more demanding. The study takes just as much account of differences as of similarities or — to more precise — it does not attempt to establish analogies between figures or legends of different types but rather to establish the relative positions of various elements within a single complex. Thus it distinguishes separations, distances, intervals and inversions as well as points of symmetry, with the final aim of establishing an ordered system. Instead of postulating as if it were self-evident that Adonis is equivalent to vegetation and so connecting this Greek god at times with deities of the *dema* (tubercules) type and at others with the oriental gods who die and are reborn in accordance with the cycle of plant life, the study tries to identify accurately the position occupied by myrrh, considerd as a species of spice, within the hierarchical classification of plants which the Greeks elaborated. This method gives rise to a number of consequences that affect questions of procedure as well as problems of content. The field of enquiry must inevitably embrace all the evidence concerning the Greeks' view of the relation of the spices to other plants. This evidence includes the writings of botanists, doctors and philosophers, the use of incense in religious ritual and of perfumed ointments in daily life. Thus, as the investigation widens it involves the progressive deciphering of a botanical code whose components range from the myrrh from which Adonis was born to the lettuce which became his death-bed. The structure of this code appears to be strictly based upon a vertical axis passing from the 'solar' plants which are hot, dry — even scorched, — incorruptible and perfumed to the plants from below which are cold, wet and raw and are closely connected with death and foul smells. In between these two extremes, occupying an intermediate position at what one might call the 'right' distance, are those plants which in the Greek view correspond to the normal life of civilised men, in other words the cereals, cultivated plants in which the dry and the wet are balanced and which constitute a specifically human type of food. Far from embodying the spirit of wheat, Adonis' position is sometimes above and at other times below the cereals; never does he belong to the same sphere as them. His destiny leads him directly from myrrh to the lettuce and this is, in a sense, an indication that he by-passes the cereals which lie quite outside his path. It thus illustrates the temptations and dangers of a way of life which would seek to elude normality.

To indicate the difference between the traditional form of interpretation and the type of study that Detienne, following Lévi-Strauss, proposes, we could say that a shift has taken place from a naturalistic symbolism of a global and universal kind to a system of complex, differentiated social coding characteristic of one culture in particular. We use such terms as 'system' and 'social' advisedly. For the botanical code does not and could not stand in isolation. It is interlocked with a number of other codes which constitute so many different levels of approach, each one complementing the others. In the first place there is the zoological code for which the evidence is, first, the stories in Herodotus, which introduce certain categories of animals to act as the necessary mediators between man and the spices and, secondly, the myths about the Phoenix, the spice bird. Then there is the dietary code where the vegetable kingdom is subdivided into the three categories of food reserved for the gods, food for the humans and pasture for the wild animals. Finally there is the astonomical code in which the spices are placed under the sign of Sirius, the Dog star, whose appearance marks the moment when earth and sun, normally distant from each other, are in the closest proximity: it is a period both of extreme danger and also of the wildest exaltation.

In this way we discover that the decoding of the body of evidence is based upon a series of oppositions linked with one another: above-below, earth-heaven, wet-dry, raw-cooked, corruptible-incorruptible, stench-perfume, mortal-immortal; these terms, which are at times united and brought together through intermediaries and at others set apart and mutually exclusive, are organised into a coherent system. The validity of this interpretation — or, to use a term from linguistics its pertinence — is confirmed by the fact that these same pairs of antimonies, arranged in the same order, reappear each time the Greeks are concerned with the power and functions of myrrh or spices, whether in their 'scientific' writings or in the most diverse myths and religious rituals. Seen as whole, this system appears to have a fundamental social significance: it expresses how a group of people in particular historical circumstances sees itself, how it defines its condition of life and its relationship to nature and the supernatural.

We are thus led to pose a second category of problems, this time not merely concerning the methodological question of 'How should a myth be read?', but of a more fundamental kind: What, in the final analysis, does this myth mean, and in what sense does it have a meaning? In order to understand how the story of Adonis is linked to the ritual of the Adonia Detienne distinguishes two central themes around which the whole body of relevant evidence is organised and which form, as it were, the keystones in the structure of the various codes which he shows to be strictly economical.

The first theme concerns foodstuffs and eating practices. It is most fully expressed in the structure of the sacrificial meal, in which spices have a definite and significant role. Sacrifice separates the man from the beast despite their common nature. Both are mortal animals; both, to survive, need to keep up their strength each day by taking in food which itself is perishable. However, man's food consists of plants which have first been cultivated, such as cereals, or of the cooked meat from domesticated animals such as the beasts that are reserved for sacrifice — in other works food this is, in every sense of the term, 'cooked'. Animals, on the other hand, feed upon wild plants and raw flesh, that is to say food left in its original 'raw' state. Sacrifice also separates men from the gods, marking the opposition between them with the very action whose purpose is to unite them. In the religion of the city state the sacrificial ritual is the normal channel of communication between earth and heaven. However, through its very form, this contact emphasises the radical disparity in status between the mortals who inhabit the sublunary world and the immortals who, forever young, are enthroned in the luminous heights of the aether. Man's share of the sacrificed animal is the dead, corruptible meat: the gods' share is the smoke from the charred bones, the smell of perfumes, and incorruptible spices. The ritual that brings men and gods together at the same time sanctifies the fact that it is impossible for man to have any direct access to the divine and to establish with it a true commensality. Thus in the context of blood sacrifice, the corner stone of the state religion, spices and myrrh represent the portion allotted to the gods alone, the portion which man could never assimilate and which remains outside their nature and alien to it despite the place they assign to it in their dietary rituals. Within the context of sacrifice, which is a model for normal human eating habits, myrrh does indeed appear as an instrument of mediation, the link between opposites, the path connecting earth to heaven. At the same time, however, its status and position in the hierarchy of plants gives it the further significance of maintaining the distance and establishing the separation between these two opposites. It represents the inaccessible character of the divine, the fact that men must renounce the far-off heavenly Beyond.

The second theme is marriage. Here myrrh and the spices again have a role to play. This time they do not take the form of fragrant incense rising up to the gods, inviting them to associate themselves with the meal of the mortals, but of perfumes whose aphrodisiac powers provoke feelings of desire and thus bring the two sexes together. Here the mediation does not operate vertically between the world below, given over to death, stench and corruption, and the world above, forever unchanging in the shining purity of the sun, but horizontally, at ground level, through the attraction that draws men and women irresistibly towards each other. The allure of erotic seduction is a part of marriage just as the spices are a part of sacrifice; but it is neither its basis nor a constituent element in it. On the contrary, it remains, in principle, alien to the tie of marriage. Although its presence is necessary — since on their wedding day young couples are crowned with myrtle and sprinkle each other with perfumes — it presents both an internal and an external threat to marriage. There is an internal threat because if the wife abandons herself to the call of desire she rejects her status of matron and assumes that of the courtesan, thus deflecting marriage from its normal end and turning it into an instrument for sensual enjoyment. Pleasure is not the object of marriage. Its function is quite different: to unite two family groups within the same city, so that a man can have legitimate children who 'resemble their father' despite being the issue of their mother's womb, and who will thus be able, on the social and religious level, to continue the line of their father's house to which they belong. The danger from this threat from within is greatest during the canicular period which is not only the time when the earth, being close to the sun, gives off all its perfumes, when the spices that have reached maturity must be gathered if they are to prove efficacious, but also when women, however chaste and pure, are in danger of abandoning themselves to the lasciviousness which totally over-whelms them at this period, and of changing, under the influence of the summer sun, from model wives into shameless debauchees. The seduction of desire also presents an external threat to marriage. One of the striking features of the Greek civilisation in the classical period is that true relationships of love, whether heterosexual or homosexual, occur outside the home. The pseudo-Demosthenes puts it as if it was an incontravertible fact: 'We have courtesans for pleasure [...] and wives in order to have a legitimate posterity and a faithful guardian of the hearth' (*Contra Neera,* 162).

It is not difficult to see then that the vegetable, astronomical and dietary codes do not apply to the sacrificial meal alone. They do indeed provide a logical framework for this meal, within which it assumes its allotted place : in an intermediary position half-way between the raw and the burned, the rotten and the incorruptible, the bestial and the divine. Its position confers upon it a status which exactly corresponds to that of the cereals which, positioned as they are in between the plants that are cold and wet and the spices which are hot and dry, stand for the truly civilised life, the type of existence led by men who are tied to the earth they must cultivate by farming in order to live. Their position is half-way between, on the one hand, the bloody bestiality of the wild beasts which devour each other raw and, on the other, the pure felicity of the Immortals who need do nothing to enjoy every kind of good, as used to be case for men in that bygone Golden Age before Prometheus' crime occasioned the institution of sacrifice — sacrifice, which is the sign of the human race's definitive separation from the race of the gods.

However, these codes also concern marriage whose position, within the same system, is strictly equivalent to that of sacrifice. Monogamous marriage is a solemn public contract placed under the religious patronage of Zeus and Hera which unites two families through the union of a man and a woman. In the eyes of the Greeks it thus raises the relationship between the sexes to the level of 'civilised' life. You could say that marriage is to sexual consummation what sacrifice is to the consumption of meat: both assure continuity of existence to mankind, sacrifice by making it possible for the individual to subsist throughout his life and marriage by affording him the means of perpetuating himself after death through his child. The 'wild' state involves first and foremost, to be sure, cannibalism and the eating of raw meat: wild beasts all devour each other, and raw to boot. But it also involves generalised sexual promiscuity: they have sexual relations with each other, crudely, in broad daylight, as chance dictates. The offspring born of these unregulated 'wild' unions have, admittedly, a mother to whom they are linked by the natural, animal bond of childbirth; but they have no father. Without marriage there can be no paternal filiation, no male line of descent, no family — all of which presuppose a link which is not natural, but social and religious. Within the system the Golden Age represents the opposite pole to the 'wild' state, its exact counterpart since, instead of living like beasts, men then still lived as gods. During this age men put no living creature to death nor ate any meat. They knew neither sexual union nor the eating of meat and since the race of women was not yet created men did not need to be either conceived or engendered but were born directly from the earth.

So the human condition is exactly like that of the cereal plants. During the Golden Age, before the institution of sacrifice, fruits and corn germinated spontaneously in the soil. It was as unnecessary to plough the land and plant it with seed in order to reap the harvest as it was to labour with women and fill their wombs with seed in order to obtain children from them. The sacrificial meal, instituted by Prometheus, has two effects. It introduces a diet in which the consumption of cooked meat from domesticated animals goes along with agricultural labour and the harvesting of cereals. Its other immediate consequence is, as Hesiod tells us, the appearance of the first woman and the establishment of marriage. The fact is that for the Greeks marriage is a form of ploughing, with the woman as the furrow and the husband as the labourer. If the wife does not, in and through marriage, become cultivated, cereal-producing land she will not be able to produce valuable and welcome fruits — that is legitimate children in whom the father can recognise the seed that he himself sowed as he ploughed the furrow. Demeter who is the goddess of agriculture is also the patroness of marriage. When a young girl enters into marriage she enters the domain that belongs to the deity of cereals. To enter this domain and remain there she must rid herself of all the 'wild' character inherent in the female sex. This wildness can take two, opposed, forms. It might make the woman veer towards Artemis, falling short of marriage and refusing any sexual union or, on the other hand, it might propel her in the opposite direction, beyond marriage, towards Aphrodite and into unbridled erotic excess. The position of the *gunè egguēté*, the legitimate wife, is in between that of the *kórē*, the young girl defined by her virginal status and that of the *hetaíra*, the courtesan entirely devoted to love. Shunning contact with males, living far from men and the life of the city, the *kórē*, like Artemis, the virgin huntress, mistress over wild animals and uncultivated land, shares in the life in the wild that is symbolised, in the marriage rites, by the crown of thorny plants and acorns. The civilised life of a wife, the 'milled wheat' life as it was called, was symbolised in the marriage ceremony by winnowing basket, pestle and bread and opposed to life in the wild as good is to evil. To accede to this life the virgin had to renounce the 'wildness' which hitherto held her at a distance from man. The yoke of marriage domesticated her, in the strongest sense of the term. By belonging henceforth to one of the family hearths of which the city was composed she became integrated, so far as any woman could be, into the civic community.

Like that of the *kórē*, the position of the courtesan is also outside marriage, but towards the opposite extreme. Her 'wildness' consists not in a hatred and intractable rejection of the male but in an excessive seductiveness and unbridled licence. As she gives herself to the passing embraces of whoever comes along she fosters in each of her men the dangerous, seductive illusion of a life all perfume and spices which, in relation to the 'life of milled wheat', occupies the opposite pole to the life of acorns. Under the beguiling mask of sweet Aphrodite, the *hetaíra* reintroduces into the very heart of the civilised world the very same general sexual promiscuity which used to reign in the 'wild' times before civilisation.

Positioned as it is between, on the one hand a radical rejection of physical union and, on the other, exaltation of the pleasures of love to the exclusion of all else, lying between sexual impotence and an excess of sexual potency, both of them equally infertile, marriage like the cereals stands for the 'right distance': this alone can guarantee that the labour of marriage will bring forth an abundant harvest of legitimate fruits of good stock.

Marriage brings us a stage further on from sacrifice in our decoding of the myth. The analysis of sacrifice was necessary to interpret every level of the code implicit in the story of Adonis and the network of oppositions on which it rests. However that analysis did not produce an intepretation capable of revealing how the story conveys a unified message, having a general significance as such, within the context of Greek culture. Marriage on the other hand leads us stright to this interpretation. Although on the face of it the myth does not appear to be any more concerned with marriage than with sacrifice its silence on these themes is not comparable in the two cases. The fate of Adonis is not directly related to sacrifice although we find the same system of codes at work in both. On the other hand it does involve the status of marriage directly. You could say that the silence of the myth on this point makes it a story about non-marriage. Implicitly it speaks of erotic seduction in its pure, fundamentally extra-marital state. Every detail in the myth acquires its significance when related to the state of marriage — this state which, to the Greeks, represented the correct norm and which for this reason does not need to be explicitly mentioned to remain the constant point of reference and essential theme of the entire story.

The author's demonstration of this point seems to be conclusive. I shall not here repeat or summarize it but only emphasise some of its important features.

We have already pointed out that in passing directly from myrrh, from which he originates, to lettuce, which becomes his death-bed, Adonis cuts the cereals out of the vegetable code on whose axis they held a central position. But put in this way this remark does nothing to further our search for the meaning of the myth. Adonis in fact has nothing to do with the consumption of particular foods. What he is is the irresistible seducer whose erotic powers of attraction are capable of bringing together the most opposite of terms, terms which would normally remain widely separated from each other. Adonis is a human being yet hardly is he born than he arouses the love of goddesses. He brings gods and men together, inspiring an equally passionate love for him in both Persephone of the Underworld and the heavenly Aphrodite. As he moves between the two of them he links heaven and earth together. He is himself the product of a union between a man and woman who are, sexually speaking, set poles apart and should never have been united: a father and his daughter. The circumstances of his birth encapsulate all the themes which are to be illustrated in the adventures of his brilliant but brief career. His mother is initially a young untamed virgin. Like the Danaids and like Hippolytus she scorns Aphrodite and rejects all the normal marriages proposed for her. Seeking revenge, the goddess inflicts upon her a passionate love which is not only outside marriage but also destroys its very foundations from within. The incestuous union takes place on the occasion when the married women celebrate the festival of Ceres-Demeter, during the days when separation between the two sexes is a ritual obligation for married couples and when, in consequence, the daughter is most closely associated with the wife who, having the status of a legally married woman, appears as a mother accompanied by her child. The very movement which brings the daughter closer to her mother separates her as much as possible from her father who, as a male, represents the other sex in the family, the sex with which erotic union, which is possible in nature, is now strictly forbidden.

First Myrrha scorns all the men who could possibly marry her; then she is fired with passionate love for the only being who cannot become her husband. Because she wanted to stop short of marriage she finds herself placed at the furthest forbidden point beyond it. The gods effect her metamorphosis into a myrrh tree. From the seed which she received when she managed to seduce her father despite the barriers between them, Myrrha gives birth to Adonis whose destiny follows, but in the opposite direction, a path that corresponds to that of his mother's. At an age when other little girls and boys, devoted to chaste Artemis, know only the games of innocence, the aromatic child who is endowed with an irresistible seductiveness is totally devoted to the joys of erotic pleasure. But when he has to cross the threshold of adolescence which, for the young man, marks the moment of his integration into society as a warrior and future husband, his career as a lover is brutally curtailed. He fails the test which normally gives a boy access to full manhood. The son of myrrh is discovered in the lettuce bed where he has either been killed or placed. Having flourished during the period which is normally innocent of amorous relationships, his excess of sexual potency disappears as soon as he reaches the age for marriage. It is arrested where marriage begins and so represents, as it were, its converse. Now we can solve the problem of the by-passing of the cereals. It is a reference not to any anomaly in food consumption but to the perversion of Adonis' sexual consummation which, because it takes place outside marriage, projects him straight from a premature excess of potency into a precocious impotence. The erotic significance of spices is balanced, at the end of our hero's career, by the lettuce which is not only a cold, wet plant but also (as so many authorities stress) one which possesses anti-aphrodisiac qualities and represents sexual impotence. And whether Adonis' powers of erotic seduction are exercised beyond marriage or fall short of it, they invariably fail to produce any fruit; whether spices or lettuce be concerned Adonis' seed remains equally infertile.

Our interpretation of the myth of Adonis is substantiated and enriched when we take into account further types of evidence. The first consists of a body of legends which, despite their different episodes and figures, are also intended to express the theme of erotic seduction and to throw light on its nature, role and effects. The second type of evidence is what we can reconstruct from both written and pictorial evidence of the ritual of the Adonis in fifth and fourth century Athens. Phaon, the ferryman, is presented — as is Adonis — as an irresistible seducer. Through the favour of

Aphrodite who has presented him with a perfume with erotic properties he acquires the power to inspire all women with love for him so passionate as to ignore the duties and prohibitions of marriage. There is another side to this limitless power of seduction. Phaon dies the victim of the jealousy of a deceived husband or — as other, highly significant, versions have it — he disappears, like Adonis, hidden in a lettuce bed. Like Myrrha, Mintha (or mint) is a fragrant plant. As Hades' concubine she shares his bed in the Underworld. When the time comes for the god to pass on to a legitimate marriage with Persephone, Mintha boasts that she, with her beauty and seductive charm, will supplant the legitimate wife within her husband's house. Demeter is angered and punishes the over-forward rival of her own child by changing her by metamorphosis into a plant which has equivocal properties: it is an aphrodisiac, for sure, and yet it procures abortions; it is perfumed but 'insignificant' and sterile. The wheat-mother, associated with her daughter in her capacity as the patroness of legitimate marriage, turns Mintha into a plant that is *ákarpos*, a term which means incapable both of bearing fruit and of having children.

The theme of the stories revolving around Iunx, whose name Mintha — according to one Alexandrian source — is held to have borne, is again one of vanity in conjunction with the powers of an entirely self-centred erotic seduction. Iunx denotes in the first place a bird: the wryneck; this bird's ability to twist its head right round, the constant motion of its tail and the piercing sound of its cry make it a creature of strange and disconcerting mobility. Just as light and shadows whirling together in an illusionary manner perplex and make one dizzy, the wryneck projects a dangerous and uncontrollable fascination. Pindar calls it the 'bird of delirium'. The second meaning of Iunx is an instrument of erotic magic which is made to whirl and whistle like a wryneck by women wishing to attract men, even against their will, to their beds. Thirdly, Iunx the sorceress nymph, the daughter of *Peitho*, the Persuasion of amorous desire or — in other versions — of *Echo*, the will-o'-the-wisp, the ghost of a sound which, being nothing in reality, can imitate all voices with equal success. The nymph attempts to cast her love-spells against the couple formed by Zeus and Hera, trying to separate them by making Zeus either desire to possess her, Iunx, or to be united with Io. Iunx is changed by Hera into a wryneck; and her male equivalent is Ixion whom Zeus punishes by fixing him, spread-eagled, to a wheel whirling in the sky.

Ixion's mythical adventures present him, systematically, as negating marriage as a social institution. Whether marrying Dia, the daughter of Hesioneus, or coveting Hera and attempting to take her by force or seduce her by guile, in every instance his behaviour manifests the same scorn for marriage as a contract, as an accepted exchange based on mutual agreement. Hesioneus gives his daughter to Ixion but Ixion refuses to reciprocate by giving him the _hédna_. This was the price paid for a wife which, in the archaic times in which the legend takes place, constituted the basis and visible sign of marriage because it publicly set the seal upon an alliance effected through marriage between two family groups. By so doing it made the daughter not just an ordinary companion for the bed but a true wife given to the husband to provide him with a legitimate line of descent. By first undertaking to pay the _hédna_ and then refusing to honour his pledge, Ixion makes a pretence of entering into marriage in order the better to destroy it from within. He does away with the distinction between the _dámar_ or legitimate wife and the _pallaké_ or concubine. He reduces Dia whom he has received from her father's hands to be his wife to the level of a companion in sexual activity like a slave captured by force in battle or carried off during a pirate raid, or like any woman installed in the house without ceremony to do her master's pleasure. However, Ixion does not simply deny Dia the status of wife, within the context of marriage. He also destroys the alliance with his father-in-law, changing it into its opposite, a relationship of hostility. When his son-in-law invites him to a feast to celebrate their reconciliation, Hesioneus goes trustingly to attend it and perishes in the trap treacherously set for him. In return for the gift of Hesioneus' daughter Ixion offers only vain and misleading words and then repays the friendly trust of the father with trickery, duplicity and murder. He negates all the forms of exchange and mutual generosity called for by marriage and, in place of the mutual exchange of gifts or — to express it in Greek terms — the _charis_, which is the basis for the marital bond, he substitutes the mere use of constraint in the form now of deceitful Persuasion or _Peithó_ and now of brutal violence or _Bía_. Although _Peithó_ may, in many contexts, be opposed to _Bía_, where marriage is concerned they have this in common that they both act in the exclusive interest of one party without the agreement of the other. *Peithó*, the persuasive power of the deceitful word or of beguiling appearances can be said, like *Bia*, to force submission upon one of the two partners instead of bringing them into agreement as does *charis*.

The second stage of the myth throws further light on this collusion between *Peithó* and *Bía* who, by moving in on either side of *Charis* and together blocking the circuit of exchanges over which it presides, unite to destroy the institution of marriage. Ixion, the first human being to shed the blood of a relative, is obliged to flee the earth. Zeus receives him in heaven and Ixion, characteristically, repays his host's kindness with ingratitude and the negation of *charis*. He covets the wife of his host within his very house. In order to gain access to the marriage bed of the divine couple who are the patrons and protectors of *hymen* he uses any means possible, resorting to violence as well as the artifices of seduction. He imagines he has already won the day once he holds Hera in his arms, apparently thereby celebrating a mockery of hierogamy, consummating with the patroness of weddings a marriage which becomes an anti-marriage since Zeus has been usurped. However, this man of misleading words, this deceitful seducer, can experience only the phantom of a true loving relationship, only the illusion of *hymen*, a marriage which is hollow because 'devoid of *charis*'. In reality Ixion caresses and embraces not the true Hera but a false ghost, a vain illusion, an empty cloud, *Nephélē*. Such a mockery of the union between man and woman can produce only the mockery of a child and *Nephélē* duly gives birth to a monstrous offspring, a being without race, family or lineage with which to identify, which remains alien to all that exists either on earth or in heaven: the ancestor to the Centaurs. Neither gods nor men will recognise it although it is not, strictly speaking, a true beast. Ixion fathers an illusory son, a creature which is, as it were, the bastard of the universe, a pure *nóthos* for whom there can be no place within an order of filiation. The apostle of brute seduction is condemned to whirl forever in the sky where Zeus has, for the edification of mankind, transformed him into a *iunx*, there to celebrate day after after unending day the virtues of the very *charis* which he presumed to deny and without which sexual union is nothing but a game of make-believe, incapable of giving rise to any authentic descendents.

Having thus cleared the ground with his analysis of the myths, Detienne is in a position to propose an entirely new interpretation of the ritual of the Adonia and one which carries conviction. The force of his demonstration does not depend simply on the concordance between myth and ritual which complement and mutually illuminate each other. Every detail in the festival, without exception, is taken into account and, in the light of the various codes previously identified, each one takes on a precise meaning which gives it its place within an ordered whole. Not a single detail is neglected or dismissed as being of secondary importance, gratuitous or without significance. First, the question of date is considered: the Adonia are celebrated during the Dog Days, the period when spices are collected, when women experience sensual abandonment, when earth and sun are in the closest proximity and when erotic seduction in all its aspects is at its height. Next, there is the question of location: the festival takes place in private dwellings, not in the public sanctuaries; and furthermore on the terraces of these private dwellings, on the house-tops so that a closer union between the above and the below is effected. Then there is the instrument which characterises the festival: a ladder set leaning towards the top of the building, up which the god's devotees climb in order to place their 'gardens' in position. Then there are the participants: these are women, concubines and courtesans, adorned and perfumed, who feast and dance with their lovers whom they have invited there to join them. Then, there is the religious atmosphere of the festival: noisy, unbridled, improper, to the point of drunkenness and sexual licence. Next, its purpose: to carry miniature gardens set in little earthenware pots up to the rooftops where they are exposed to the intense heat of the summer sun. In these imitations of true agriculture, the mere ghosts of real plantations, there are lettuce and fennel (which here assumes the role of substitute for the spices, a gardener's version of myrrh) and also seeds of wheat and barley which the women treat as garden plants. Exposed directly to the sun as they are, in their pots, the seeds take only a few days to germinate, grow and become green and thereupon immediately die, completely dried up. The women then cast the pots and their contents into the cold water of springs or into the barren sea. These pseudo-gardens which pass in a few days from greenness to dessication, from vigour to exhaustion, do not merely evoke the young god, born of spices, whose precocious career of seduction ends up in the cold and sterile lettuce bed. They also, at every level, represent an anti-agriculture: a make-believe game rather than a serious and useful occupation, a pastime for women, not the work of men, in which a cycle lasting only eight days takes the place of the eight months that elapse between the normal time for sowing and the harvest; in which the plants are abruptly and forcibly roasted instead of ripening slowly and naturally. The canicular period alone takes the place of a harmonious and balanced collaboration of the different seasons and ludicrously tiny receptacles replace the vast mother earth. The gardens of Adonis which never come to maturity, which have no roots and bear no fruit are indeed sterile, infertile 'gardens of stone'. Their rapid, illusory blooming simply serves to emphasise more strongly the productivity of the ploughed field in which Demeter, having received the seed at the propitious time, in due course makes the cereals, on which men live, germinate, ripen and be fruitful.

This first set of oppositions is overlaid by a second. Or rather, the same characteristics which set Adonis' gardening and Demeter's agriculture in diametrical opposition on the astronomical and botanical levels, also set up an opposition, on the social level, between on the one hand the unbridled licence of the Adonia and, on the other, the solemn gravity of the Greek festival of Demeter. According to myth it was the Latin equivalent which Myrrha's mother was celebrating at the very moment when her daughter was carrying out her guilty attempt at seduction. The Adonia represent more than simply an inverted agriculture. They must also be seen as a counter-Thesmophoria. On the one hand, with the lover of Aphrodite, we have the lascivious heat of summer, courtesans and concubines met together with their lovers, in intimacy in their own houses; revelry, carousing and sexual licence; the climb up the ladder to place the gardens on the rooftops; a profusion of perfumes heightening the atmosphere of erotic seduction. On the other, with the mother of Persephone, we have the season of autumn rains when the sky makes the earth fertile, which at the onset of winter and at the time of sowing marks the beginning of the period that is propitious for marriage; married women, mothers of families, celebrating as citizens accompanied by their legitimate daughters an official ceremony in which they are, for the time being, separated from their husbands; silence, fasting and sexual abstinence; they take up an immobile position, crouching down on the ground; they climb down into underground *megara* to collect talismans of fertility to be mixed in with seeds; a slightly nauseous smell prevails and instead of aromatic plants there are clumps of willow branches, the willow being a plant with anti-aphrodisiac qualities.

At this point, however, we are faced with a difficulty. The parallelism to be seen in this table of strict oppositions appears to raise a problem. By reason of their status or profession, the devotees of Adonis — concubines and courtesans — are relegated to a position outside the family. So how can it be that they celebrate their god and his power of seduction with a ritual whose every characteristic constitutes a negative imprint of the model forms of conjugal union created by the very institution from which these women are excluded? How can they glorify sexual attraction, the power of eroticism and the pleasures of love with a language and within a framework borrowed from a religion which refuses to recognise anything but the procreation of children and the establishment of a legitimate line of descent within marriage? Why do they honour their god with gardens whose significance appears to be purely negative, whose sole raison d'être seems to lie in the contrast that they set up with true agriculture and which can only be defined in the negative terms of their deficiencies — as lacking serious purpose, rootless, fruitless, good for nothing but to be thrown away?

We may find part of the answer to the problem in considering the nature of the evidence which portrays this aspect of the Adonia. It comprises texts from the authors of comedy, remarks made by philosophers or scholars, maxims and proverbs — all of which, on the whole, represent the prevailing views of the city, the official line of thought, the opinion of citizens well integrated into the public life. It is quite possible that the point of view of the devotees of Adonis was quite different. Indeed this seems all the more probable given that there is another aspect to the Adonia, this time an altogether positive one and, far from having no connection with the ritual creation of the gardens, it forms the necessary counterpart to it. At the same time as they hold their celebration with their friends and grow their short-lived gardens for Adonis these women carry out on the rooftops what seems to be an imitation of the collection of spices, carrying these down the very ladder which they previously used to carry up the gardens. Frankincense seeds and loaves fashioned from myrrh are then depositied in incense and perfume burners and serve both to honour the lover of Aphrodite and to promote the power women exert over men through their seductive wiles.

Seen from this point of view the gardens of Adonis appear in a different light. The inverted image of agriculture turns out not to have a purely negative significance after all. On the contrary, it appears as a necessary preliminary condition in order to gain access to spices. One can only enjoy the life of perfumes and taste its precious, short-lived delights at the price of having no earth in which to put down roots and no fruits as end product. The ritual of the festival does indeed express the incompatibility of Adonis and Demeter, of seduction and marriage, but it does so in order to choose and glorify Adonis and seduction. The Adonia thus have a place within the same system of codes that is at work in the official city religion. But it is a code which can be approached, so to speak, from two different, diametrically opposed points and which can be interpreted in two different ways depending on which of the two poles one chooses to make the positive one. Although they employ the same language within the framework of the same religious system the adherents of the official cult and the devotees of Adonis use it to convey truths that are different or even opposed. Once the plants that have been forced too quickly to be fertile have been cast into the springs or the sea, the Adonia, the festival held to grieve for the lover, reaches its culmination with the joy of perfumes, the promise of pleasures to come and the assurance of seduction. At the end of the Thesmophoria, held to grieve for the daughter, the matrons abandon their silence, mourning and abstinence and celebrate the joy of reunion. The last day of this festival which held husband and wife ritually apart from each other went by the name of *Kalligéneia*, betokening assurance and promise, in this case the assurance of a good harvest and the promise of a fine offspring.

We have been considering the question of the meaning of the Adonis myth. In our view Detienne's analysis resolves this question. His reading of the myth and ritual of this god provides the modern interpreter with a meaning, that is it reveals a well-defined position for them within the Greek religious system, (even if — as we have seen — this is a somewhat marginal position), which determines where erotic seduction stands in relation to the other elements in the system as a whole. However, a third category of problems remains to be tackled, concerning the organisation of the system of codes discovered by Detienne, how it is balanced and where there are internal distortions and tensions. The structure of the system would appear at first sight to be startingly assymetrical. Sacrifice and marriage appear to occupy the same position at the centre of gravity of the system, this being exactly comparable to that of the cereals which, placed between the wet rawness of grasses on the one hand (the food of animals) and the incorruptible dryness of the aromatic plants (the food of the gods) on the other, represent the mid-way position, the human norm. So far as the consumption of meats is concerned sacrifice stands in between cannibalism in general (as in a state of wildness) and the refusal of any food in the form of meat (as during the Golden Age); and with regard to erotic consummation marriage stands in between general promiscuity (as practised in a state of wildness) and total abstinence (as during the Golden Age). Sacrifice and marriage are also the two human institutions where spices have a part to play — in sacrifice to bring gods and men together, and in marriage to bring men and women together. But the union does not, in the two cases, have the same meaning and value. In sacrifice the spices have a purely positive quality. They represent the share of the gods, a super-food for which men can only yearn without themselves ever attaining to it. So, in a sense, to have the spices predominate to the exclusion of everything else in sacrifice (as Empedocles does when he replaces the ox to be slaughtered by little figurines fashioned from spices, which the participants divide amongst themselves instead of each eating his portion of roasted meat) is to destroy the sacrifice by making it reach beyond itself. In contrast, in marriage the role of myrrh and perfumes is dangerous and negative. If they are allowed to predominate in the conjugal union — instead of their effects being first restricted and later totally eradicated (a matron is supposed to eliminate all perfumes both on her own person and on her husband's) — the marriage is destroyed, not by over-reaching itself but by being perverted. Thus when spices are seen not in the context of sacrifice but in that of marriage their meaning and value are inverted.

At the beginning of his enquiry Detienne examines the figure of Adonis somewhat indirectly and from a particular angle since he takes sacrifice as his starting point and this is not a subject with which either the myth or the ritual connected with the god are directly concerned. The full light of his enquiry is brought to bear upon sacrifice since, in order to distinguish its meaningful elements, he considers the subject not from the standpoint of the official religion but from the point of view of a sect, the Pythagoreans, whose attacks on sacrificial practice questioned the very foundations of the public religion. The Pythagoreans either rejected all forms of blood sacrifice or else they excluded oxen and sheep and allowed the slaughter only of pigs and goats which were to be eaten. Which they did depended on whether they saw themselves as a religious sect quite outside the city or as a brotherhood committed to political life and seeking to transform it from within. In both cases the purpose of the religious challenge to sacrifice, to the murder of domesticated animals and the eating of meat was to establish a more or less vegetarian diet which should ideally bridge the gap separating men and gods and thus wipe out the original, insuperable distance between them which sacrifice was supposed to have established and which, in the official religion, was celebrated, confirmed and consecrated each time that an animal was ritually slaughtered and subsequently eaten. The Pythagoreans thus sought to outflank sacrifice by going one better than it and to replace it with a way of life and of eating which could restore the community of existence, the total commensality with the gods which used to exist in the olden days before the crime that Prometheus committed against Zeus which was currently commemorated by sacrifice. In order to live in the company of the gods they were, as far as possible, to eat like the gods themselves did. They were to consume vegetable plants that were altogether 'pure' like the foodstuffs eaten in the Golden Age and now offered up to the deity on altars that were not bloody, that had never been defiled by the murder of sacrifice. And holy men, such as Pythagoras or Epimenides would even be able to nourish themselves from nothing at all, to live on fragrant perfumes just as the Immortals did.

By the end of his analysis Detienne is thus led to emphasise the positive character of spices. In the context of the consumption of foodstuffs the 'life of spices' represents an ideal, an ideal which, according to the official religion, men must necessarily forgo and which, according to the Pythagorean sect, they must seek to attain by giving up the portions of meat which in sacrifice are allotted to men as their share. However, when Detienne considers marriage, the institution to the heart of which he is led by the religion of Adonis, he has to characterise the spices as negative. These perfumed and incorruptible essences bring together both earth and heaven, and men and gods. But when they unite men and women too closely they break up a marriage instead of cementing it. In the context of marriage they represent, not the ideal, but the kind of erotic seduction which in itself bodes ill and is evil. How then can one explain how, in such a precise and consistent system of codes, the same element can take on opposite values in the contexts of two similar and parallel institutions? For Detienne the problem is all the more crucial in that it is within Pythagoreanism, chosen by him to throw light upon the significance of sacrifice, that the contradiction appears in its most startling form. The sect aligns itself with spices to the point of refusing all forms of blood sacrifice and the eating of meat; yet to defend the institution of marriage it aligns itself with lettuce. When the Pythagoreans condemn all kinds of seduction together with the use of perfumes, harass concubines and courtesans, and forbid illegitimate love affairs it is not the element of myrrh in their diet that they are celebrating but that of lettuce whose anti-aphrodisiac qualities they extol. Within the framework of Greek religion they thus occupy a position which is the extreme opposite to that of the devotees of Adonis. It is as if the choice of spices in the one case was incompatible with their choice in the other, as if their being prized in the context of sacrifice and the consumption of meat implied their necessary depreciation in the context of marriage and sexual consummation.

How does Detienne account for this asymmetry? We should first point out that the picture is, in fact, not as simple as we have made out. In both the forms in which we have come across them — as incense bringing men and gods together and as perfumes uniting men and women — spices have ambiguous aspects in their role as mediators, aspects which Detienne quite rightly emphasises. They are plants 'of the sun', dry and incorruptible, and as such are related to the fire above and the divine; yet they grow here below, upon the earth of mortal men. And it is only under particular conditions of time, place and harvesting that they acquire their fully fiery quality. The role of the spices is to bring opposites together and it would be impossible for them to fulfil it if they were once and for all totally on the side of one of the terms to the exclusion of the other, in the couple they are supposed to unite. In order to unite earth and heaven they must shuttle between the below and the above; to bring men and gods together they must be in some way connected to the former even while they are close to the latter. This equivocal status of the spices explains the extraordinary stories in Herodotus of the ways in which they are collected. These are really myths although disguised as accurate accounts, and in various forms they were later echoed throughout Greek literature, from historians and geographers to botanical writers. Spices grow in a land that is both quite real and at the same time utterly mythical, in Arabia, a country which, like any other, can indeed be described and located on a map but which is also (like the homeland of the Ethiopians known as the Long-Lived, the most just, beautiful and pious of men) a land of the Sun — as it were an enclave of an age of gold preserved within our own corrupted world. Part of the spice harvest is for men to use while the rest is placed on the altar of the Sun where it bursts spontaneously into flames. The spice harvesting — one might even call it the spice hunt — is carried out according to two opposed methods which, through their very contrasts, emphasise the ambiguous nature of the quarry and the role as mediator that it plays. Men cannot procure it directly. Intermediaries are necessary in the form of animals some of which are hostile, others benevolent, some chthonic, others heavenly. In some cases the spices grow 'below', in the waters of a lake or in a deep ravine. In order to collect them it is necessary to overcome the animals that guard them — chthonic beasts, monstrous bats or snakes, all related to the realm of the wet, the earthy, the corrupt. To do so the collectors must use the pelts of flayed oxen (that is the outermost, incorruptible, inedible part of the animal) to cover their entire bodies except their eyes which are, as it were, the luminous, sun-like, element in a man. In other cases the spices are to be found 'above', in the nests of birds of the heavens, perched on top of inaccessible rocks. In order to bring them down, these creatures related to the fire from 'above' are lured by pieces of meat which, in contrast to the pelts, represent the internal, corruptible, edible part of the animal. The heavenly birds swoop down and grab the hunks of dead flesh; they carry them up to their nests which collapse under the weight of the meat, meat which can be said to be doubly *out of place*, being carried up from below to the heights where it is incongruous and whence it returns to where it should be, bringing down with it as it falls the spices which the hunters are then able to seize. Thus for collecting spices men have at their disposal two methods whose means and modalities are the reverse of each other. In the one case the spices are brought up from the depths, in spite of the chthonic beasts thanks to a dried pelt which repulses the attacks of these creatures which are putrid albeit sometimes winged. In the other they are made to fall from up above with the help of heavenly animals thanks, this time, to the hunks of bloody meat which attract these creatures that are related to the fire above although they still need foodstuffs that are 'wet'. In both cases emphasis is laid on this tension between opposite terms which is the characteristic feature of the status of spices and which causes them to oscillate between the above and the below, the dry and the wet, the incorruptible and the putrid. This constant shuttling to and fro is most strikingly expressed in the myth of the Phoenix, the spice bird which, oscillating suddenly from the fiery to the corrupt, and thence returning to its original incandescent nature, simultaneously and, as it were, with the same movement, emphasises both the antimony that exists between two mutually exclusive orders of reality and also their necessary conjunction in the earthly world. The Phoenix occupies in the hierarchy of animal life a position equivalent to that of the spices in the hierarchy of plants. It is a creature of the Sun, belonging to the highest sphere. Each day it accompanies the fiery star in its course, regenerating its strength from this contact and being fed by its purest rays, and it thus escapes the mortal condition while yet not acceding to the immortality of the gods. It is perpetually reborn from its own ashes. The power of celestial fire which is pure, incorruptible and spontaneous is forever sufficient unto itself; it perpetuates itself in a constant, imperishable youth. Human fire, stolen by Prometheus and given to mortals in the form of a 'seed of fire', a fire that must be generated for the purpose of cooking the meat from the sacrifice, is a hungry fire: it must be constantly fed or else, like man himself, it will die for lack of sustenance. The Phoenix's incandescent life follows a circular course, waxing and waning, being born, dying and being reborn. This cycle carries the spice bird, which is closer to the sun than an eagle of the heavens, to the state of a worm, which is putrid, a creature even more chthonic than the snake or the bat. From the ashes of the bird which is consumed at the end of its long existence in a nest of fire made from spices a tiny grub is born, nourished on dampness and eventually, in its turn, becomes a Phoenix.

This myth makes it quite clear that if they are to bring together the above and the below and fulfill their role as mediators between the gods and men, spices must occupy an intermediary position between the two opposed terms. The gods enjoy an eternal form of existence outside time, in the permanence of an unchanging youth. Men live within a limited time, always facing in the same direction, namely towards death; they are born, grow old and disappear forever. To perpetuate themselves they must unite with a creature of the opposite sex and produce a child which is a continuation of themselves in a new being, different from themselves. The Phoenix lives in boundless, cyclical time, alternately facing in opposite directions. It perpetuates itself without being physically united to anything, without producing another creature that is not itself but by being born from its own ashes. So it can be said that, according to the logic of the myth that expresses in the most condensed form the mediatory role of spices, these perfumed essences have the power to bring together earth and heaven, and men and gods, to the extent that they represent in the botanical and zoological codes a form of life which is self-renewing, which has no need of a union of opposite sexes, no need consequently of marriage and the procreation of children. In a way the Phoenix's mode of existence recalls that of men in the Golden Age before the introduction of sacrifice, before the use of corruptible and generated fire, before agricultural labour, before the creation of women and marriage, when mankind — exclusively male — still led a pure life, a life incomparably longer than nowdays, knowing neither old age nor death in the strict sense of these terms, being born spontaneously from the earth just as the Phoenix is from its own ashes.

These remarks will perhaps enable us to supplement Detienne's explanation concerning the mismatch that we have noted between the positive function of spices used as incense and their negative role when used as perfumes.

Detienne makes the point that, in the eyes of the Greeks, there is a good way of using spices — namely in sacrifice — and a bad one — namely in erotic relationships. This is because once perfumes are principally used for erotic ends they are 'diverted' from their proper religious and ritual purposes. They are 'withdrawn from their correct role which is to return to the gods the substances with which these have particular affinities'. But where and why does this diversion occur? There are two possible answers. One is simply that in using perfumes for erotic seduction there is none left for sacrifice, that one neglects to sacrifice, one fails to do so at the very moment when one indulges in any sexual enjoyment. But this is obviously untrue. In the matter of sacrifice lovers, voluptuaries and sensualists are neither more nor less scrupulous than those who are chaste or prudish. Besides, as the Adonia show well enough, even spices used for erotic purposes have a ritualistic and religious role to play. Alternatively, there is a more complex explanation: because the aim and significance of spices are reversed in the two cases of sacrifice and seduction one cannot give unqualified support to them in both cases at once. A Pythagorean celebrating the Adonia is as unthinkable as a devotee of Adonis being converted to the Pythagorean way of life and vegetarianism. And of course this opposition which takes the form of a radical incompatibility at the two extreme poles of the religious system is also expressed at its centre, in official ceremonies, by a tension between the spices that are an integral part of sacrifice and the perfumes that are an integral part of marriage. According to the method which, with Detienne, we have followed, the solution should, first and foremost, be a structural one. It should account for the disparity in terms of the overall structure of the system. The Phoenix myth gives us our first clue: the spice bird is the embodiment of a form of existence which corresponds in Greek philosophical terms to a moving image of eternity and in terms of Greek mythology to the life of the men of the Golden Age. In the context of sacrifice the role of the spices is positive since they point towards this Golden Age. It is true that sacrifice commemorates the passing of this happy state of former years but within its context spices represent the share that, even now, is truly divine. To give them a heightened, or even exclusive, role is to promote a religious experience which stands for a return to the Golden Age; it is to make oneself aromatic in order to find once more that original condition in which one used to live and eat in company with the gods. In marriage however spices point in the opposite direction. They preside over sexual attraction without which marriage cannot be physically consummated and thus, at the very centre of this institution, they consecrate the break with the Golden Age, the duality of the sexes, the need for a sexual union, for birth through generation and, correspondingly, also for old age and death. Sacrifice and marriage occupy analogous positions on the same level. But in sacrifice spices are connected with what, in myth, preceded the need for meat as food. In marriage they are connected with what, in myth, led man to sexual consummation. The greater the part played by spices in sacrifice, the greater the apparent power of spices to unite gods and men. The more limited the role of perfume and seduction in the union between man and woman, the more their marriage is legitimately established. From a religious point of view the justification for sacrifice is the offering of spices which are thus enabled to return to the deity. The religious justification for marriage lies in the very definite restrictions it imposes upon the sexual attraction that is stimulated by the use of perfumes. If it were possible, indeed, marriage would do without perfumes altogether but the human condition that resulted from man's separation from the gods forced it to make, as it were, a virtue of necessity.

This does not solve our problem but it enables us to rephrase it in the following manner: given the role that they play in sacrifice why is it that spices also preside over erotic seduction? Hesiod provides us with the answer in the two versions he gives of the myth about the introduction by Prometheus of blood sacrifice. Originally men and gods live in the closest proximity, feasting together. When the moment comes to establish their respective shares Prometheus kills and cuts up a huge ox, dividing it into two parts. The men receive the meat and all that can be eaten while the gods are left with the bones and a little fat, the very portions still assigned to them, in the form of rising smoke, in the sacrifices made on perfumed altars. Zeus takes his revenge by hiding his fire from men — the heavenly, pure, inexhaustible, ungenerated fire which men had presumably enjoyed hitherto. So it is now impossible to cook the meat. Prometheus steals the seed of fire, hidden in the hollow stalk of a fennel plant, and presents it as a gift to men. So the flame of sacrifice burns on earth where men are now able to sustain their failing strength by eating the cooked meat. Zeus, cheated, counter-attacks. He hides the seed of wheat from men and buries it in the depths of the earth: it will henceforth be necessary to labour in the fields in order to harvest grain and eat bread. At the same time he creates the first woman, with whom it will be necessary to labour in order to produce children. Hephaistos models her out of clay moistened with water. She is a chthonic creature, damp and earthy, and not only is her condition mortal but also close to bestial by reason both of her insatiable appetite for food and also of her sexual appetite unleashed during the Dog Days when, being better protected against the burning heat of the sun then her husband, whose constitution is hotter and dryer than hers, she literally roasts her man; 'without any torch she dries him up', delivering him over, even while still green and raw, to the dessication of a premature old age. Pandora is, through her excessive animal sensuality, a fire to make men pay for the fire that Prometheus hid and stole from the gods. But she is more than this. She is herself a hidden trap, a double being whose appearance disguises and masks the reality. Hephaistos makes her out of clay and water but he fashions her in the image of the immortal goddesses and the beauty which shines forth from her body as if she were divine strikes not only men but gods too with wonder. The cunning of Zeus' vengeance lies in his having endowed with erotic seduction, that is a divine appearance, a being whose soul is that of a bitch and who hides her gross bestiality beneath the winning gentleness of her smile and the deceitful flattery of her lips. Pandora is an evil but an evil so beautiful that men cannot, in the depths of their hearts, prevent themselves from loving and desiring her. The seductive attraction of her physical appearance is further enhanced by the grace with which Aphrodite endows her whole body and the clothes, flowers and jewels with which Athena and Hephaistos adorn her. Pandora emerges from the hands of the gods as a young bride leaving the women who have prepared her for her wedding, anointed with perfumes, crowned with myrrh and clothed in the wedding tunic and veil; and she makes straight for Epimetheus, the Thoughtless One, who despite the warning of his brother Prometheus, the Foreseeing One, receives her into his house as his spouse. An irresistible enchantment emanates from her and illuminates her whole being; yet her first action is to lift the lid of the jar and release all the evils men had hitherto not known: hard labour, sickness, painful old age and death.

In the world of men erotic seduction is embodied in the equivocal figure of Pandora, the poisonous gift sent from Zeus as a counterpart to fire, as the opposite of the good thing that Prometheus fraudulently presented to them. And seduction — like Pandora — is a dual and ambiguous thing. In virtue of what it imitates it is divine. All beauty comes from the gods and the grace of a human body can only be a reflection and emanation of theirs. The perfumes are divine too. The gods smell fragrant; their presence is made manifest not only by intensely bright beams of light but also by a marvellous smell. So the attraction exercised by beauty and stimulated by perfumes has in itself a fully positive significance; it is an impulsion towards something divine. However, in erotic seduction it is a perverted impulsion towards a false semblance of the divine, towards the deceptive appearance of beauty disguising something in reality quite different: female bestiality. Just like Ixion who embraces the ghost of a goddess in the form of *Nephélē* who has the appearance of Hera, the man who yields to the call of desire falls into the trap Zeus laid in the person of Pandora; because he is clasping at an illusion his prey eludes him as he grasps at a shadow and is left empty-handed. Because he has desired to taste the divine life of the spices in the illusory guise of erotic seduction he forfeits, in the union of the sexes, man's rightful share which allows beings now become mortal to perpetuate themselves through marriage in a line of descent, and which makes of woman — who is divine in virtue of her seductively beguiling appearance and a beast in her true appetites — the companion, if not the equal, of her husband. Together they form a couple whose condition of life is neither that of the gods nor that of the beasts, neither the Golden Age nor a state of wildness but something between the two: the life of man as it has been defined ever since the separation of mortals and immortals through sacrifice, agriculture and marriage.

In finding a solution to the difficulties that arise from the presence of spices in both sacrifice and marriage where their roles are parallel but inverted one is paradoxically led to formulate a new, and final, category of problems. We have tried in our consideration of Detienne's work to emphasise the analogy between the two institutions and to distinguish as accurately as possible the implications and consequences of this symmetry. However, when the two institutions are replaced within the total system to which they belong, a radical difference between them becomes apparent which affects the entire harmony of Greek religion and culture. Sacrifice is the corner stone of the religion of the city. Yet it is attacked from both sides, both where it establishes a gap between men and gods and where it separates men and beasts. In both cases the attack is prompted by a desire to use different approaches (that while being opposed to each other may nevertheless be common to the same sect) in order to attain a religious experience which is unlike that offered by the official religion and which confers upon the devotee the privilege of a more direct contact, a closer union with the divine. We have seen how the Pythagoreans outflank sacrifice by going one better than it, by giving up eating meat, in an attempt to bridge even during life the gap separating gods from men. They are not alone in making such an attempt. A whole current of religion and philosophy follows the same trend, from those who were known as the Orphic sect to the greatest thinkers in classical Greece, Plato and Aristotle. For them, the object of the philosophical life is to make man like a god to the greatest extent possible, as opposed to the teaching of the official religion which can be expressed in the Delphic maxim: 'Know yourself' or, in other words, 'Recognise your limitations, know that you are not one of the gods and do not seek to equal them'.

But sacrifice can also be outflanked on the other side. There were groups of the devotees of the Dionysiac religion which practiced a form of worship in which the central rite was 'omophagy', the devouring of the absolutely raw flesh of an animal not led ritually to the altar to be slaughtered, cut up, roasted and boiled according to the rules, but captured as it ran wild, cut up, torn apart while still alive and consumed while life was still warm in it. Here the frontier that is wiped out is that separating man and nature in the wild, the aim being to abolish the barrier between humanity and bestiality. Instead of feeding on pure foods and, ideally, aromatic smells like the gods, these people eat raw flesh like wild beasts. This retrogression to a state of primitive wildness which is, as it were, the reverse of the Golden Age is also expressed on other aspects of the cult. Dionysus is seen as a wild hunter leading to their quarry a group of women who have themselves become wild, who have abandoned their homes, their domestic duties and their husbands and children in order to roam the wild, uncultivated countryside among woods and mountains far from the towns with their sanctuaries and far from the cultivated fields. The animals which these women track down and then eat alive are presented as being at times wild — lions, tigers or fawns — and at others domesticated — such as cows or goats — as if the difference between them had disappeared. Yet this difference between the two kinds of animals is recognised and consecrated by the usual form of sacrifice in which, unlike in the hunt, only domesticated animals are killed and — in principle at least — not until they have given some sign to indicate their acquiescence. Cannibalism is added to 'omophagy'. The frontier between men and beasts is abolished. In the myths in which they appear there is nothing left to distinguish Dionysus' frenzied maenades from the wild animals that they hunt down even in their lairs. They themselves become the very vixen, does and panthers whose blood they are about to lap up. Or else the reverse is the case: those whom they in their madness believe to be the wild dwellers of the forest turn out to be, in reality, their own race, their own family, of all living creatures those that are closest to them and most like them, — their children, their parents, their brothers. And they tear at them with their teeth without realising what they are doing — humans devouring other humans as birds eat the flesh of other birds.

This foray into wildness has a positive, religious significance: once the barriers within which man is enclosed (being confined as well as protected by them) are down, a more direct contact with the supernatural can be established. The maenades, beyond them-selves, overwhelmed by *mania*, the divine delirium, accede to a state that the Greeks call 'enthusiasm'; they are taken over by the gods who (in a religious sense) ride and possess them. The Dionysiac religion, in the savage form of possession, and Pythagoreanism, in the intellectual and ascetic form of spiritual purification, both — in opposite ways — bypass sacrifice in order to draw nearer to the gods. The aim they share explains how it is that, despite their mutual opposition, omophagy and vegetarianism are (as there is evidence to show) in certain instances practised within a single sect: eating raw flesh and a vegetarian diet reinforce each other, the one serving as necessary condition for the other, the one falling short of and the other going beyond sacrifice. Perhaps it could be said, to use a distinction sometimes used by anthro-pologists, that where it is a question of falling short of sacrifice, on the side of wildness, of omophagy and maenadism, it is the gods who take charge and draw near to men, descending to their level in order to take possession of their devotees. Beyond sacrifice, on the side of vegetarianism, asceticism and inner purification, it is men who take the initiative and strive to develop their own spiritual resources in order to be able to rise to the level of the gods, to reach them by an internal effort to pass beyond the normal limitations of human nature. At all events, by taking up a position outside the framework imposed by the practice of sacrifice both these 'mystical' experiences shaped the religious world of the Greeks and had a decisive effect on the orientation of ancient thought.

There is nothing comparable so far as marriage is concerned and yet, from a structural point of view the same possibilities existed here. Marriage, like sacrifice could have been outflanked in two different ways. This could have happened either in the name of total chastity, with a rejection of sexual consummation along with the rejection of the consumption of meat in order to find again the Golden Age in which both were unknown; or, on the contrary, in the name of sexuality and eroticism seen, in their brutish form, as religious forces which can no more be limited and regulated in man than in wild beasts. Why did the Greeks not exploit this double possibility which appears to us to be implied in the architecture of their religious system? In their quest for a life that is totally pure — alien to anything concerned with death and generation — the Pythagoreans could have adopted towards marriage the same dual attitude as they adopted towards sacrifice. On one level, as a brotherhood integrated within the city and seeking to transform it from within, they could have cut their losses by accepting sexual union only in the form of legitimate marriage and rejecting concubinage and prostitution in the same way as they accepted sacrifice only for goats and pigs and not for oxen and sheep. On a second level, as a religious sect, they could have taken up a more radical position and refused sexual union in all its forms just as they totally rejected blood sacrifice. Although there is much evidence to show that on the first level such an attitude was adopted, it does not seem that the sect ever defended the second attitude. The Pythagoreans are not religious extremists where marriage is concerned. The need for descendants is never directly questioned despite the fact that the procreation of even legitimate children fuels the cycle of rebirths which, from a Pythagorean point of view, is to some extent an evil. Nor do they appear to have had the idea that sexual activity is impure; they only considered it to be so if the union was an illegitimate one. The married couple remained pure in the carnal act which unites them as husband and wife. The ideal of *hosiótēs*, of complete sanctity and the hope of a return to the Golden Age did away with sacrifice but bypassed the institution of marriage without attacking it, for there was no tendency — not even a sectarian one — to reject this. Marriage does not appear ever to have been challenged from a religious stand point in Greece. Figures such as Hippolytus who, in tragedy, are the embodiment of a religious insistence on total purity, are presented with such equivocal features and display a puritanism so ambiguous in its very excesses that there is a whole side to their characters that tips the scales over towards wildness. Hippolytus whom his father, Theseus, considers as a devotee of Orpheus and as a fervent follower of the vegetarian diet desires and claims at the same time to be as chaste as a virgin. He rejects carnal union with the same intransigent disdain as a vegetarian rejecting animal flesh. He is a strange vegetarian though for he also appears to be very close to the wild beasts which he devotes his time to hunting and slaughtering and which then, once the hunt is over, he shares as a meal with his male companions, — a meal which he enjoys with the best of appetites. While he speaks of marriage only to reject it with indignation and horror, this young man, believed to be all modesty and reserve, has difficulty in masking under the artifice of a sophistic rhetoric the brutish violence of his true temperament. As for the Danaids who flee from marriage like timid doves escaping from the hawk which seeks them as its prey, the first time the king of Argos comes across them he compares them to the Amazons, 'the women who devour raw flesh', and the full force of this comparison becomes apparent when one considers the treatment they later mete out to their husbands, actually slaughtering them on their wedding night. For Greek thought in general, as well as for the Pythagoreans in particular, purity consists not in the rejection of marriage but in the rejection, in the name of marriage, of all illegitimate sexual relationships. And to renounce marital life altogether is not to beat a path towards the Golden Age but rather to detain boys and girls in the primitive state of wildness from which marriage can deliver them by introducing them into the very heart of civilised life.

Marriage is equally successful in resisting such attacks as could assail it from the opposite quarter. All that we learn from Detienne about the religion of Adonis indicates clearly that it does not attack marriage head-on. There is nothing in either the myth or the ritual which constitutes a challenge to its legitimacy or denies its religious value. In the religion of Adonis the attitude remains defensive. It goes no further than asserting the rights of erotic seduction, not claiming that it should take the place of marriage but that it should be practised alongside marriage and apart from it. This happens within the framework of a religious system that revolves around legitimate union and no attempt is made to deny the wife's recognised and proper privileges, namely her capacity to produce true fruits, to engender a line of descent firmly rooted in the earth, fixed to the very hearth of the house, a line of descent which is, in this way, directly continued and perpetuated with every birth of each new generation. Sacred prostitution which is commonly practised in the East is significantly absent from the Greek world. Even where, as in Corinth, there is evidence that it existed, it is a matter of a phenomenon that is in some way atypical, a reflection of oriental influences which remains profoundly alien to the Greek mentality. And the Greeks did not consider erotic activity to be a religious experience in itself any more than they consecrated total sexual abstinence. Unlike other civilisations they never made erotic activity a discipline for the body to acquire and develop, a kind of inverted asceticism. It is the fact that they consecrated neither abstinence nor eroticism that assures the undisputed legitimacy of marriage and that establishes it, alongside cereals, at the centre of the religious system. There were some sects for whom men were not considered to be those who ate the cooked meat of a sacrificed animal; but nevertheless they remained those who ate bread and practised a form of marriage without which there could be no civilised life, no *pólis*. At the same time, the fact that the Greeks did not consecrate either sexual abstinence or eroticism raises problems. By providing a solution to long-standing disagreements Detienne's study, like any work which is truly original and which marks a turning point in scholarship, alters the entire field of traditional views and suggests new areas of enquiry. To solve these new problems it would no doubt be necessary to enlarge the investigation beyond a mere structural analysis of the religious system. We should have to examine, this time from a historical point of view, how marriage became instituted in archaic Greece, how it developed from infinitely more open and free forms and how, within the institutional framework the city imposed upon it, marriage was transformed as, in part, it became established but, in part, continued to seek its own identity. As the author indicates in his last pages, one might formulate the hypothesis that religious thought was all the more insistent in consecrating the unique significance of marriage by opposing it systematically to erotic seduction since, in default of an unequivocal legal definition, the distinction between concubine and legitimate spouse remained in the fifth and fourth centuries somewhat hazy and uncertain. However, that is another story which we can but hope to see told in its turn one day following the same lines as those indicated by Detienne. In this way this book, which is full of seductive attractions and which is bound to prove seminal, would have the effect of uniting the two opposite qualities, and of reconciling the hostile figures, of Adonis and Demeter.

J.-P. Vernant.

Translator's Note

The translations from ancient texts are my own (from Detienne's French) except in the case of the following:

Aristotle, *Part. anim*: The Oxford translation of Aristotle (Ross).
_____ , *Problemata*: The Oxford translation of Aristotle (Ogle).
Aristophanes, *Peace*: (longer passages): Loeb (adapted).
_____ , *Lysistrata* (longer passages): Loeb (adapted).
Herodotus: Loeb (adapted).
Homer: Andrew Lang (adapted).
Ovid: Loeb (adapted).
Plato, *Laws*: Loeb (adapted).
_____ , *Phaedrus*: Hackforth (adapted).
Pliny: Loeb.
Plutarch: Loeb (adapted).
Theophrastus: Loeb (adapted).

Foreword

In introducing *Adonis*, the first volume of *The Golden Bough*, to the French public, James George Frazer confessed that he had wished to spare his readers from being lost in 'a dark labyrinth of crude, unformed, and savage customs and ideas (dans un sombre labyrinthe de coutumes et d'idées crues, informes et sauvages)'. Dismissing the 'hideous phantoms' whose evocation seemed inevitable in tracing the origins of rites designed to 'reanimate nature', he strove from the outset to reveal the 'graceful figure' of one of those deities whose death, as emotive as the fall of autumn leaves, alternates with the vibrant youthfulness that reawakens nature at the first burgeoning of spring. The triumph of Frazer's Adonis, a compound of pathos and grace, was all the more assured given that the vast erudition of anthropology appeared to echo the random suggestions of certain symbolical writers of the fourth century A.D. who saw the brief life of Adonis as the cycle of 'ripe ears of corn and harvested wheat'.[1] What Andrew Lang called 'the savage intellectual condition'[2] could be confronted without alarm in this exquisite Hellenistic youth who played the handsome lover abandoning himself in the arms of his mistress from whom death is soon to wrest him. The magic rites to 'revive the failing energies of the gods' had been stripped of their violent, savage character to be replaced by enchanting scenes of gardens and romance which testified to 'the growth of humane feelings' which used to be considered Greece's special legacy.[3]

The spell which Frazer cast over the principal historians of Greek religion was so great that the author of a recent book devoted to the Greek Adonis still proved unable to shake off the influence of Frazer's model even when he himself strongly criticised its conceptual limitations.[4] And yet we have only to read the myth of Adonis in the version given by Panyassis of Halicarnassus[5] (who was related to Herodotus), to see at once that Adonis — like so many others dealt with in this way — has been surreptitiously taken out of his true context and distorted by scholars applying an unchecked comparative method in which they are so carried away by the resemblances they believe they have discovered that they ignore the differences which might have set them on the right path.

'Thias, king of Assyria had a daughter, Smyrna (or Myrrha). In consequence of the wrath of Aphrodite, for she did not honour the goddess, this Smyrna conceived a passion for her father and, with the complicity of her nurse she shared her father's bed without his knowledge for twelve nights. But when he was aware of it he drew his sword and pursued her and, being overtaken, she prayed to the gods that she might be invisible; so the gods in compassion turned her into the tree which they call *smyrna* (myrrh). Ten months afterwards the tree burst and Adonis, as he is called, was born, whom for the sake of his beauty, while he was still an infant, Aphrodite hid in a chest unknown to the gods and entrusted to Persephone. But when Persephone beheld him she would not give him back. The case being tried before Zeus, the year was divided into three parts and the god ordained that Adonis should stay by himself for one part of the year, with Persephone for one part and with Aphrodite for the remainder. However, Adonis made over to Aphrodite his own share in addition; but afterwards in hunting he was gored and killed by a boar'.[6]

Frazer knew this Greek myth of Adonis better than anyone. It is, moreover, confirmed by a whole series of versions, some Greek, some Latin, which differ from each other only on minor points (geographical details, the nature of the quarrel between Aphrodite and Myrrha, the circumstances of Adonis' death.[7]) Paradoxically however, the author of the *Golden Bough* only wanted to see in it Adonis' connection with vegetation. Frazer's view was that if he passed one third of the year in the lower regions and the rest on earth surely this proved that he was the incarnation of the spirit of wheat. In a society in which the cereals had for a long time provided the staple diet Adonis could only stand for the most important cereal of all, the one which was the best to eat.[8] He could hardly have been more mistaken. The whole body of Greek mythology into which the story of Myrrha's son fits revolves around a fundamental opposition between the sphere of Adonis and that of Demeter: spices are as diametrically opposed to cereals as seduction to marriage. Spices and seduction are, in effect, the two explicit terms used in the myth. Just as Myrrha, spurred on by Aphrodite, sets out to seduce her father in secret, Adonis openly seduces first Aphrodite, then Persephone. Also, Adonis is produced by the myrrh tree whose form his mother has taken. But it is not a question of substituting one concept for another, of putting 'spices' where Frazer has 'spirit of wheat, and 'seduction' in the place of 'dying god'. To do so would be to share the illusion that in ancient mythology a divine power can be defined by one particular essence and that every myth itself contains a meaning which has only to be revealed. To attempt to decipher one myth on its own is as mistaken as to wish to identify a particular plant or animal in myth, without taking the entire ethnographical context into account. Around the story of Adonis and Myrrha, within which it is first necessary to distinguish the different levels of meaning, or codes, (the botanical, the sociological, the astronomical), a whole series of myths (concerning Phaon, Mintha, Ixion and the Lemnian women), gradually coalesce to form, in conjunction with the original myth, a group whose coherence depends upon two factors. The first is the interaction of a limited number of oppositions linking a series of stories which appear, on the face of it, to have nothing in common.[9] The second is the subject matter, for all these myths refer more or less explicitly to seduction or to spices, or even to particular features in the way these were represented in Greek thought. At this juncture a further point should be made. Even the historical evidence seems to underwrite the search for a code common to the whole body of spice myths centering on Adonis. Most of the evidence — both archaeological and literary — relating to the Adonia seems to be particularly homogeneous with regard both to time and to place. It comes from Athens in the fifth and fourth centuries. And it is no doubt relevant to the image Greek society had of Adonis that the vogue enjoyed by this exotic, marginal god was roughly contemporary with the popularity of various foreign and at times disturbing deities such as Sabazios, Bendis and Cotytô, and Hermaphrodite — all of them powers whose emergence is one symptom, among others, of the crisis which was tearing the social body apart and splitting the citizen in two, into the private citizen on the one hand, and the political man on the other.[10]

Thus, some aspects of the myth of Adonis can be set in a concrete historical context. Yet it can also be related, through its various levels of meaning, to the overall framework of Greek social and religious thought. In effect, to define the meaning and functions of spices is to pose the whole problem of the system of foods, of dietary behaviour, and ultimately of sacrifice, — in other words, different types of relationships between gods and men. Similarly, to decipher the meaning of the Adonia is to determine the position of this ritual in relation to the festival of the Thesmophoria dedicated to Demeter. It is also to establish the relationships between the different sociological statuses of women and between the various types of sexual relations that range from perversion to legitimate marriage and include seduction and concubinage. Through the myth of the precocious adolescent, the seducer who died young, we can discover as it were the mirror-image of a politico-religious order based on the interdependence of civilised life, marriage and sacrifice. However, to restore Adonis to the place he had in the story as the Greeks told it, we must take as our starting point the myrrh tree whose form its namesake, Myrrha, adopts, and whose exceptional fruit bears the name Adonis. The botanical characteristics of the species, the affinities of myrrh with other aromatic products, the status of spices, the function of perfumes: these are the problems and questions by means of which the botanical code that illuminates the whole of this mythology can be deciphered.[11]

I

The Perfumes
of Arabia

Although Panyassis' account appears to set the metamorphosis of Myrrha into a myrrh tree in Assyria, other versions locate it in the Land of Spices. Antimachus of Colophon[1], a contemporary of Panyassis, sets the story in Syria and Arabia. According to Ovid's *Metamorphoses*, Myrrha's flight, lasting a whole nine months, took her from Cyprus across an Arabia covered with palm trees, as far as the land of Saba where she was transformed into the plant from which the child named Adonis was later born.[2]

Like the legendary Hyperboreans[3] and the peoples inhabiting the furthest extremities of the earth, the Arabs occupy an area which, even as late as the geographical tradition of the fifth century, is privileged as 'receiving as its lot all that is most beautiful'. Herodotus, in fact, makes this remark in the course of his description, in Book III of his *History*, of the most distant lands stretching away to the East and the South. On the one hand there is India where the animals, whether winged or quadruped, are larger than anywhere else, where gold flows in the streams and is extracted from the ground by ants as large as foxes, and where wild trees bear, as their fruit, a wool that is more beautiful and stronger than that which is produced by sheep. To the South, on the other hand, is Arabia, 'the only country which yields frankincense, myrrh, cassia, cinnamon and ladanum'.[4]

To Greek thought, all the aromatic plants mentioned by Herodotus belong to the same land and their distinctive botanical characteristics tend to become blurred in the mythical accounts in which they are linked together, encompassed by a single boundary.

From Herodotus' descriptions to the treatises of the botanists, the picture remains unchanged. Even for Theophrastus, frankincense and myrrh, and cassia and cinnamon all grow together in the Arabian peninsula in the vicinity of Saba, Hadramyta, Kitibaina and Mamali.[5] Alexander's expedition enriched geographical knowledge and gave it a new framework but it did not radically alter the Greek's idea of the Land of Spices. In modern botany the name myrrh is reserved for the product of trees of the *Balsamodendrum Kunth* group, belonging to the Burseraceae family[6], which are to be found especially in the Yemen and in Abyssinia, while the oleo-resinous gum from the shrub *Boswellia Carterii Birdw*, which grows in Arabia and also belongs to the Burseraceae, is known as frankincense. However, the naturalists of the ancient world tended to confuse these aromatic plants which grew so far away, to the point of claiming not merely that myrrh trees and frankincense trees grew together in the same forests[7] but even that frankincense and myrrh were both secreted by the same tree.[8]

The affinities between these two aromatic substances, so closely associated as to become confused with each other, are revealed by a whole body of Greek and Roman evidence in which can be discerned a model for mythology concerned with spices and perfumes. Frankincense and myrrh, both precious substances which had long been sought after, were the object of commercial exchanges which were the prerogative of certain individuals and which took place according to ritually established procedures. According to the Elder Pliny, three thousand families among the Minaeans of Arabia had the hereditary right of exploiting the frankincense forests. Those who collected the frankincense were called 'sacred' and were forbidden any contact with the dead or with women while they were engaged in gathering the crop. The trunks and branches of the myrrh and frankincense trees were slashed with a kind of axe at the places where the bark, being very thin and distended, seemed to be the most swollen with sap. 'From this incision a greasy foam spurts out which coagulates and thickens, being received on a mat of palm leaves ... but in other places on a space round the tree that has been rammed hard'.[9] The most sought after frankincense was formed by a second secretion coagulating on top of an earlier one that had adhered to the trunk. The Roman naturalist recalls a time when men were less greedy for gain and would patiently wait for one of these lumps of frankincense, described as 'breast-shaped' and large enough to fill the hand, to form by itself.[10] Myrrh was collected in the same way as frankincense, and it took a similar form of irregular small lumps formed from the concretion of a whitish juice that was easy to melt.[11] But it is in Theophrastus' account of the Sabaeans, the just men who owned the mountain where frankincense and myrrh trees grew together, that the ritual nature of the collection of these spices is shown most clearly.

'The myrrh and frankincense are collected from all parts into the temple of the sun, which is the place which is by far the most sacred in the Land of Saba. It is guarded by certain Arabians in arms. When they have brought it, each man piles up his own collection of spices and leaves it with those on guard; and on the pile he puts a tablet on which is stated the number of measures it contains, and the price for which each measure should be sold. When the merchants come, they look at the tablets and whichever pile pleases them they measure and put down the price on the spot from which they have taken the wares. Then the priest of the sun comes and, having taken a third part of the sum for the god, leaves the rest of it where it was, and this remains safe for the owners until they come and claim it.'[12]

The sun is patron not only of the silent frankincense and myrrh transaction but also of other aromatic products such as cinnamon. Theophrastus writes, not without scepticism, about the extraordinary way it is collected:

'They say that cinnamon grows in deep glens, that in these there are deadly snakes that have a deadly bite. Against these they protect their hands and feet before they go down into the glens and then, when they have brought up the cinnamon, they divide it into three portions, one of which they leave behind as the lot of the Sun. And they say that as soon as they leave the spot they see this take fire.'[13]

The same legend reappears in the *Natural History* of Pliny the Elder:

'The wood being divided into three portions, a share is assigned to the sun. Then lots are cast to assign the shares and the share that falls to the sun is left and bursts into flames of its own accord'.[14]

Collected in this way into the Temple of the Sun, divided out by the Sun priest and offered as tribute to the fire of the sun by which they are immediately consumed, the spices appear in these Greek myths as substances whose nature is related to the fiery power of the Fire Above.[15] But the affinities between spices and the Sun are even more clearly emphasised in the traditions concerning the most favourable time for the collection of these products. When Theophrastus describes the plants that contain sap, he is careful to mention that neither are they cut nor do the sap and gum naturally flow at the same time of the year in the case of all plants. He adds: 'The frankincense and myrrh trees should be cut at the rising of the Dog star (*hupò kúna*), on the hottest days.'[16] These astronomical details are confirmed in Pliny's *Natural History*:

> 'It used to be the custom, when there were fewer opportunities of selling frankincense, to gather it only once a year, but at the present day trade introduces a second harvesting. *The earliest and natural gathering takes place at about the rising of the Dog Star when the summer heat is most intense* ... The frankincense from the summer crop is collected in the autumn; *this is the purest kind, bright white in colour.* The second crop is harvested in the spring, cuts having been made in the bark during the winter in preparation for it; the juice that comes out on this occasion is reddish and not to be compared with the former taking'.[17]

As for the myrrh tree:

> 'This also is tapped twice a year at the same seasons as the frankincense tree, but in its case the incisions are made all the way up from the root to those of the branches that are strong enough to bear it. But before it is tapped, the tree exudes of its own accord a juice called stacte (which flows drop by drop) which is the most highly valued of all myrrh, ... *the best type of myrrh is that which is tapped in summer.*'[18]

There might seem to be a considerable difference between these indications about the most suitable moment for harvesting[19] the spices and the traditions we have mentioned relating to the ritual nature of these collections. On the one hand we have reports of a mythical or legendary nature which are echoed in the writings of certain botanists while on the other we have astronomical or calendary data which appear to belong to a would-be 'scientific' description. But we have only to compare this data with the geographical and botanical facts to see that we are mistaken: the collection of frankincense actually took place in February or March[20], that is to say four months earlier than the date given by Pliny and Theophrastus.[21] If the mythical character of the reference to Sirius should still remain in any doubt, there is another argument to dispel it: according to Theophrastus, it is not only frankincense and myrrh that must be collected 'when the heat is most stifling, at the rising of the Dog Star',[22] but also the product of the balsam tree. The collection of spices under the sign of Sirius resembles and is no less mythical than the sharing out of perfumed substances in the presence of the Sun. The fact is that, in Greek thought, the brightness of Sirius is simply a metaphorical reference to the sun's fire.

The most brilliant star in the constellation of the Dog is the 'fire-bearing' (*purphórus*) one.[23] Each year, its appearance on July 27th, a few moments before the rising of the sun, marks the beginning of the canicular period, the time which 'increases the radiation of the sun'.[24] Sirius, which burns with a bright fire and sheds a killing light,[25] is described by both Hesiod and Archilochus as a 'dessicating Sun' (*seiriân*).[26] It burns up the plants, makes the fields sterile and deprives the seeds buried deep inside the earth of food:[27] the animals die of thirst, vines are 'burnt to a cinder'[28] and men are prostrated with fevers.[29] It is a time of the most cruel heat and of total drought: Sirius burns the skin and men are parched with thirst and dessicated[30] like those unfortunates who, while dying of thirst are afflicted with hydrophobia as a result of being bitten by dogs said to be driven mad by the heat of the dog days.[31] The appearance of the dazzling constellation that the Greeks imagine in the form of a bounding dog with lolling tongue and bulging eyes, its head encircled by the rays of the sun[32] marks the beginning of the period of the year when the Fire of the Sun comes most dangerously close to the Earth.[33]

Being the products of Sirius, spices can obviously not grow in just any region of the Earth. There is no doubt that the reason why most Greeks agree with Theophrastus that cassia and cinnamon originate, like frankincense and myrrh, in the Arabian peninsula, [34] is that substances showing so many affinities with the Sun could only grow in that region of the world which is most exposed to the burning heat of the Fire from Above. The Land of the Arabs, which is the domain of spices, is described in Herodotus'

History as a burning, dry land which, under the beating southern Sun, gives off a 'marvellously sweet fragrance' in which every aroma is mingled.[35] It is a fragrance so pervasive that, it is said, Alexander's fleet could smell it when they were still far out to sea, even before they could make out the coast of Arabia.[36] Herodotus is not alone to prove that the image of the Land of the South is an integral part of the mythical view of spices. Theophrastus, whose account is reported by Plutarch, also reveals the underlying categories and concepts in question. Plutarch writes:

'I have read in the *Memoirs* of Aristoxenus that the mouth of Alexander and all his flesh exhaled a fragrance so sweet that his garments were filled with it. Now the cause of this, perhaps, was the temperature of his body which was a very warm and fiery one. For fragrance is generated, as Theophrastus thinks, where moist humours are concocted (*pépsis*) by heat. This is why the dry and parched regions of the world produce the most and best perfumes, for the sun draws away the moisture which, like the material of corruption (*húlē sēpedónos*) abounds in bodies.'[37]

The same theory is expressed, in almost the same form, in Plutarch's *Table Talk*: 'Cassia and frankincense are produced in the dryest and hottest part of the world for fragrance, according to Theophrastus, comes from a sort of concoction (*pépsis*) of moistures when their harmful excess is removed by heat'.[38] These same, fundamental oppositions of wet and dry, and rotten and fragrant guide Theophrastus' analyses in his *Treatise on Odours* and are the basis for the explanations given, also in this field, in the Aristotelian *Problemata*. Two examples drawn from the latter should suffice to make this point. First, in the 'problem' of why the inhabitants of hot climates live longer than others, 'it is because their nature is dryer and that which is dryer is less liable to putrefaction and more lasting, death being, as it were, a kind of putrefaction (*sêpsis*)'.[39] In another 'question' (Why does no living animal except the panther have a pleasant smell?), the bad smell can only be explained by inadequate concoction: the humour is a source of putrefaction unless it is evacuated by concoction: 'This is why, in hot regions, such as Syria and Arabia, the earth is sweet-smelling and everything that comes from these countries has a sweet smell; everything is hot and dry and nothing is liable to decay'.[40] In the works of the botanists and of the 'physicists', as in the legends, aromatic substances are produced by a dry, baking soil in which the wet principle is submitted by fire to the most intense concoction. Whatever their form and context, all these accounts appear to be constructed upon the opposition between two groups of complementary concepts: on the one hand the cold, the wet, the principle of corruption, putrid smells and remoteness from the fire of the sun; on the other the hot, the dry, the principle of incorruptibility, fragrant smells, and proximity to the heavenly fire. The dividing line between these two groups depends on the sun since the degrees and methods of 'cooking' are governed by its proximity or remoteness. Indeed, the relationships between all the different natural products, from wild grass to perfumed substances and including fruits and cultivated plants, can only be defined in these terms of concoction or cooking.

SUN	
+	−
Dry	Wet
Hot	Cold
Incorruptibility	Corruption
Fragrant smells	Putrid smells

The position of the Sun

There is whole tradition, systematised by the Aristotelian school, according to which the production of edible plants results from several types of 'cooking', each of which operates at a different level: the cooking of the earth by the fire of the sun; the internal concoction of the juices in fruits and plants; concoction promoted by agriculture; and finally, the cooking of plants by fire in the kitchen. The first type represents the most general level of agriculture in Greece. In Xenophon's *Oeconomica*, preparing the unploughed land is not simply a matter of turning the soil over in the spring time or getting rid of the weeds with either a hoe or a plough, but above all of allowing the 'raw' part of the earth to be baked by the Sun (*optân*).[41] But the Sun's action is not limited to this preliminary baking; it also operates in concoction through ripening or *pépansis*[42]: as it ripens in the rays of the summer sun, the fruit undergoes a cooking process which softens it and which, given its wet nature, resembles cooking by boiling.[43] However, at this second level, concoction only takes place given certain conditions determined both by the degree of cultivation of the plant and by the particular type of farming involved. In point of fact, the sun only appears to operate as a culinary agent to the degree that it can prolong a purely internal concoction which it is the business of agriculture to recognise and promote. We must now attempt to illuminate this view of agriculture.

One of the 'problems' in the Aristotelian collection uses a technical term from culinary vocabulary to define agriculture: to cultivate plants is to cook them (*péttein*), to make them soft and good to eat.[44] Even more explicitly, agriculture is described as the art of educating (*paideúein*) plants.[45] But just as in the kitchen one does not cook everything indiscriminately, in agriculture not every species of plant can be cultivated. There is a clear cut distinction between two types of plant: one grows and develops from well-cooked nourishment (*pepemménēs ... trophês*)[46], while the other derives its sustenance only from that which is uncooked and is a principle of corruption.[47] Although farming succeeds in educating and cooking the former type, the latter plants are intractible to its effects; these are wild (*ágria*) plants that will not grow in cultivated earth.[48] If the attempt to domesticate them through farming is made they simply die. The caper plant is an example, flourishing when it grows on tombs yet incapable of growing in cultivated ground.[49] The distinction between uncultivated and cultivated earth is not only a matter of the cultivation of plants. Cultivation can only succeed within the limits already determined by a more ancient opposition — between plants that are raw and plants that are cooked. In other words, agriculture can only 'soften' (*hēmeroûn*) plants that are already subject to concoction; it can only cultivate those species which are, in a sense, already part of it.[50]

The final level, that of domestic cooking, can only be defined in close relation to the three preceding ones which must be regarded as a kind of pre-cooking. It seems in fact that the only role of the culinary fire can be to provide certain species with the extra cooking which makes them edible and good to eat (*brōtá*).[51] Similarly, cooking in the strict sense of the word, is not able to make edible those plants whose juices, in the raw state, are not susceptible to concoction.[52] Thus, the scope of domestic cooking is restricted precisely to the limits established by the natural concoction of plants and by farming. Consequently, according to this conceptual system of the Greeks at the end of the fourth century, the truly wild plant is shown to be raw in three ways: it is intractable to internal concoction, it cannot be cultivated and it cannot be cooked domestically. In the same way, the perfectly cultivated plant in principle undergoes three degrees of cooking: [53] internal concoction, the cooking provided by cultivation and, finally, culinary preparation.

WILD PLANT		CULTIVATED PLANT
—	Internal concoction	X
—	Cultivation	X
—	Domestic cooking	X
3 x raw		3 x cooked

Degrees of Concoction

In accordance with these criteria, the whole gamut of natural products can be set along a vertical whose top and bottom are correlated with hot and cold, dry and wet, the principle of incorruptibility and that of corruption, perfumed smells and putrid ones, and proximity to and remoteness from the fire of the sun. At the lowest point, next to the earthly element and what is rotten, comes the plant that is wet and cold for example, wild grass which grows spontaneously (*botánē ek gês*)[54], a raw food, untreated and suitable for animals, which man rejected following the invention of agriculture and cooking.[55] The wild nature of such cold and wet plants is illustrated forcefully in the venomous character of the snakes that feed upon poisonous roots and grasses, produced in those lands that are remote from the Sun[56]: not only does their venom, when spat from a distance, kill a man instantaneously, but mere contact with them is enough to make things rot. Aristoxeus of Tarentum records the case of a man who died through having touched a snake with his bare hands and whose clothes, being contaminated by the reptile, very soon rotted away.[57]

In the middle range, situated at a fair distance from the fire of the sun, are the edible plants in which the dry and the wet are equally balanced, the cereals and the fruits. Their intermediate position is illustrated, especially, in the dual status of the fruit of the vine. This is sometimes a moist and refreshing food, when the first grapes are gathered in early July for eating, and sometimes a fermented drink of a fiery nature that is made from the riper grapes picked after the Dog Days, at the rising of Arcturus.[58] Here we have two types of ripening for the same fruit, representing two methods of cooking by boiling. In one case there is a concoction where the external balance of the hot and wet is ensured by the regular alternation of sun and rain; and in the other, the emphasis is placed on the internal boiling, a bubbling similar to that of sweet wine when the juice is subjected to a greater heat during the period of the *Opôra*, the season of ripe fruits[59], whose position in relation to Sirius is symmetrical with that of the harvest period.

Finally, beyond the fruits, even beyond the dryest of them — for example, the Arabian dates whose outer covering is, as a result of the great heat, really more of a bark than a skin[60] — comes the sphere of the aromatic plants whose proximity to the Sun causes their products to be so dried up that they are burned. Only in reference to this system of representations does Theophrastus' information about the most favourable time for the collection of spices take on its full conceptual meaning. Incisions must be made in the myrrh and frankincense trees at the heliacal rising of the constellation of the Dog because the dried up substances produced by the fire of the sun from the baked earth are ripe and ready at the moment when the Sun is at its closest point and the earth is at its dryest.

There is confirmation of the strange and marvellous nature of spices in Herodotus' *History*, in the various accounts of how the inhabitants of Arabia acquire these perfumed substances. Here, for

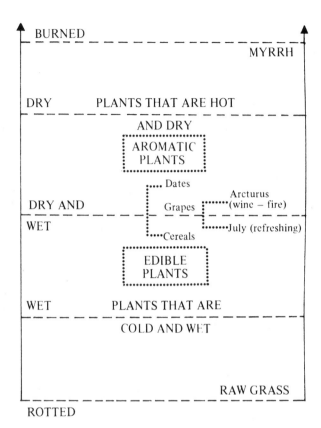

Natural products and cultivated products

instance, is a description of how the Arabs obtain cassia and cinnamon bark:

'When they seek it they bind ox hides and other skins over all their bodies and faces, leaving only the eyes. Cassia grows in a shallow lake. Round this and in it live certain winged creatures, very like bats, that squeak shrilly and make a stout resistance. These must be kept from the mens' eyes if the cassia is to be plucked. As for cinnamon, they gather it in an even stranger fashion. Where it grows and what kind of land nurtures it they cannot say except that it is reported, reasonably enough, to grow in the lands where Dionysus was reared. There are great birds, it is said, that take these dry sticks that the Phoenicians have taught us to call cinnamon and carry them off to nests built of mud and attached to precipitous crags to which no man can approach. In this situation the Arabs use the following device: they cut into the largest possible pieces dead oxen and asses and other beasts of burden, then they set these near the eyries, withdrawing themselves far off. The birds then fly down and carry the pieces of the beasts up to their nests which, not being able to bear the weight, break and fall to the ground; and then the Arabs come up and collect it. Thus is cinnamon said to be gathered and so to come from Arabia to other lands.'[61]

We are prompted by such accounts of Herodotus to observe how important it is to realise the extent to which the Greeks' idea of these spices was at variance with the geographical and botanical facts. Although most of the ancients believed that cassia and cinnamon, which were paired together in the same way as frankincense and myrrh, came from the Land of Spices, Southern Arabia, these two kinds of cinnamon are in fact of far-eastern origin. Cassia, whose name is derived from the Chinese *kewi-shi* and is often connected with the name Khasi, denoting the inhabitants of Northern Assam, is an aromatic plant belonging to the Lauraceae family (the *C. Cassia Bl.* of southern China) whose properties were well known as far back as the time of the Emperor Shön-nung, that is to say since time immemorial. As for cinnamon, known as *kayu manis* in Malay and as *quinnamon* in Hebrew, this is a member of the same botanical family (the *C. Zeylanicum Breyn*, native to Ceylon) and had belonged to Chinese pharmacopeia ever since the period of the Shang or Yin, whilst in Egypt it had been used for embalming ever since the fifteenth century B.C. Cassia and cinnamon were carried from Indonesia to Rhatpa via Madagascar and then, under the control of Southern Arabia, brought to the ports of Somalia from where they were distributed through the trade routes of the Mediterranean world.[62] From that time on these spices were collected in China and South-Eastern Asia by a technique whose essential features appear to have remained unchanged and which was still used until quite recent times by the natives of Ceylon. The cinnamon trees were cut in May and in October when the rains were heaviest and when it was easy to remove the bark from the stems swollen with sap. Once stripped of their leaves the stems had circular incisions cut through the bark into the wood at the bases of the internodes. The incisions were then connected lengthwise by others cut one on either side of the stem. Then the bark was tapped with a short, thick stick of hard wood. It came away from the stem and was detached by means of some kind of copper blade inserted between the wood and its covering. The bands of bark were then dried for twenty-four hours and their epidermis was scratched, and then they were cut into thirty centimetre lengths and dried, first in the shade and then in the sun. As they dried out they furled over so that they looked like a series of tubes fitted into each other.[63]

A comparison between these geographical, botanical and technological facts and the two accounts given by Herodotus in his History shows that Pliny the Elder was quite right to describe the reports of the old historian as fables and tales aimed at 'increasing the price of spices'.[64] However, the cynical sting in the remark should be ignored and it should rather be understood in the figurative sense: these are tales of a kind to reveal the mythical values of these fragrant substances. And indeed, Herodotus' two accounts can only be deciphered by means of the oppositions and categories that are in play in the marvellous stories of the Land of Spices.

Cassia and cinnamon are rare products, difficult to harvest, whose collection involves operations halfway between hunting and gathering. Cinnamon is obtained through the mediation of huge birds which must be lured to participate whilst cassia has to be won from bats against which the collectors must protect themselves. Neither is a simple matter of harvesting nor yet of a real hunt since there is no question of either killing or catching the huge birds or the bats. Cinnamon and cassia which are closely linked — in this two-fold mythical account as in all the Graeco-Roman tradition — are opposed to each other on a series of points. In the first place there is an opposition between water and air: cassia grows in a lake while cinnamon is to be found up in the sky. This opposition is correlated with one between below and above: cinnamon is used by the great birds as a material for constructing their nests which they build at the summit of steep mountains. Cassia, on the other hand, grows in a shallow lake which is water of the region Below. In the first case the spices are brought down from above; in the second they are brought up from below. Although the spices follow opposite paths in the two accounts this does not affect their significance in any way, as is proved by the account that Theophrastus gives of the collection of cinnamon. Here the spices grow in ravines infested by legions of snakes whose bite is deadly. But once they have been collected and one third dedicated to the Sun, these spices from Below, which might have seemed but one step away from the cold and the wet, reveal their true fiery nature by spontaneously bursting into flames through internal combustion. [65]

The animals in the two stories express this difference of direction. Where the cinnamon is concerned we have huge birds that nest at the summit of rocky cliffs. Herodotus does not indicate their species but Aristotle and Pliny the Elder, who both echo the same tale, write explicitly of Spice birds. According to Pliny, they belong to the species of the Phoenix.[67] In the story about the cassia, they are the winged animals 'which closely resemble bats', that is to say animals that the Greeks defined as chthonic creatures with wings. Aristotle holds that the bat belongs to two different genera: it has as much in common with the bird as with the land animal, sharing characteristics with both without wholly belonging to either: 'Bats, if regarded as birds are anomalous in having feet, if regarded as quadrupeds in not having feet. Furthermore, they have neither a quadruped's tail (because they are fliers) nor a bird's tail (because they are land animals). This, their lack of a tail like a bird's, is a necessary consequence since they have membranous wings and no creature has a tail of this sort unless it has barbed feathers; such tails are always made out of barbed feathers. And a tail of the other sort, growing among feathers, would be a definite impediment.'[68] The birds that guard the cassia are diametrically opposed to the cinnamon birds: they have wings of skin instead of feathers and they flutter heavily and clumsily, close to the ground. These bat-like creatures are indeed chthonic birds as is indicated in particular by their habit of living in dark, damp places.[69] If further proof were needed Pliny's *Natural History* would provide it for there he maintains that 'cassia is guarded by a terrible kind of bat, with their claws, and by winged snakes'.[70] In effect, these winged reptiles which Herodotus elsewhere reports as guarding the frankincense tree[71] resemble water snakes with bat's wings.[72] Winged snakes and bats correspond to one another in that the former are winged chthonic creatures, the latter chthonic winged ones.

There is one more opposition that is part of the structure of the two myths about the collection of spices. This time it concerns the method chosen to obtain the precious substances. For collecting cinnamon the Arabs use bait, hunks of meat, pieces as large as possible from dead oxen and asses and other beasts of burden.[73] When these pieces of meat are placed at the foot of the mountain they attract the huge birds who carry them away to their cinnamon nests where they cause the spices, perched on the top of the inaccessible cliffs, to fall to the ground. In contrast, when harvesting cassia, the Arabs do not seek to attract birds to act as mediators but rather to repulse flying creatures which thwart their attempts to collect the fragrant essences. Equally, in this case it is not the internal parts of the animals, their meat, that mediates between the collectors and those that stand guard over the spices but rather their outer covering, their skins which the collector wears to cover his entire face and body, excepting the eyes. Although they differ in the method of procedure they use, the two methods share a common end, to bring together the above and the below, to mediate between what is near and what is far away.

As the versions about the collection of the spices become briefer and more schematic their framework emerges more clearly.

Cinnamon	Cassia
air	water
above	below
birds from the heights	bats
to be lured	to be kept off
by means of meat (internal)	by means of a pelt (external)

Harvesting cinnamon and cassia

Thus, in Aristotle's *Historia Animalium* harvesting the cinnamon is described as a kind of hunt with a bird's nest built in a tall tree as the quarry, and with a weapon in the shape of a bow whose arrows do not kill but instead bring the cinnamon to the grasp of the hunger-gatherer. Mediation between the Above and the Below, between the inaccessible spices and the men rooted to the earth is effected by the weighted arrow which combines the heavy and the light and by this piece of technology brings about a synthesis between the two poles of the vertical axis upon which this myth of spice collecting, like the others, is structured.[74]

In these myths, the mediation between opposites provides the linking factor. In this connection, there is one detail in Herodotus' myth about cinnamon that is particularly striking, namely, the meat which serves as bait for the birds from the heights. In order to define the relationship between the spice-bird and the dead flesh, we must compare another myth concerned with hunting and gathering, constructed on the same vertical axis and employing similar terms, — that is, a bird from the heights on the one hand and raw meat on the other. In the twelfth part of Antoninus Liberalis' *Metamorphoses* Phylios is the unhappy lover of a young misanthropic hunter named Swan who rebuts him by imposing upon him a number of trials. He must kill a lion without the use of arms, capture some monstrous vultures alive and seize hold of a bull and carry it to the altar of Zeus. In all three exploits Phylios, because of the methods imposed, acts as an anti-hunter.[75]

This is how he sets about capturing birds of a quite exceptional size and ferocity, without any weapons:

'Phylios was wondering how he was to carry out his lover's order when he noticed an eagle which had caught a hare and then, at the instigation of some god, let it fall, half-dead to the ground. Phylios immediately seized it, tore it apart, covered himself with its blood and lay down on the ground. Seeing him lying there, the vultures took him for a corpse and swooped down upon him. Phylios watched closely; he seized two by the feet, captured them and offered them, living to Swan'.[76] In this type of hunt where a totally unarmed hunter from Below confronts a powerfully armed bird from Above, the hunter captures his quarry by himself playing the part of the prey: Phylios is at the same time both quarry and hunter. This double role is strikingly reminiscent of the eagle hunt among the Hidatsa of North America. As Claude Lévi-Strauss' analysis has shown,[77] the eagle hunter hides in a ditch while the bird is lured by a bait placed above him. When it flies down to seize the bait, the hunter catches the bird with his bare hands. As in Phylios' hunt, the man is simultaneously hunter and quarry: in order to capture the eagle he must descend into the ditch, thus taking up the position of an animal caught in a trap. Among the Hidatsa the eagle hunt is preceded by a ritual whose complexity appears to be occasioned by the exceptional nature of a type of hunt in which there is a maximum distance between the hunter and his quarry: the hunter takes up the lowest position in order to capture a quarry occupying the highest. Mediation between them is effected by the bait, that is by the piece of meat, bloody flesh that is going to rot. Among the Hidatsa the eagle hunt is preceded by a preliminary hunt, for a small animal must be killed to serve as bait for the eagles. This first hunt is the pre-requisite for the second hunt in which, in contrast to the first, no blood is shed. The eagles are taken alive, for their feathers. Instead of their throats being cut, they are strangled. The eagle is not good to eat but is, on the other hand, the most splendid finery. The first hunt is an indispensible preliminary whose function is to ensure the conjunction of hunter and quarry: in other words it provides 'the means of effecting a union between what is so distant that it looks at first as if there is a gulf which cannot be bridged — except, precisely, by means of blood'.[78]

There are three points of resemblance between Phylios' vulture hunt and the eagle hunt among the Hidatsa. In the first place a preliminary hunt is the condition for the one that follows. Secondly, in each example, in the first hunt blood is shed, in the second it is not. Like the eagles, the vultures are captured alive and Phylios makes a present of them to his lover. In the Greek myth, as in the American ritual, it is not so much a question of hunting an animal as of obtaining some finery. Lastly, Phylios, like the Hidatsa eagle hunters, combines the roles of quarry and hunter. He lies on the ground like a corpse and thus lures down a bird from Above which believes itself to be the hunter only to find that it is the quarry. However, differences between the two hunts are to be found at the very heart of their similarities. First, where the preliminary hunt is concerned, whereas the Hidatsa hunter himself kills the small animal that is to serve as bait, it is an eagle that catches the hare that Phylios then uses to lure the vultures down. In fact the whole story makes it quite clear that the eagle half-kills the hare and Phylios finishes off the hunt: the eagle attacks a living creature which it then drops, half-dead, to the ground instead of carrying it off to its eyrie. Phylios immediately seizes possession of it, tears it to pieces and smears himself with its blood. This difference in the preliminary hunt is balanced by a difference in the second. Among the Hidatsa the hunter gets down into a ditch on top of which he places a bait. But although he thus seems joined to the animal he has hunted and although he takes up a position that is essentially 'below', the Hidatsa hunter is nevertheless not completely identified with the quarry in the way that Phylios is as he waits for the birds, lying motionless on the ground, covered in blood, like a lifeless hare. These two differences must be connected with the use, in the Greek myth, of categories that are not present in the American example. First there is the category of the 'half-dead' and 'half-alive'; and secondly the eagle-vulture couple. The hare is described as being half-dead (*hēmithnēs*) while Phylios is a living man behaving like a corpse (*nekrós*).[79]

	Eagle Hunt	Phylios' Hunt
The first hunt:		
● actor	hunter	hunter and eagle
● type of hunt	blood-shedding	blood-shedding
The second hunt:		
● object of attraction	small hunted animal	man/corpse
● type of hunt	not blood-shedding	not blood-shedding
Object of hunt	finery	gift-finery

The Hidatsa Eagle Hunt and Phylios' Hunt

In the story of Phylios, the two categories of the living-dead and the dead-yet-alive depend upon the switch from eagle to vulture, the former striking down the animal that the latter then prepares to devour. The eagle and the vulture are birds that are similar in some ways but different in others. Both are birds of prey, hunting by day, but the eagle feeds on fresh meat and living animals, the vulture on carrion and dead flesh. The myth about Phylios exploits the ambiguity of these two birds. The vultures that have to be caught behave like eagles; they are bloodthirsty animals that attack human beings; when Phylios confronts them they have already killed several victims.[80] But at the same time they are birds of prey that eat dead flesh; it is as vultures that they swoop down upon Phylios as soon as he has disguised himself as a bloody corpse. Furthermore, the ambiguity of the bird from the heights is perfectly matched by the ambivalence in the position of the hare in the first hunt and of Phylios in the second: both oscillate in a similar way between two different roles, that of living prey and that of dead flesh. Clearly, the main interest in the comparison between the story of Phylios' hunt and that of the collection of cinnamon centres on the couple formed by the eagle and the vulture. The significance of the mythical relation between spices and dead meat lies in the differences that separate the two birds of prey. We must therefore analyse the ethnographical and mythical representations of these two birds more closely.[81]

Throughout the Greek tradition, the vulture, like the eagle, is a bird from the heights: it builds its nest on inaccessible cliffs; no man can reach its lair nor discover its young.[82] Herodorus of Heraclea, the author of a Heracles story written in the fifth century B.C. drew from these facts the extreme conclusion that, given that nobody has ever seen a vulture's nest and that these birds of prey appear quite suddenly out of nowhere in the wake of armies, they must come from a different earth from ours, that is invisible to our eyes. According to Herodorus, this 'other earth' must be the moon which, following a Pythagorean tradition, he calls the 'aetherial earth'. In this Heracles story the vulture appears in the unusual guise of the 'most just of carnivorous creatures' (*dikaiótatos tôn sarkophágōn*). It is the most just, Herodorus claims, because it does no harm to crops or plants or to animals at pasture; it neither attacks nor kills any living thing and feeds only on corpses.[83] However, Herodorus' argument does not appear to have succeeded in gaining acceptance for this sophisticated image of the virtuous carrion-eating bird. For most Greeks the vulture remained the bird most detested both by gods and by men, the flying creature that Hermes and Ares inspired with an insatiable desire for the flesh and blood of men.[84] The vulture, consecrated to the god of war and to carnage, is not a bird of the heavens as the eagle is. The far-away place from which it appears is, rather, a sinister Beyond. In the Homeric Epic, there is no more horrible fate for a warrior than to hear his conqueror condemn him to be devoured raw by the carrion-eaters instead of being consigned to the desired flames of the funeral pyre: 'the birds that eat flesh raw shall tear you, shrouding you in the multitude of their wings.'[85] Because the vulture devours a man's corpse, it is more than simply an eater of dead flesh, it is a bird of death and a bloodthirsty predator. The excessive horror that it inspires in men places it both beyond and below the eagle which is also a bird from far away, but unlike the vulture, one that lives close to the Sun.

But it is not merely what they eat and where they live that differentiate the two birds of prey. They also differ widely in their positions on the axis constituted on the opposition between the fragrant and the rotten. The ornithological treatise attributed to Dionysus Periegeta notes that the eagle never touches any corpse except that of the animal it has just killed,[86] whereas it is said that the vulture arrives three days in advance on the scene where it will be able to eat its fill of carrion.[87] As soon as it has caught a whiff of putrefaction nothing can stop it, or rather nothing except a smell diametrically opposed to the first one: the fragrance of spices. The same ornithological treatise tells us that 'whereas vultures are delighted by the putrid smell of corpses, they detest perfumes (*múra*) so much that they would never touch a dead creature whose body was covered with spices'.[88] The carrion-eater's horror of perfumes corresponds exactly with his passion for corruption for, whereas the latter is a source of life and strength to it, spices are reputed to kill it on the spot. Conversely, for the eagle, contact with spices and perfumed oils is life-giving. One of Aesop's fables tells how the feathers of an eagle that had been ill-treated by a man who reduced it to the state of a farmyard bird grew anew when it was rubbed with myrrh.[89] For the bird from the heavens that has been transformed into a bird of Below spices provide a remedy as effective as the fire of the sun in the case where an ageing eagle approaches it in order to singe its feathers and so regain its youthful splendour.[90] The same contrast appears in parallel traditions concerning the marvellous properties of the feathers of each of these two predators. It is said that when eagles' feathers are placed in contact with those of other birds they make the latter wither and rot away, while they themselves undergo no change at all. It is as if, being so radically different in this way, the feathers of the eagle demonstrated the great distance between the bird from the heavens and all other flying creatures.[91] In contrast to this incorruptible plumage, the feathers of the vulture are the only ones which smell so foul when burnt that they attract reptiles, making them emerge from their holes.[92] There is a correspondence between the feathers of myrrh which clothe the eagle and the rotten plumage of the vulture which, here again, is seen as an inverted eagle.

	EAGLE	VULTURE
HABITAT	Above, near the sun	Beyond, in the other world
FOOD	Fresh meat	Carrion and what is rotten
SMELLS	Restored to life by spices	Killed by spices
PLUMAGE	The only incorruptible plumage	The plumage smells rotten enough to attract reptiles

Differential features of the Eagle and the Vulture

This relationship between the two birds of prey is confirmed in the representations of two other animals which find a place within the same schema, namely the snake and the dung beetle. While the snake adores the smell of the vulture it loathes the eagle, a sentiment that is mutual. The eagle and the snake are mortal enemies — according to Aristotle[93] because the eagle feeds on snakes, according to Pliny because the snake tries to destroy the eggs of the eagle.[94] As for the dung beetle or scarab, it forms a clearly defined triangle together with the eagle and the vulture. Its position is defined by several of its characteristics: the scarab, an insect with membranous wings, lives among filth and excrement; it cannot tolerate the smell of myrrh; finally, it is the enemy and rival of the eagle. All these features are mentioned in one of Aristophanes' comedies in which a scarab appears. In order to reach Olympus and the gods, Trygaios uses as his steed a giant dung beetle, a stinking creature which feeds on excrement and hibernates in a ball of filth.[95] When the scarab is about to take flight towards the heavens, its rider in pathetic tones begs the inhabitants of the earth to restrain themselves from evacuating their excrement: 'If my steed from on high gets wind of some putrid odour, it will head straight down to feed upon it'. There is only one way to neutralise the attaction of the stench.

'Dig it down in the ground, scatter perfumes around,
Heap, heap up the earth on the top,
Plant sweet wild thyme to encircle the mound,
Bring myrrh on its summit to drop.'[96]

Nothing fills the dung-beetle with so much horror as spices; myrrh is as fatal to it as to the vulture.[97] But the scarab seems not only to be like a chthonic vulture but also acts as an anti-eagle.[98] In the fable, the dung beetle, like the snake, seeks the eggs of the eagle in order to destroy them by making them roll out of the nest. As it is the sworn enemy of the eagle so it can also be its rival, for the reason why Trygaios uses a scarab to travel to Olympus is that he cannot find an eagle, the bird of Zeus having withdrawn in the company of the gods to the very furthest point on the dome of heaven.[99] There is one detail in this same play by Aristophanes that illustrates the degree of complicity operating in the rivalry between these two creatures: when Trygaios is about to bring back to earth with him *Opôra* and *Theōria*, the two deities of the Festival that he went to seek up in the heavens, he wonders where his steed is and is told by Hermes that the scarab has been promoted to the position of thunderbolt carrier and that it will henceforth feed upon the ambrosia of Ganymede.[100] The bird of excrement is transformed into its opposite and becomes a bird of spices, thus confirming in another way that the vulture is none other than an inverted eagle just as the latter is the reverse of an eater of carrion.

However, this inverse relationship of the two birds of prey should be judged against the background of the resemblances between them where the eagle and the vulture are so close as to appear to be confused with one another. Some classifications produced by ancient zoologists stress these affinities in order to distinguish intermediary species which have as much in common with the eagle as with the vulture. One such, for example, is the *perncopteros* described by Aristotle: this ˌis an eagle which resembles the vulture in that, because it has great difficulty in finding food, it carries carrion up to its eyrie.[101] Another bird classified in the *Historia Animalium* as half-way between the eagle and the vulture is the *phēnē*, known in Latin as the *ossifragus* and which has been identified since Cuvier as the Bearded Eagle or Bearded Vulture, better known as the Bearded *Gypaetus* or *Lämmergeyer*.[102] It is given this name by virtue of its peculiar hunting technique: if it sees a kid or other quadruped perched on the edge of a steep cliff, it swoops down upon it, knocking it off by its weight; it then glides down and tears its prey to pieces at its ease. This is the bone-breaker (*ostoklástēs*) or bone-crow (*ostokórax*) as it is called in a number of Latin glossaries.[103] The bearded *gypaetus*, half-eagle, half-vulture, combines the feeding habits of both birds of prey: it attacks living animals as does the eagle, but it devours its prey at the foot of a precipice like a true carrion-eater.

The same dual behaviour is a feature of the mythical birds that collect precious stones, in a story that appears in the *Treatise on the Twelve Gems*.[104] This story completes our comparative analysis of the myth about the collection of spices and the account of Phylios' hunt. In the desert of Great Scythia there is a very deep valley lying between rocky cliffs. Nobody can reach or even see the bottom of it. This is where the gems are to be found. In order to obtain them, the kings of the neighbouring regions employ the services of those who are condemned to death. These wretched men climb to the top of the mountains bordering the valley of precious stones, driving lambs before them. Once they have arrived at the edge of the precipice they slaughter the lambs and, having flayed them, hurl them into the abyss. The precious stones stick to the flesh that is still fresh and bleeding. The eagles nesting on the cliff tops are then attracted by this meat, descend to the bottom of the valley and bring the flayed lambs back up to their eyries. The condemned men have then only to seek out the eyries and, when the eagle has satisfied its hunger and abandoned its post, to appropriate the gems that have been left there among the bones. In collecting these precious stones the birds of the heights behave like vultures even though they belong to the eagle species. They are attracted not by living prey but by victims which, although freshly slaughtered, are nevertheless already more or less destined to rot. There is an obvious resemblance between this myth about collecting precious stones and the one about the collection of cinnamon. It is the more striking in that the precious stones picked up by the eagle-vultures are not jacinths, as the author of the Treatise seems to believe, but rather aetites or eagle stones,[105] as is proved in particular by their being so unaffected by the action of fire that they extinguish, through their own fiery strength, the lighted coals upon which they are placed.[106]

These three myths — about collecting cinnamon, gathering precious stones and hunting monstrous birds, all present the same structure. An apparently unbridgeable gap separates the men from Below, whether collectors or hunters, from the 'finery' of Above, whether these be spices or quarry-finery. In each case mediation is effected by a bird from the heights coming into contact with dead flesh. However, union between these two extremes is itself only made possible through a second mediation operating within the bird from the heights, this mythical creature in which we find a tension arising from the complementary opposition between an eagle from Above and a vulture from Below. In the myth about Phylios' hunt, this second mediation within the bird from the heights is repeated at the level of the human partner who has the double role of being both quarry and hunter and of being alive while yet being a corpse. In the story about the collection of cinnamon, the same mediation involving the ambivalence of wings of myrrh and wings of rotting matter, is further illustrated by a feature which appears to relate exclusively to the cunning of the collectors but which, in fact, serves to remind us of the significance of dead flesh at the very point when the latter is found in close proximity to spices. The hunks of meat break the nests made from spices but they do so not only because of their weight and size but also because dead flesh is something from Below and too strongly marked by its belonging to the world of death and corruption for it to remain Above, in the heavens where the spices are.

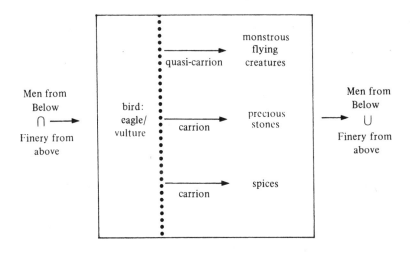

Structure of the three myths

This interplay of oppositions and mediations between antithetical terms is again to be found in the myth about a magic bird, the Phoenix.[107] The significant features of this bird form a circular framework which synthesises this entire area of the mythology of spices. In our study of the different versions of the myth about the collection of cinnamon, we have seen that the name of the bird from the heights, which was not mentioned by Herodotus, was given by Aristotle and Pliny in three forms: the cinnamon-bird, the 'cinnamologue' and the Phoenix.[108] This definition of the Phoenix as a flying creature from Above and a collector of spices is in complete agreement with the account of it that is given in Herodotus' description of Egypt.[109] It is not important that the Phoenix is a Greek transposition of the Bennu bird of the Egyptian

world[110] or that Herodotus has, for the first time, situated a
Greek Phoenix legend in Egypt.[111] The point is that when the
Phoenix makes its appearance in Greek thought, it is as a bird of
the Sun as well as of spices.

The Phoenix is a bird of the Sun in two ways, as is testified firstly
by the colours of its feathers: 'His plumage is partly golden, partly
red'.[112] In Greek colour terminology, *phoinix* means a reddish
purple, a purple which can, in some instances tend towards golden
and which indicates the most intense bright light.[113] But the links
between the Phoenix and the Sun are also revealed in the place that
it inhabits: the Phoenix only leaves the Land of the Arabs to travel
to the sanctuary of Helios or the Altar of the Sun. Throughout an
entire tradition, this connection with the fire of the sun appears in
one of two forms, each corresponding to one of two cycles, the one
a daily cycle and the other annual. In the former, the Phoenix is
closely associated with the course of the Sun and escorts it each
morning like a mobile screen protecting the earth from the burning
that it might otherwise inflict. In the latter, the Phoenix follows the
rhythm of the Sothic year, the Egyptian cycle originally of 1461
years, reduced to 500 years in Greco-Roman sources and defined
by the simultaneous occurrence of, on the one hand, the Heliacal
rising of Sirius (Sothis) and, on the other, the appearance of the sun
and the beginning of the Nile floods.[114]

The bird of the Sun must necessarily be a bird of spices, as the
myths that we have already examined show. From Herodotus to
Lactantius and Claudian, from the fifth century B.C. to the fourth
A.D., the Phoenix always possesses myrrh and frankincense, using
them to build its nest, even moving them from one place to
another, and finally being consumed on the pyre that it has built by
heaping together perfumed substances of all kinds.

All these features amply justify the Phoenix's constant
reputation of being a bird of extreme rarity. 'I myself have never
seen it, but only pictures of it' admits Herodotus.[115] But even if
it is the only representative of its species, the Phoenix cannot be
dissociated from the other winged creatures that we have
considered and whose reciprocal relationships we have defined in
the course of our study of the myths about spices, namely the eagle,
the bat, and the vulture. It is only within this system of meanings
that we can decipher a whole series of details in the myth of the
Phoenix, the unique bird whose identity never changes. Some of

these details are connected with the Phoenix's relations with the eagle while others have to do with its peculiar metamorphosis into a worm.

Herodotus writes that the shape and size of the Phoenix are exactly comparable with those of the eagle.[116] The comparison is borne out by the status of the eagle which not only dwells in the heavens but also has a fiery nature and has certain affinities with the fire of Above. The eagle, as fire-bearer, *purphóros*[117], is characterised by its ability to look straight at the sun. Some Greek naturalists even claimed this to be the test by which the eagle assures itself of the nature of its offspring. It was said that there is one kind of eagle that forces its young, even before their feathers have grown, to look fixedly at the sun. If any one of them refuses to do so the eagle by its blows forces it to face the sun and if the young bird's eyes start to water, the parent kills it. The eagle will only rear the young birds which pass the test and thus qualify themselves to be future eagles.[118] In a more humorous tradition, the fiery nature of the eagle is also indicated by the fact that if it did not take care to place a particular stone said to be extremely cold among the eggs it is hatching, there would be a danger of turning them into hard-boiled eggs since its natural temperature is so high.[119]

Nevertheless, the affinities the eagle has with the fire from Above are not sufficient to make it the Phoenix's rival. The eagle is, without doubt, the largest, the most powerful and the highest of birds but its royalty is called into question as soon as the Phoenix makes its appearance. When this happens the eagle, followed by the falcon, places itself at the head of the procession all the birds form to accompany the Phoenix wherever it may go.[120] The distance between these two birds from Above is indicated in the first place by certain details in the process of renewal for which both periodically feel the need, despite the exceptional longevity they both enjoy. When the eagle grows old, its body becomes heavy and its wings can support it only with difficulty. When this happens, in order to escape the attraction that the world Below increasingly exerts upon it, it is said to gather its strength and soar upward towards the 'heaven of the Sun' where it approaches the Sun in order to burn its feathers:[121] 'Its old age derives new vigour from this change in its plumage'.[122] The fire of the Sun is as effective as myrrh in rescuing the eagle from the decadence which has transformed it into a chthonic flying creature.[123]

The example of the Phoenix demonstrates this even more clearly. Throughout a tradition from Statius to Claudian the decline of the Phoenix is recognised by the same symptoms as that of the eagle: it grows heavy, sclerosis threatens and its wings 'which formerly cleft the clouds' are barely strong enough to lift it from the ground.[124] The Phoenix is no longer able to follow the course of the sun nor reach it at its zenith. It can barely flutter along at ground level. Like the eagle it is reduced to the status of the bat. And, again, the remedy is the same: only the perfumed flame of spices can restore the full vigour of the Phoenix who has been separated further and further from the Sun by the progressive onset of old age.

This cycle of transformation through which the eagle and the Phoenix both pass also reveals the differences between the two birds. There are three main differences, relating to length of life, degree of combustion and type of food and all of them reveal the Phoenix to be a super-eagle. Whereas the eagle's life span is not more than a hundred years, the Phoenix lives for five hundred or a thousand.[125] Similarly, whereas the eagle merely has its feathers burned by the Sun, the Phoenix must be utterly reduced to ashes; the one is singed while the other is burned to a cinder.[126] The difference between these two kinds of burning corresponds to the relationship that each of these two birds has with spices: the eagle only needs to be rubbed with an ointment of myrrh, while all the most precious spices must be heaped together when the Phoenix is cremated. A kind of identity of substance exists between the Phoenix and spices to which the bird's entire behaviour bears witness. When the end of its life draws near, the Phoenix makes for the hottest regions of the earth (Arabia, Ethiopia, Heliopolis), there to construct the nest that will serve as a pyre, either in some high place at the top of huge trees or else close to the city of the Sun. Lying on a heap of spices and very dry wood, the bird bursts into flames either because of the heat generated within the spices which catch fire of their own accord or as a result of the direct action of the fire of the Sun which the Phoenix has longed for and sought to be near.[127] Although these two methods of cremation appear to be different they form a single type: whether the flame comes from the Sun or is generated from the spices, what it manifests is the fiery power of perfumed substances. It is thus possible to counter objections brought against this interpretation on the grounds that it does not take account of the history of the myth or of the changing forms of the legend. It was long ago noticed that there was until the first century A.D. no tradition that described the process by which the spice bird regenerated itself and that the image of the perfumed pyre on which the Phoenix is consumed and then reborn from itself does not appear until Martial, Pliny the Elder and Solinus.[128] This long silence led some historians to distinguish two phases in the history of the Phoenix myth: they hold that before it became the bird on the pyre it was simply a bird connected with spices.[129] But this distinction is a gratuitous one as our whole enquiry proves. The increasing importance of the pyre in the Phoenix myth is sufficiently explained by the development, at the beginning of the Roman Empire, of a politico-religious ideology associating the deification of the Emperor with the custom of cremation.[130]

One further point confirms that the Phoenix is indeed a super-eagle: the food on which it lives. Whereas the eagle feeds on the animals that it hunts, the Phoenix has a quite exceptional diet. It eats no ordinary fruits or plants.[131] According to some writers it eats nothing at all: 'Nobody has ever seen it take any food', writes the Roman senator, Manilius, who devoted an entire book to the bird.[132] Others believe that the Phoenix eats only magical foods: the purest rays of the Sun, the ethereal mists blown by the sea breezes,[133] or the drops formed by frankincense and from the sap of *amonne*.[134] Like those who lived in the Golden Age and the beings which subsist on super-foods,[135] the Phoenix produces no excrement at all except 'a worm which turns into the cinnamon used by kings and princes', as Pseudo-Baruch writes.[136]

This transformation from excrement to perfumes is not as surprising as it seems. The link is established by the go-between in the form of a larva which appears as the natural consequence of the cremation of the Phoenix. We know this from a series of accounts which fall within the same semantic field as those already mentioned, to which they form an exact counterpart. All the versions, from Manilius to Lactantius, follow the same pattern: within the ashes of the bird consumed by the spices a worm is formed which grows and becomes a Phoenix. To explain the presence of this lowly insect in the Phoenix myth, J. Hubaux and M. Leroy have appealed to the possible assimilation in Greek thought between the Phoenix bird and the word 'phoenix' used to denote the date-palm (*phoînix*).[137] They suggest that the worm is simply a transposed and corrupt memory of the small fly held to be responsible for the artificial fertilisation of the date-palm. According to Herodotus, the fruit of the male palm trees, like those of wild fig trees, carries within it a small fly which enters the dates and makes them ripen without making them fall.[138] However, this insect cannot be confused with the worm which, before assuming the gold and purple plumage of the Phoenix, passes through a series of states which together trace a precise path leading from the Below to the Above.

According to Manilius, the bones and marrow of the Phoenix that died amid the spices produce a kind of worm which turns into first a fledgling and then a fully grown Phoenix.[139] In Apollonius, the worm which appears in the ashes already resembles the Phoenix: as soon as its wings have grown large enough[140] or as soon as the Sun has warmed it[141], the insect flies off towards the Sun. The worm and the fledgling mediate between the ashes and the new Phoenix. But there are two more versions to enrich this model. In Lactantius' poem on the Phoenix, the worm is only formed in the ashes once nature has made them damp and fertilised them.[142] The *Physiologus of Vienna* gives further details: three days and three nights after the burning of the Phoenix and the spices a winged worm appears; it flies away from the high rock on which the Phoenix built its nest 'outside our world and close to the Ocean'. The winged worm flies to the Ocean shore and there it lives for some time 'drawing its subsistance from the wet and the dry'.[143] The two versions are complementary: in one a wet element appears and fertilises the charred remains of the old Phoenix while in the second, the winged worm that has emerged from the ashes develops and grows by feeding upon the wet and the dry, before becoming the new Phoenix. The mediations between the two extremes are expressed sometimes in zoological terms (the worm, the fledgling) and sometimes in terms of 'elementary' qualities (wet, dry and wet, dry), and these terms form two, parallel, graduated scales between the two extremes.

A final version in the same series, which includes most of the above-mentioned features, completes this interaction of the worm and the Phoenix. Here the transformation of corruption into its opposite shows that the relationship between the two creatures takes a circular form. In the account given by Clement of Rome, the sun bird lies down to die on a nest of frankincense and myrrh.

Its flesh rots (*sēpoménēs tês sarkós*) and from the corruption emerges a worm which feeds upon the humour (*ikmás*) of the corpse from which it was born, and gradually becomes covered with feathers. When it is full grown the Phoenix seizes the nest containing the remains of its father and heads for Heliopolis where, in broad daylight, in the sight of all, it lays its burden on the altar of sun and then returns to Arabia and its perfumes.[144] It is clear, therefore, that in this version the worm born from the putrefaction finds within it the wet vital element, thanks to which the insect takes on the size and plumage of the Phoenix. The spice bird is produced from the putrefaction in which a worm grows just as, similarly, it is from the Phoenix at the end of its life that the worm and putrefaction are produced. Furthermore, this same account which emphasises the aromatic nature of the container (the nest) within which the putrefaction produces a worm, clearly refers back to a version of the myth about the collection of cinnamon which we have not yet mentioned. In this, the twigs of the cinnamon tree, which are broken into tiny pieces, are sewn into a freshly flayed skin where the putrefaction gives birth to worms which eat away the wood but leave the bark intact because of its sour and bitter taste.[145] But the comparison between these two stories is above all important in this context because of the differences that it reveals. In the cinnamon myth the worm is what marks the radical separation between what is rotten and the spices, while in the other account the same insect shows where putrefaction and spices become identical in the course of the two-way transformations effected between the Phoenix and the worm.

If the Phoenix is a super-eagle, it is also an infra-vulture, and these accounts of the metamorphosis of a larva into a Phoenix are simply the converse of those in which the bird is degraded into a kind of bat.[146] From its birth to its rebirth then the Phoenix accomplishes a complete cycle in a double movement between two extreme terms representing opposite poles, in the tension between which is comprised the entire body of spice myths.[147]

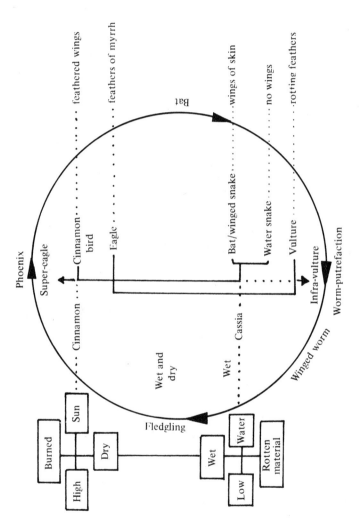

The Cycle of the Phoenix

II
The Spice Ox

Spices, which are the product of an exceptional union between the earth and the fire of the sun, are a gift of wild nature. Men take possession of this gift using methods whose purpose is to mediate between the near and the far-away and to link the above and the below. Although some of these aromatic plants are really cultivated species, in the eyes of the Greeks, who knew them as products brought from far away, they were plants which needed no cultivation; they only had to be collected. In the Greek world, where spices were used from the seventh century B.C.[1], their functions were threefold: culinary, religious and erotic. They were natural plants that were held to be 'beyond' cultivated plants and were only eaten in the form of seasonings or condiments. Minute amounts of these substances were sufficient to flavour large quantities of either food or drink. However, although many kinds of spices were used as flavouring in ancient Greek cooking[2], those of the frankincense and myrrh type were used almost exclusively[3] either for making ointments and perfumes or else in sacrifices that were part of the worship of the divine powers.

There is a frankincense myth that enables us to identify one significance of spices in the context of these cults. In order to get her revenge against the Sun who has unmasked her illegitimate love affairs, Aphrodite makes him fall in love with Leucothoë, the daughter of Orchamos, king of the Persians, who rules over the Land of Spices.[5] He, however, is furious that the Sun should have had the effrontery to sleep with his daughter and so decides to put Leucothoë out of reach of her lover and his designs upon her. He buries her in a deep trench which he has covered over with sand. By the time the Sun tries to rescue her, it is too late: his rays are

powerless to revive the girl. The Sun then covers Leucothoë's body
with fragrant nectar, and promises her that despite everything she
shall rise to the skies.

'Straightway the body, soaked with the celestial nectar, melted
away and filled the earth around with its sweet fragrance. Then
did a shrub of frankincense, with deep-driven roots, rise slowly
through the soil and its top cleared the mound.'

The punishment that the father inflicts upon the seduced daughter
whom he desires to separate from her lover and consign to the
position furthest removed from the Sun is matched by the
metamorphosis of the body that had been consigned to corruption
into its opposite. It becomes an aromatic plant whose product,
being born of the Sun and destined to be reunited with him, makes
it possible for the lover and his mistress to be together once again,
even more closely united than previously. From this time on the
spices — frankincense in this case — are invested with the privilege
of uniting the Below with the Above.

Such is the significance of the offerings of frankincense and
myrrh with which the ritual of a blood sacrifice opens in Greece. As
is noted by an ancient commentator, the 'scholiast' of the orator,
Aeschines, 'the purpose of the spices is to attract the gods'.[6]
Frankincense and myrrh which are thrown into the sacrificial fire in
the form of little loaves or finely ground grains, establish a
communication between two worlds that are necessarily separate
from each other: the world of men and the world of gods. Far from
their purpose being simply to offset the unpleasant smell of burnt
meat and fat, the vapour from the burning spices[7] represents an
essential aspect of the Greek sacrifice, as is proved by the
importance of the concepts of smoke and of smell in the most
ancient representations of the worship of divine powers.[8] A
whole series of words which are part of the technical terminology
connected with sacrifice are constructed on the root *thu which
forms a semantic group including *thúō, thusía, thúos,* and which
expresses the all-important role played by fire and smoke in
conveying offerings to the seat of the gods. Thus it has been noted
that one of the most ancient terms used in the Homeric epic to refer
to offerings to the gods, namely *thúos* (plural, *thúea*) originally had
the sense of 'substance burned in order to obtain fragrant
smoke'.[9]

These linguistic points are fully borne out by the evidence of the
'antiquarians' who, in effect, developed a whole theory of sacrifice
at the end of the fourth century B.C. Theophrastus' treaty *On piety*

mentions that, long before spices were introduced into Greece, the most archaic type of sacrifice consisted in burning pungent shrubs. This is proved, he claims, by the custom of selecting perfumed essences as fuel which was still observed by his contemporaries in certain rituals.[19] According to Philichorus of Athens[11], a diviner, interpreter of omens and expert on sacrificial practices, it was 'thyme' (*thúmos*) that was burned in the most ancient of sacrifices, the *nēphália*, in which there was no libation of wine nor any burning of the wood of the vine or of the fig-tree. The only reason why it should have been 'thyme' — which in Greek denotes a type of savory[12] — in preference to the cedar[13] or the bay or even the barley meal that Plutarch[14] says the ancient Pytho used to burn on the altar of Apollo, was that the name *thúmos* clearly makes it out to be the shrub most likely to produce the smoke (*thumiân*) that is the basic principle underlying the act of sacrifice.[15]

In that the perfume of the spices burned on the altars establishes a vertical line of communication between men and gods, its role is apparently similar to that of the pungent smoke from the fatty meat[16] burned in honour of the Olympians. In Lucian's *Icarominippus* Zeus's workroom has a floor pierced with openings covered by circular lids. When the Father of the gods lifts one of these lids he listens carefully to the names borne on the smoke of those who are making offerings to him, while he blows angrily on wisps of smoke that bring him evil prayers, thus denying them entry to Olympus.[17] An identical model of communication is crucial to one of the Aristophanes' comedies.[18] When the birds, at Pisthertairos' instigation decide to seize power over the world from the gods of Olympus, the immediate prize for which they are fighting is the smoke from the sacrifices as much as the perfume of the spices. Once Pisthetairos has succeeded in persuading the birds to found a city half-way between the earth and heaven, in between the men and the gods, he forbids the inhabitants of earth to send up the slightest wisp of smoke to the gods through the city of the birds. Not a whiff of meat can henceforth reach Olympus. Prometheus is sent in secret to tell mankind that the gods are 'as during the Thesmophoria': deprived of offerings and compelled to fast.[19] The blockade is successful. Zeus is forced to grant the birds *Basileía* or sovereignty. Now, at the moment when Pisthetairos, celebrating his marriage to *Basileía*, advances dazzling as a star, bearing a thunderbolt in one hand and leading Sovereignty with the other, then, at that very instant 'an ineffable fragrance ascends to the highest vault of heaven and light winds scatter the wreathes of incense'.[20] Communication between the Below and the Above is reestablished; the smell of spices takes over from the fumes of the burning meat which the new kings of heaven can well do without.

The fragrance of spices and the aroma of meat were mixed up with one another to the point where they were more or less indistinguishable in the practice of daily sacrifice, yet they did not have exactly the same significance. In order to define the difference between them and thus establish an essential aspect of spices we must digress to consider the dietary system adopted by one particular social group. Thanks to the marginal position of this group in the Greek world we find certain contrasts emphasised and are able to discern oppositions often undetectable in other contexts. In the Pythagorean sect we find a system of representations of the various food-stuffs.[21] Its complex network of relationships enables us to see how the position of spices varied in relation to a series of natural products. The Pythagorean sect was founded at the end of the sixth century BC in the city of Croton in Magna Graecia.[22] It was, simultaneously, a religious sect, a political group and a philosophical enclave, distinguished by a number of characteristics one of the more peculiar of which was their adherence to a strict food diet.[23] Right up till the time of Plutarch dietary taboos were automatically taken to suggest a disciple of Pythagoras.[24] Most foodstuffs were divided into groups, some being good to eat while the rest were strictly forbidden. Rather than merely see in these strange taboos and customs 'the debris of a folk-lore in which there is nothing to be understood', as a historian of philosophy once put it[25], we can try to show that the selection of some foodstuffs and rejection of others were complementary features of a unified system whose meaning cannot be understood except in the context of the social group that, throughout its history, preached and practised adherence to these diets.

At the end of the fourth century B.C., there was a controversy between the two historians best informed about Pythagoreanism, over the question of whether or not Pythagoras and his disciples ate animal flesh. It shows clearly that the problem of diet was a fundamental one.[26] Timaeus of Tauromenium, the historian of Sicily and Magna Graecia, is responsible for the tradition according to which Pythagoras refused to eat meat and at the same time rejected all blood sacrifice. In Timaeus' work, this account of a vegetarian Pythagoras appears to be closely connected with his veneration for the altar to Apollo *Genétōr* at Delos[27], an altar upon which no animal victim could be sacrificed. In fact, several informants associate the prohibition of meat as a food and the rejection of all blood-shedding sacrifice closely together. Iamblichus writes that Pythagoras abstained from eating meat and respected altars that were not tainted with blood. And here the refusal to eat meat follows on from the prohibition against sacrificing (*thúein*) animals in honour of the gods, which Iamblichus had just mentioned.[28] In a similar prohibition reported by Diogenes Laertius[29], the eating of meat is not even mentioned; it is blood sacrifice that is strictly forbidden. Moreover, it is forbidden in terms that betray a kind of horror. The technical term used is *sphágia*[30], reserved for sacrifices in which blood is the principal offering, and it is intended in this context to emphasise the equivalence between sacrifice and murder. It is again Diogenes who confirms and pinpoints the Phythagoreans' attitude to the slaughter of animals: he reports that Pythagoras forbade his disciples to *phoneúein*[31] which means, literally, to commit a murder. Now here the master is not attempting to discourage his disciples from shedding the blood of a citizen or a relation but rather from lifting a hand against animals 'who share with us the right to live and who possess a soul'. To eat meat is to commit murder, *phoneúein*. The equivalence between the two terms is so strong that, according to Eudoxus of Cnidus, Pythagoras refused any contact with cooks and hunters, considering both categories to be criminals, *phoneúontes*.[32] This threefold refusal — to eat the flesh of animals, to offer blood sacrifice and to shed the blood of living creatures[33] — is counter-balanced, in Pythagorean circles, by an obligation to offer to the gods sacrifices in which no blood is shed, *thusíai anaímaktoi*, and to present them with simple and pure offerings[34]: figurines made from barley-cake (*psaistà*), honeycombs (*kēría*) and frankincense (*libanótón*). These are the offerings Pythagoras encourages the women of Croton to make with their own hands instead of honouring the gods with blood and murder.[35] All of them fall into the same category as the ritual gifts of wheat, barley and cakes which are proper to the altar that Pythagoras most respects, that of Apollo *Genétōr* at Delos.[36] In both cases they are diametrically opposed to the animal victims used for blood sacrifice.

Timaeus' picture of a vegetarian Pythagoras is in strong opposition to the account of the Pythagoreans given by the musicologist, Aristoxenus of Tarentum. Aristoxenus describes the type of life led by the latest members of the first brotherhood, those at Plius whom he claims to have known personally.[37] While on the subject of the communal meals — the *syssities* — he gives a detailed account of the kind of foods the Pythagoreans ate together.[38] Included in the menu for the principal meal, the *deîpnon*, along with the wine, the barley bread, *mâza*, the wheaten bread, *ártos*, a seasoning, *ópson*, and cooked and raw vegetables, Aristoxenus mentions animal meats referred to as *thúsima* meaning that they were suitable for sacrifice and for eating.[39] Aristoxenus refers on several occasions to the Pythagoreans' tolerance of meat: he describes Pythagoras as living on young kids and sucking pigs[40], and elsewhere declares that he enjoyed eating all kinds of meat with the exceptions of the flesh of sheep and of working oxen.[41] These meat-eating Pythagoreans are also described by Aristotle as 'abstaining from eating the womb and heart of animals ... but they eat everything else'.[42] Plutarch also mentions them in his *Table Talk*, saying that they admit to being meat-eaters, especially on the occasions of sacrifices.[43] They are also described as the group known as *'acousmaticoi'* or *'politicoi'* whom Pythagoras advises to make sacrifices, although not in excess, and to offer less important animals but never the ox.[44]

In thus attributing two different diets to the Pythagoreans, Greek fourth century historiography was simply transposing into a kind of debate the ambiguity of a truly Pythagorean tradition in which there are two conflicting figures, the master and his first disciple: on the one hand Pythagoras of Samos who fed exclusively upon strange substances 'which suppressed hunger and thirst', and on the other Milo of Croton whose exploits as a meat-eater were well-known throughout Greece. Both types of diet belong to a single type of social behaviour.[45] When Pythagoras settled in Magna Graecia in about 530 Milo was one of the most important figures in the city of Croton.[46] Not only was he a member of one of the most powerful families [47], but he was also both a priest of Hera of Lacinia, the guardian deity of Croton[48], and a famous athlete who had several times been victor at the great games in Greece.[49] In the aristocratic manner, he entered into a close relationship with the founder of the Pythagorean movement: he is said to have married Pythagoras' daughter[50], and he became one of the eminent members of the sect.[51] Now, this prominent Pythagorean stands in violent contrast to the philosopher from Samos in a number of ways, his diet being, on the face of it, the most surprising example. Whereas Pythagoras is received in Croton as a 'holy man' (*theîos anér*), passing for another Hyperborean

Apollo living on magical foods, Milo of Croton, in contrast, was well-known throughout antiquity for his exceptionally huge appetite. When Aristotle wants to quote an example of a man who eats to excess Milo naturally comes to mind.[52] His main gastronomic exploits are recounted in the *Deipnosophists* by Athenaeus.[53] On a single day he consumed more than ten kilos of meat and an equal quantity of bread and drained more than ten litres of wine. At Olympia, where he was six times victor in the games, he once lifted on his shoulders a four year old bull, carried it round the stadium, sacrificed the animal and then, totally unaided, consumed the entire creature down to the last mouthful. On another occasion he made a similar meal, seated comfortably at the altar of Zeus, as the result of a bet.

Milo's gluttony could be taken to be purely anecdotal. But this would be to overlook one essential aspect of this character, his Heraclean quality, that is made quite clear by his social status and his impact on the history of his city.[54] At Croton Milo acts as priest of Hera of Lacinia, the guardian deity and warlike power, *hoplosmia*,[55] whose cult is closely linked with that of Heracles. This is why, in 510, at a pitched battle between Croton and Sybaris, Milo appeared at the head of the city's troops disguised as Heracles, wearing a lion skin and holding a club.[56] In this context the significance of the appetite for meat of Pythagoras' son-in-law becomes clear: it exemplifies eating habits worthy of Heracles, a voracious appetite which can bear comparison with the *boulimia* of the hero who was taken as a model for the priest of Hera. Furthermore, Milo's eating habits cannot be dissociated from his warlike activities in Croton, in which he follows the example of Heracles associated with Hera *hoplosmia*. It is as a warrior that Milo leads the men of Croton to victory against the Sybarites. He is the war leader not only by virtue of his position as priest to the divine warrior-protectress of the city but also because he is a member of the aristocracy which are the traditional holders of political power. Milo is at the same time a great eater, a famous athlete, a victorious warrior and an exceptional citizen and he holds a central position in the Pythagorean movement as is shown clearly enough by the selection of his home as the seat for the deliberations that Pythagoras and his disciples engaged in concerning the affairs of the city.[57]

Milo of Croton's eating habits are an integral part of this character who is both athlete and warrior and at the same time Pythagorean and citizen. This leads us to consider a type of behaviour which is no doubt very different from that of Pythagoras but which nevertheless characterises a whole other side of Pythagoreanism, in which the members of the sect appear this time not as a circle of ascetics subjected to rules of holiness orientated towards the purification of the soul but as an action group engaged in politics and bent on introducing reform into the city. Pythagoras is the extatic Magus, the sage seeking purification, eating only supernatural foods; Milo, on the other hand, is the active citizen, the man of war, the robust meat-eater; and the opposition between these two types of behaviour reveals two different orientations of Pythagoreanism which may appear contradictory but which are, at a deeper level, complementary. On the one hand we have an insistence on individual salvation, on the other a desire to reform the city; on the one hand an introspective religious sect comprising the Three Hundred Pythagoreans living on the margins of society and of the city, on the other a society in which political careers are possible: the Two Thousand Crotonians whom, according to one tradition, Pythagoras at one stroke converted and won over to his project of political and religious reform.[58]

The choice between eating meat and vegetarianism involves more than just a diet. For the Pythagoreans what they ate was a way of accepting or renouncing the world. What, in fact, did eating or not eating meat mean to a Greek? In a society in which the consumption of meat was inseparable from the practice of making blood sacrifices — a practice which constituted the most important ritual action in the state religion — the refusal to eat meat cannot be regarded as a purely personal form of eccentricity or one confined to eating habits. On the contrary, it implies a wholesale rejection of an entire system of values which found expression in a particular type of communication between gods and the world of men.[59] Behind blood sacrifice there lies an ideology whose main features need to be outlined. It is not by chance that, in Aristophanes' *Birds*, it is Prometheus who comes to tell Pisthetairos, the founder of Cloud-Cuckoo-Land, about the straits to which the gods are reduced as a result of the 'Thesmophoric' fast imposed upon them by the birds' blockade. As the inventor of the fire used in cooking and of the sacrificial meal, it was Prometheus who was responsible for the first distribution and for the beginning of the separation of gods and men. On the day when, at Mekone[60], he distributed the shares from the first sacrificial animal, Prometheus established the diet which differentiates men and gods. To men, whom he wished to favour, the Titan allotted the best share, all the meat from the huge ox, leaving to the gods only the smells rising from the burned fats and roasting meat. In making this unfair allocation Prometheus was unconsciously recognising the vital need for the human species to eat meat. He was fulfilling the will of Zeus who condemned men to experience hunger and death. Similarly, by allotting to the Olympians only the bones and fat, thus leaving them nothing but the smoke and smells, the first sacrificer was consecrating the superiority of the Immortals over their human partners. Since the need to eat is in inverse proportion to vital energy and since Hunger and Death are seen as twin brothers, the gods demonstrate their supernatural condition by insisting upon super-foods which are inaccessible to creatures of flesh and blood who can no more live on the smell of meat alone than subsist on the perfume of myrrh and frankincense.

By their refusal to eat meat the Pythagoreans were, like the Orphics, rejecting the original allocation which defined the human condition by setting it in opposition to that of the gods. Simultaneously they placed themselves outside the city[61] all of whose religious practices, inextricably bound up with political activity, were organised around this primary relationship between men and gods. However, unlike the Orphics whose behaviour was confined to pure renunciation, the Pythagoreans assumed two different attitudes to blood sacrifice and in social practice they accepted both types of diet equally. Food that is meat and food that is not meat: the opposition here seems to be sufficiently important to provide the clue to an understanding of the system of Pythagorean foods in which myrrh and frankincense are two essential terms.

In the first place, a whole section of the Pythagorean diet is based on their refusal to kill, sacrifice and eat animals. It is a threefold refusal expressing one and the same renunciation of sacrificial meat. This is the starting point from which there evolved a number of types of eating habits answering the need for a regimen that did not open up insurmountable distance between men and gods but which aimed, in various ways, to establish a real fellowship between the two parties, a true *syssitie* as the Pythagoreans themselves would call it.[62] The principal ways of eating with or like the gods are revealed in the composition of the so-called 'pure' sacrifices made each day by the members of the order. The canonical offerings were either pure cereals or spices.[63] The latter were myrrh and frankincense, the former wheat, barley and millet or barley meal and paste cakes. The cereals were placed on the altar without being burned[64] while the spices were consumed in flames. The true significance of these two types of customary sacrificial offering only becomes apparent when we compare other mythical material, a body of data concerning both the foodstuffs peculiar to Pythagoras and the model sacrifice that he is said to have made to Apollo. At Delos there was an altar to Apollo *Genétōr* on which it was forbidden to make any animal sacrifice. It was said that here Pythagoras placed barley, wheat and cakes, the offerings that befitted the ritual for Apollo Genétōr.[65] These offerings, placed on the altar to Apollo were not merely 'simple and natural' but, in this ritual at Delos, were held to be 'souvenirs and specimens of primitive foods'. Plutarch[66] who gives us this information adds that as well as wheat, barley and cakes Apollo was offered mallow and asphodel, two plants that — we are elsewhere told — the Pythagoreans valued exceptionally highly and believed to be 'primitive foods'. All the traditions connected with Apollo *Genétōr* indicate clearly that this was a power who generously provided the fruits of the earth: Apollo *Genétōr* was considered a 'dispensor of fruits' (*karpôn dotḗr*).[67]. The Delian myth of the *Oinotropoi* provides an illustration of his bounteous provision of food. Anius, who is the son of Apollo, is a mythical king whose three daughters have the power of making nature's products appear at will. Oino dispenses wine, Spermo provides cereals and Elais makes the oil flow. They are powers from the Golden Age, deities who assure for men an abundance of food ready to eat while they, for their part, need make no effort at all.[68] Like the *Oinotropoi*, Apollo *Genétōr* rules over mankind's Golden Age.[69] He guarantees civilised life in its earliest form at a time when the earth makes its products grow spontaneously for men, offering them fruits that are 'natural', *autophuḗs*, growing of their own accord without the intervention of the technique of agriculture and without any need for hard labour on the part of men. True, to us these products of the Golden Age — cereals such as wheat and barley and plants such as the mallow and the asphodel — seem to be two different types of food, the former being cultivated and the latter wild. Nevertheless in the mythical thought reflected in this evidence concerning Delos they were considered as products of the same kind; here, the wheat and barley are, like the mallow and asphodel, spontaneous fruits of the earth, foods that are perfectly 'cooked' and that men can eat directly without using fire to prepare them. Thus the Pythagoreans considered the ritual offerings to Apollo *Genétōr* as a paradigm: they represented the foods that men once used to share equally with the gods.[70] Clearly, in the age of the city, when oxen were used for ploughing, cereals could not entirely retain their status as natural products of the Golden Age and as food common to both gods and men. For this reason it was rather the mallow and the asphodel that the Pythagoreans considered as perfect foods. These two plants which can be eaten in their wild state[71] play a large part in the composition of the *álima* and the *ádipsa*, the foods which can suppress hunger and thirst, the super-foods which it was the privilege of the extatic magi such as Pythagoras, Epimenides and Abaris to consume. Epimenides' refusal to eat like other men went hand in hand with the need to eat like the gods. Each day this famous purifier took nothing but a kind of pill which prevented him from experiencing either thirst or hunger.[72] Now this astonishing food was composed of a mixture of mallow and asphodel, both plants whose magical qualities had been discovered by Epimenides while taking part, as Pythagoras had also done, in the sacrifice in honour of Apollo *Genétōr*.[73] According to Pythagorean tradition these *álima* and *áeipsa* are regarded as substitutes for human foods, revealed by the gods themselves. Demeter, the food-producing power, was held to have invented them in order to make it possible for Heracles to cross the desert and reach Libya.[74] Although in this instance the preparation of these substances seems more complex[75] and involves several types of seeds (poppy, sesame, cucumber, etc.), cereals (barley and wheat), and even a particular local cheese, the leaves of the mallow and of the asphodel still play an important part in the composition of these foods which suppress hunger and thirst. Pythagoras was held to have lived on them, especially during the long visits that he paid to the gods, in caves and caverns.[76]

In the diet of the Pythagoreans, mallow and asphodel, together with cereals, are an important aspect in the art of eating like the gods where the Pythagoreans combined several religious ideas connected with the Golden Age. Both plants are specimens of the very earliest food and are spontaneously produced by the earth. They are placed upon the altar of Apollo in the purest of sacrifices and eaten by holy men whose style of life enables them to get back to the Golden Age.

Alongside the pure cereals which, as we have seen, are connected with the mallow and the asphodel, the Pythagoreans would offer another type of sacrifice to the gods: spices, namely frankincense and myrrh. Although they are closely associated in ritual the difference between the cereals and the spices might seem considerable. Not only are cereals offered up without being burned while spices have to be consumed in the flames but furthermore the former are plants cultivated by men as their principal food while the latter are the products of wild nature, inedible by men and, as it were, reserved for the gods. But these differences become insignificant as soon as the spice offerings are interpreted according to the model we have already used in connection with plants used as food. We must refer to certain mythical traditions concerning the foodstuffs used by the Pythagoreans. Alongside the stories about the *álima* and the *ádipsa* we must consider the Pythagorean legends about the exceptional beings who live on smells and effluvia. There is evidence in Aristotle's *De Sensu*[77] that the Pythagoreans were interested in this kind of nourishment and a whole set of texts produced by the ancient Academy and summarised by Plutarch in his *Dialogues*[78] describes strange beings who neither eat nor drink: they are the inhabitants of the moon, an aetherial earth, people without mouths (*ástomoi*) who feed on smells alone. They are daemonic creatures whose feeding habits these traditions explicitly compare with those of Epimenides.[79] Here we can glimpse another schema, parallel to that of the mallow and the asphodel, in which the spice foods of certain superhuman beings correspond to the sacrifices of frankincense and myrrh made by the Pythagoreans.

Spices answer even better than mallow and asphodel to the religious needs of the Pythagoreans. They are food for the gods as are ambrosia and nectar and furthermore they are a constituent element in the nature of the gods. Anything in any way connected with the Olympians, — altars, temples, clothes, — is fragrantly perfumed.[80] Just as flashing eyes, majestic stature or youthful limbs denote the divine to the Greeks, a sweet smell, *euōdía*, is a specific feature of the gods, a sign of their supernatural condition. The most delicious perfumes emanate from the powers of life which dwell on Olympus just as, conversely, the powers of death give off a nauseous smell. We have an example in the stench given off by the demon Harpies (sometimes associated with vultures[81]) when they swoop from the skies and befoul the food set on Phineas' table, leaving to the guilty king as they depart nothing but a revolting smell of corruption and putrefaction.[82] Thus when men allow the smoke from their sacrifices of myrrh and frankincense to rise up to heaven they are, in a way, simply returning to the world of the Olympians those substances which are most intimately related with the powers from Above. There is a whole current of fourth century pietist thought which reveals yet another reason why the Pythagoreans valued sacrifices of spices so highly; frankincense and myrrh are the gifts most acceptable to the hearts of the gods because, once consumed in the flames, they belong to them wholly and utterly, leaving nothing to be shared.[83] It is here that the difference between the smoke from spices and the smoke from other sacrifices shows most clearly: on the one hand the smell from the roasting meats appears as the most manifest sign of the circumstances of the original allocation of shares[84], and the odours from the sacrifice rising straight up simply emphasise the distance that separates the world of men from the world of gods so radically; on the other, the smells from frankincense and myrrh represent for the Pythagoreans a type of sacrifice in which the super-foods establish a genuine commensality between men and gods.

These parallel traditions relating to pure cereals, to mallow and asphodel, and to frankincense and myrrh thus reveal the entire system of dietary and sacrificial practices all of which, in the context of Pythagoreanism are expressions of the same absolute refusal to eat meat. Of the three types of vegetable products — cereals, 'wild' plants and perfumed species which, in the Pythagorean system, represent three forms of anti-meat, spices are without doubt the most extreme term. This is both because they are diametrically opposed to the aroma from the sacrifice which appears to become confused with their own smell in a traditional city sacrifice and also because, far from emphasising the difference between Mortals and Immortals, through this rediscovered commensality they bring about the surest means of communication between men and gods.

To confirm what the super-foods mean we must contrast them with a foodstuff the eating of which represents for the Pythagoreans the opposite attitude to the one we have just defined. To a disciple of Pythagoras the most absolute way of eating meat is to partake of the fruit of a leguminous plant, namely the broad bean. We know that the bean was the subject of the strictest prohibitions. Not only did the members of the sect refuse to eat it but they harboured a genuine revulsion for this foodstuff for a number of interconnected reasons on which our sources write at length.[85] The first of these reasons is botanical: the bean is the only plant whose stem is totally devoid of nodes (*agónaton*).[86] This feature makes the bean plant a special means of communication

between Hades and the world of men. Two lines in one of the
Pythagoreans' *Sacred Speeches* describe the function of the bean
plants as follows: 'They serve as support and ladder for the souls
[of men] when, full of vigour, they return to the light of day from
the dwellings of Hades'.[87] These bean plants with their hollow
stems are the route through which there is a continuous interchange
of living and dead. They are the instruments of metemsomatosis
and of the cycle of births. The further reasons the Pythagoreans
adduce for their revulsion for the bean are extensions of this first
one and they too stress the plant's mixed character of the living and
the dead. First, there are the peculiar experiments carried out by
certain members of the sect: a bean, enclosed in a sealed box or pot,
was buried in the earth or hidden under a pile of dung. After some
days, numbered at forty or ninety in different sources, the
receptacle was dug up and, in the place of the bean, was found
either a fully formed head of a child or a female sexual organ or a
man's head or else blood.[88] Such experiments, which later
survived in Graeco-Egyptian magic[89], might be taken to be the
inventions of a later age. However, there are two arguments to
counter that interpretation. In the first place there is evidence for
such practices as early as the fourth century BC.[90] Secondly,
Aristotle testifies to the genuinely Pythagorean nature of the
significance attached to the beans in these experiments for he
reports that, to Pythagoras' disciples, beans resembled sexual
organs.[91] Lucian takes up the same idea when he remarks, more
succinctly, 'in these aspects beans are generation itself'.[92] These
strange experiments aimed at proving that the bean and generation
are identical must be considered in the context of certain
cosmogonic images which lead the Pythagoreans to see the bean as
the first living thing to emerge from the original putrefaction at the
same moment as the first man.[93]

> 'At the time of the confusion that reigned at the beginning and
> origin of everything, when many things were mixed with the
> earth in germination and putrefaction[94], when little by little
> birth came to be and whole-formed animals were distinguished
> from plants which at that time germinated in the same decompo-
> sition, man was formed and the bean grew.'

In the representation of the bean which emerges from this
cosmogony, two features stand out. The first is that the bean
belongs to the order of what is putrified and rotten. The reason for
this vegetable evoking putrefaction and appearing as a horrible
mixture of blood and sex is that, in the Pythagorean system of

symbols, it represents the pole of death — the death connected with inevitable rebirths. This was opposed to true life which is reserved for the immortal gods whose bodies are not made of flesh and blood but remain forever incorruptible as do spices and perfumed substances. The second feature that emerges from the cosmogony is that the bean growing on its stem is like the human plant; it is man's double, his twin brother. One last version of the 'bean experiment' reveals all the consequences ensuing from this view: if a bean which has been bitten or slightly broken with the teeth is exposed to the sun's heat for a few moments, it is shortly after found to be giving off the smell of human semen or, according to another version, the smell of human blood shed in a murder.[95] In this last case to eat the bean is tantamount to shedding a man's blood. The full measure of the violence inherent in such a view is expressed in a Pythagorean saying which became more vulgarised than any other in the literature of the sect: 'To eat beans is a crime equal to eating the heads of one's parents'.[96] Here we have the most profound meaning attached to the eating of the bean: it is equivalent to cannibalism.[97] This is made explicit in the Pythagorean tradition which attributes to Pythagoras the prohibition against 'eating beans as much as against eating human flesh'.[98] To eat the bean is to devour human flesh, to behave like a wild beast, to condemn oneself to a type of life that stands in extreme opposition to the Golden Age.

Thus it is that, in the system of Pythagorean foods, eating the bean is seen as an original, secret and exclusive way of symbolising the eating of meat and the practice of blood sacrifice.[99] For the Pythagoreans eating beans is the same as eating meat and this they absolutely forbid themselves to do when they value as super-foods such things as the spices, the mallow and the asphodel, and the pure cereals. The Pythagorean system of foods thus appears to be constructed around the opposition between two polar terms: the positive is represented by the spices, the negative by the bean. The fact that these are indeed two antithetical terms is proved by two features of these two types of plant. First, the bean plant with its nodeless stem establishes with the Below and the world of the dead the same direct communication that spices, for their part, establish with the Above and the world of the gods. Secondly, the bean belongs to the order to what is rotten as clearly as the spices belong to the order of the dry and the burned.

The opposition between the bean and the spices illustrates one major element of the system we are studying. But now we must define the relationship between this first type of foods and other dietary practices of the Pythagorean movement. How are foods defined in the meat diet characteristic of the so-called 'political' Pythagoreans? What is the position of the working ox in relation to spices and the bean? It is as strictly forbidden to eat this animal as to eat beans; and this brings us to the very heart of the problems raised by the eating practices of those Pythagoreans who operated within the context of the city. Although the disciples mentioned by Aristoxenus do eat the flesh of animals, they do not eat all meats indiscriminately. Some are permitted while others are strictly forbidden. According to Aristoxenus, kids and sucking pigs may be eaten but sheep and the working ox are absolutely forbidden. Such a distinction between two types of sacrificial victim is not the result of an arbitrary decision nor is it an element of folklore 'in which there is nothing to be understood'. The XVth book of Ovid's *Metamorphoses* sets out the mythical and religious reaons that form the basis for this classification.[100] In a summary of the history of mankind ascribed to him by Ovid, Pythagoras 'in person' puts the matter as follows: After a Golden Age during which men needed nothing but the cereals, fruits and plants which the earth produced in abundance[101], the first blood to be shed was that of wild animals, harmful beasts which could be killed but which should not have been eaten.[102] The second stage involved the sacrifice of domesticated animals. At this point Pythagoras establishes a clear distinction between guilty victims and innocent animals. The first animal victims to deserve death and the first to be sacrificed were the pig and the ram — the pig because it was the enemy of Demeter, rooting up seeds and trampling on growing plants, and the ram because it offended Dionysus by eating the vines and spoiling the grapes.[103] Pythagoras sets in contrast to these two guilty victims two others which are perfectly innocent and should never have been offered in sacrifice: the sheep and the working ox.[104] The sheep provides wool and gives milk with a generosity equal to that of the earth when it produces the harvest. The ox is man's working companion; it is the farmer's closest relative, his double, another self. Pythagoras says that to kill the ox is 'to slaughter the labourer', and lines 120 to 145 in Book XV consist of a veritable 'lament for the soul of a working ox'.[105]

These mythical traditions which confirm the division between two types of sacrificial victims that Aristoxenus attributes to the Pythagoreans, belong to the same sphere of religious thought as several legends of Athens and Eleusis relating to the first animal sacrifice. According to these, the pig and the goat were put to death for having committed a wrong towards Demeter and Dionysus. The pig trampled on the harvest[106], that is attacked the gifts of Demeter; and the goat cropped the vine of Icarios[107], ravaging the fruits of Dionysus. Because pigs and goats are destructive and harmful, *lumantikoí*, they are condemned to serve as victims in the sacrifices in honour of the divine powers that they have offended. However, although the Pythagorean traditions relating to blood sacrifice agree with certain mythical views shared by the Greeks as a whole, they are organised according to a theory which is quite original and whose main lines can be detected through a number of indications afforded by the literature on the sect. First, this doctrine underlies the obligation imposed upon the Pythagoreans not to seek to harm or to destroy (*méte phtheirein méte bláptein*) the animal that causes no harm to the human race and to respect it as they would a cultivated plant or fruit tree.[108] Secondly, the point is made explicitly in an account of the first animal sacrifice related by a Pythagorean, for although Plutarch is our source for this account, it relies on both the traditions and the practices of the 'ancients'.[109] He says that for men in the olden days 'it was a sacrilegious and criminal act (*érgon enagès dai áthesmon*) not only to eat but to kill an inoffensive animal. However, when men found themselves under pressure from the growing number of animals and the oracle at Delphi encouraged them — so it was said — to come to the aid of the fruits of the earth which were threatened with destruction, then they began to sacrifice animal victims'. The first sacrificed animals were guilty of an injustice towards the human race and civilised life: they devastated the harvests, devoured the vines and destroyed the seeds.[110] In this way they behaved like wild animals and forced men to treat them as such. All these traditions refer to a single vision of society — a state in which man felt himself to be at one with the growing plants and animals, a Golden Age when the earth spontaneously produced the most perfect fruits and when men and beasts lived together in harmony with each other.[111] The Pythagoreans share with Hesiod and with all the Greek tradition which draws on him this representation of man's Golden Age, a representation which alternates in Greece with a picture of the first human beings in a wild state.[112]

This same 'official' and political line of religious thought lies behind the distinction the Pythagoreans made between two types of sacrifical victims: the pig and the goat on the one hand and the working ox and the sheep on the other. When offering three

animals together in a *trittye*, the sacrificial practice of the City was
to take the largest victim from among the cattle and the smaller
ones from among the goats and sheep.[113] The only difference
between the Pythagorean classification and that of the city lies in
the position of the sheep. Whereas it is usually one of the minor
victims in a classical *trittys*, the Pythagoreans associate it with the
working ox. There is a simple explanation for this difference. In
Pythagorean thought the distinction between the two classes of
victims is not made on a purely economic and religious basis; it is
also affected by the degree of domestication of the animal, in other
words by its closeness to, or distance from, man. The pigs and
goats live in herds in the open spaces of the uncultivated ground at
some distance away from the human group and its dwellings and
are considered to be the wildest of the domesticated animals. The
sheep and the ox, on the other hand, are the domesticated animals
that are closest to the household. The working ox, in particular, is
traditionally a part of the farming unit and the family, a member of
the *okos*.[114] It dwells under the same roof as the farmer and is his
most faithful working companion. The fact that the degree of
domestication was an essential criterion in the Pythagorean
classification of beasts of sacrifice is borne out by the way
Pythagoras and his disciples justify the slaughter of the first
animals to be killed: the pig and the goat were sacrificed because of
their harmfulness which goes with their semi-wild nature.

There is further evidence to support this interpretation, within
the Pythagoreans' representation, of the working ox and of its
place among the sacrificial victims. Here again Pythagorean
thought proves to be in agreement with religious attitudes
fundamental to the Greek city. It is indeed in the status of the
working ox that we find one of the major problems of blood
sacrifice expressed in the city. On the fourteenth of the month of
Skirophorion, Athens celebrated the festival of the *Bouphonia*,
meaning literally 'the murder of the ox'.[115] A dramatic sacrifice
lies at the heart of the ritual. A working ox, taking advantage of its
master's distraction, approaches the altar of Zeus *Poliéus* and sets
about eating the offerings placed there, the cereals and cakes being
offered to the god of the city. At this sacrilege the priest of Zeus, in
his anger, seizes an axe and strikes the beast, killing it. Then,
horrified at what he has done, the 'murderer of the ox', the
bouphónos, flees in haste, leaving the murder weapon behind him.
There are two parts to the second half of the ritual. In the first,
judgement is passed in the Prytaneum by the tribunal competent to

deal with crimes involving bloodshed[116]: the guilt of the axe being established, it is expelled from the territory of Attica. In the second part, the flesh of the victim is ritually consumed by the entire city while what remains of the ox is stuffed with straw, set up and harnessed to a plough to simulate the operation of ploughing.

The whole of the *Bouphonia* ritual hinges on the sacrilegious character of this blood sacrifice: to offer an animal victim to the gods is to shed blood, actually to commit murder. Animal sacrifice is seen as a defilement in the city, but an inevitable and necessary defilement, for slaughtering the ox is an act that is essential for the establishment of the city's relations with the divine powers. The city comes to terms with its distress in the face of the bloodshed and killing of this animal through a ritual dramatisation which emphasises and exploits the ambiguity of the victim and the sacrificer.[117] The working ox is an innocent animal but at the same time it is guilty for, although it is the guarantor of cereal foods, it eats these very cereals and is thus condemned to be eaten in its turn. Similarly, by approaching the altar to eat the consecrated foods upon it the ox proclaims itself as the victim for the sacrifice. The man who strikes it down is equally ambiguous. He is the 'murderer of the ox' but at the same time the priest of Zeus *Polieús*, hence the qualified sacrificer. In one version of the myth connected with the *Bouphonia* ritual, the ambiguity of this figure is even more strongly emphasised by the varying status of his position at different points in the drama. The man who kills his own ox is a farmer and a foreigner. This 'ox murderer' takes refuge in Crete but is then recalled by the city at the order of the Delphic oracle, for he alone can avert the famine brought about by the animal's death. He must now — and this time with the status of a citizen — celebrate the sacrifice and division of the victim which will make the earth fertile and rich in cereals again. The whole of this dramatic ritual turns upon the peculiar status of the ox which belongs to the animal kingdom but is also, in a manner of speaking, a part of mankind. It is because the working ox is, of all the animals, man's closest companion[118] that, at a particular point in the history of the city[119], its execution in the sacrificial ritual gave rise to such deep distress.

We can only interpret the Pythagoreans' attitude towards the working ox by reference to this ritual and against the background of these religious beliefs in the city. By strictly forbidding the sacrifice of such a victim Pythagoreanism, within the framework of the city, took over all the distress occasioned by blood sacrifice.

But, even more important, this makes it possible to distinguish the original position of this movement. Its character as a sect found expression both in an Apollonian mysticism directed towards an existence of perfect purity and in a horror of cannibalism and the life of bestiality. Within the city the whole of religious practice was founded upon the sacrifice of the ox. But, even when active within the political system, the Pythagoreans refused absolutely to eat the flesh of such a victim. This was the first point on which they differed from the city's official sacrificial practice. There were two others, and they indicate the exact measure of the compromise made by Pythagoreanism as a political movement. These were two restrictions the Pythagoreans made with regard to eating sacrificial meat. The first was that they would eat only the flesh of animals recognised as guilty and harmful; the second, that they would eat only the less 'vital' parts of such victims, that is they abstained from eating the heart, the womb and the brain — the parts that the Pythagoreans referred to as the 'seats of life'.[120] In the opposition that Pythagoreanism thus establishes between two types of sacrificial victims, we can recognise the division which seemed to be the basis of their system of foods, namely the distinction between meat and non-meat.The 'political' Pythagoreans considered the edible parts of minor victims to be food that is non-meat[121] and only the working ox was considered to be meat in the fullest sense. Within the context of the city to show respect for the working ox was, for these Pythagoreans, the same as to refuse absolutely to eat meat. And, conversely, to put the working ox to death by sacrificing it was to adopt a diet diametrically opposed to the Pythagorean way of life.

So it is that, in the Pythagorean system of foods, the working ox comes to represent the third important term, joining the first two, the spices and the bean. There are two legends elaborated by the Pythagoreans on the theme of the working ox which show clearly that the third of these three terms occupies a special position in between the other two. The first legend tells the story of Pythagoras' sacred ox.[122] One day at Tarentum Pythagoras noticed an ox, peacefully grazing in the middle of a field of beans, watched by the cowherd. The philosopher called to the cowherd and asked him to stop the animal from eating beans. When the cowherd mocked him, saying that he did not know the language of oxen, Pythagoras went up to the animal and spoke so persuasively into its ear that not only did the ox stop eating the beans but furthermore it was never again seen to eat these vegetables. It was said that this ox lived to a ripe old age in the sanctuary of Hera at Tarentum. It was known as 'Pythagoras' sacred ox' and was fed on 'human food'.[123] Whenever it may have been invented, such a story[124] is only meaningful in the context of the categories of the Pythagorean foods. To stop the ox eating beans and induce it to eat the same foods as human beings was to effect a concrete change from a wild state to a pure, undefiled way of life. The starting point was cannibalism: an ox eating beans manifests its cannibalism as clearly as does one man eating another. The final situation is a conversion to the Pythagorean life: to this animal that has lapsed into a state of wildness Pythagoras reveals the human status which is accorded to the ox by the whole tradition that considers it to be man's closest companion. Henceforth the ox of Tarentum will eat nothing but food suitable for men, which means, no doubt, those pure foods that constitute the diet of a good Pythagorean.

But the metamorphosis of the ox does not stop there. There is a second story, as mythical as the first, which adds the finishing touch. It is the anecdote about the sacrifice offered by Empedocles, following an Olympic victory in the chariot race.[125] According to this legend, Empedocles,[126] who was a disciple of Pythagoras, abstained totally from eating meat. In order to comply with the custom according to which victors in the games offered and sacrificed an ox, he resorted to a memorable device: he had an ox[127] made from myrrh, frankincense and the most precious spices and divided this among the gathered assembly in the ritual manner. Thus the eater of beans is elevated to the condition of spices; the cannibal ox is transmuted into a substance all of perfume. By showing that there is a third term that mediates between the opposition between spices and the bean these traditions surrounding the working ox provide decisive proof that the Pythagorean system of classifying foods is constructed around three essential terms, — spices, the (working) ox and the bean, and also depends upon the opposition which underlies these three terms, — between food that is meat and food that is not. Because of its double orientation, in that it is both a religious sect and also a society involved in politics, the Pythagorean group is at the centre of a conflict between two models the opposition between which we have emphasised. On the one hand there is the anti-city reflected in the behaviour of the religious sect, on the other the reformed city which finds expression in the actions of the political group. The Pythagorean system of classifying foods expresses and translates this tension. It does so not by juxtaposing diets that are diametrically opposed, but by combining two food models. The first shows the maximum distance between meat and non-meat as expressed in the opposition between the bean and the spices. The second minimises the separation between these very terms by means of the distinction between two types of sacrificial victims: the working ox on the one hand and the pigs and goats on the other. And the overlapping of the two dietary models shows clearly that the Pythagorean system stems from both these attitudes towards the eating of meat and blood sacrifice.

Each of these two legends confirms that the Pythagorean dietary system constituted a language through which the aims of the social group were expressed and its contradictions revealed.[128] But the last of these stories, which tells of the metamorphosis of an ox into the substance of spices, does not only show the contrast between two types of sacrifice. It pushes to its limits the antithesis between on the one hand the smells rising from the sacrificial beast and on the other the smoke from the myrrh, by suggesting that the latter smell emanates from the very offering that should have produced the former. Thus it is from the dietary system of a marginal group that the religious significance of aromatic perfumes in Greece emerges most clearly: frankincense and myrrh are diametrically opposed to chthonic putrefaction as represented by the bean, and because they rate as super-foods they alone are able to unite men and gods in the rediscovered fellowship of a shared meal.

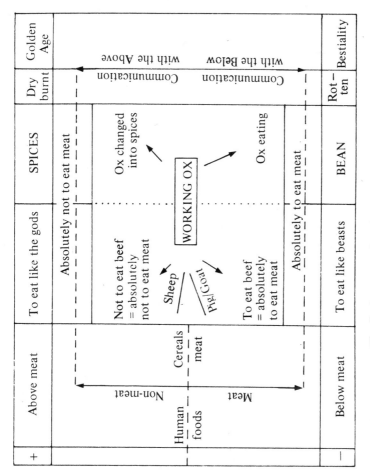

The Pythagorean classification of foods

III
From Myrrh
to Lettuce

Spices are employed in the ritual making of smoke and in sacrifices; but they are not used for these religious ends alone. In the form of ointments, perfumes and other cosmetic products they also have an erotic function. However, whereas in sacrificial practices spices, in the form of solids, that is loaves or seeds, are consigned to the flames to be consumed, in perfumery aromatic essences are doubly protected from the effects of fire. In order to make perfumes which take the form of oils, the *murepsós* or boiler of ointments undertakes a culinary operation to thicken and condense the liquid.[1] Theophrastus tells us that to do this he uses a receptacle half-immersed in hot water, thus avoiding any direct contact with the flames of the cooking fire.[2] In the same treatise, *De Odoribus*, Theophrastus explains that the perfume-makers also take another precaution: they never expose perfumes to the heat and brightness of the sun. This is the reason why these artisans always live in houses that are cool and situated in the shade.[3] Both of these precautions provide confirmation, if this be necessary, that myrrh and spices are set in opposition to those plants whose own internal concoction has to be supplemented by their being cooked over a fire which is a substitute for the power of the Sun which is too far away. Because spices result from a most active concoction, both internal and external, they do not have to be submitted directly either to the power of the cooking fire or to that of the sun. In the case of the first precaution water acts as mediator; in the second, shadow or the lead or alabaster receptacles which enclose and protect the perfumes. In this way the spices to be used as cosmetics are, as it were, withdrawn from the vertical line of communication in which they are necessarily involved when used in religious ritual. However, even when changed into the form of ointments and perfumes, they still retain the same powers as the myrrh and frankincense burned in honour of the gods. In this case, operating as they do on a horizontal axis, these spices used for erotic purposes make it possible, through the power of their perfume, to bring together beings normally separated from each other.

Perfumes and spices are substances endowed with mysterious powers. When the gods are attempting to persuade Hephaistos to leave Lemnos and come and rescue Hera from the invisible fetters of an enchanted throne, Dionysus alone succeeds where all others have failed. He does so either by making the blacksmith drink intoxicating wine or by rubbing his limbs with myrrh whose perfume casts a spell over him and lures him unresisting to Olympus.[4] Apuleius gives another example of this magic power possessed by perfumes. Pamphile is dying of love for a young man of great beauty whom all her philtres and spells have failed to lure to her bed. So she decides to don the plumage of a bird and to fly to the object of her desire:

'When she had taken off all her clothes, she opened a coffer from which she took several boxes. She removed the lid of one of them and took out a perfumed ointment with which she anointed her whole body from the tips of her nails to her head, rubbing it in for a long time. Then, after sitting in the lamplight for a long time, she moved her limbs rhythmically. While they were gently beating the air, a soft down could gradually be seen to wave, strong feathers to grow, a beaked nose to harden, and curved nails to thicken. Pamphile took the form of an owl. Then, with a plaintive cry she practised leaving the ground with increasingly high leaps and soon she soared into the sky and her wings bore her strongly away'.[5]

A love-lorn girl is transformed into a bird by a magic ointment, and is thus enabled to join her lover through the sole power of spices.

For an entire moralistic tradition for which Plato of the *Republic* is the most powerful spokesman, the scent given off by perfumes at banquets and the seductive attraction of ointments rubbed on to limbs represent a kind of life given over to the delights and pleasures of the senses. The very evocation of spices is, by itself, enough to conjure up a succession of images of luxury and sensuality — flowing dresses, exquisite dishes of relishes and sweetmeats, wreaths of flowers, courtesans and women of pleasure — in sum, all the refinements of life lived in the Persian manner,

at least as the Greeks imagined it.[7] Dissolute pleasures are
inseparable from clouds of frankincense and heady perfumes.
Hēdonḗ, Sensual Pleasure, is the name under which Aphrodite,
smothered in perfumes, appears at the judgement of Paris[8], 'all
proud of the power of desire'.[9] However, the perfumed
Aphrodite is not only the patroness of the sensuality (*makhlosúnḗ*)
of courtesans when 'with their hair and breasts covered in perfume
they would arouse the desire even of an old man.'[10] She is also
the protectress of marriage who stands beside Hera and Demeter
and who, on a religious level, represents the sexual desire and the
pleasures of love (*aphrodísia*) without which man and woman's
union in marriage could not be fulfilled.[11]

Spices and perfumes are ritually used, in Greece, by newly
married couples. Before leading the bride to the house of her
husband, the womenfolk who have dressed her in richly coloured
fabrics, rub her with ointments and anoint her, drop by drop, with
the most precious perfumes.[12] The young husband who awaits
her, adorned in white clothes and crowned with crimson flowers, is
also covered in myrrh.[13] The perfume of spices is given off from
the bodies of the young couple and its fragrance is the outward sign
of the attraction which draws them irresistibly together. However
much Xenophon's Socrates[14] reproaches women for their use of
cosmetics and tells young brides that they have no need of perfumes
since their own bodies exhale a fragrance of their own, the fact is
that, in Greece, the pleasures of love cannot do without either.
Plutarch points out[15] that most men will only consent to make
love to their wives if they come to them covered with perfumes and
powdered with spices.

This erotic function and significance of spices is particularly well
illustrated by an episode in the *Lysistrata* of Aristophanes. Desiring
to force their men to bring the war to a close, every woman in
Greece has solemnly pledged to refuse to make love with her
husband. Encouraged by Lysistrata, they set out with all the arms
of their sex, 'your saffron dresses and your finical shoes, your
paints and perfumes and your robes of gauze'[16], to excite their
husbands, or rather — as they put it — to roast them (*optân*) and
grill them (*statheúein*).[17] The girl who gives a perfect demonstration of their methods is called Myrrhina. Pretending to yield to her
husband's desire, Little-Myrtle allows herself to be coaxed into the
grotto of the god Pan, next to the Acropolis[18], but she then finds a
thousand excuses for procrastination. A mattress is the first excuse,
then a plait of hair, then a pillow, then a blanket. Finally, just as

she uncovers her breasts, Myrrhina remembers that they have both forgotten to rub themselves with perfumes. Despite the protestations of her husband, she runs off to fetch a flask of balm and carefully rubs herself with it, inviting her husband to do likewise. Then just as the wretched man, by now consumed with desire, thinks he will at last clasp his wife in his arms, Myrrhina slips away, this time for good.[19]

This woman's powers of seduction are emphasised by the fact that her name, Little-Myrtle, carries heavy erotic overtones. The branches of this aromatic shrub are used, in Attica, to weave the crowns worn by marrying couples.[20] The name of this plant which is consecrated to Aphrodite is used to refer to either the clitoris or the pudenda of the woman.[21] Thus the perfume in which Myrrhina smothers herself is simply the ultimate expression of the seductive attraction emanating from a woman totally committed to Aphrodite.

The resemblance between this Myrrhina and the Myrrha who seduces her father is all the greater in that in one of the versions of the myth of Adonis, his mother is transformed by metamorphosis into not a myrrh tree but a sprig of myrtle.[22] In this semantic context, Adonis — whether thought of as the product of the myrrh tree or the fruit of the myrtle — thus takes on one of his fundamental meanings. Two more direct proofs may be added to the evidence already provided. First, in Greek love terminology, Adonis is synonymous both with perfume and with lover. 'My perfume, my tender Adonis': these are the names by which a courtesan addresses her lover in an epigram from the *Palatine Anthology*.[23] Secondly, in a Latin variation[24] of the myth of Myrrha, Adonis is connected with the Greek word *hēdonē*, meaning sensual pleasure, and it is stated quite explicitly that Aphrodite's passion for Myrrha's son is provoked by the sap of the Myrrh tree, a juice whose perfume makes the drinker burn with passion. Adonis, who is both the son of Myrrha and the product of the Myrrh tree, is literally as well as figuratively both lover and perfume.[25]

Once the overall symbolism and significance attached to spices by the Greeks have been deciphered, it is impossible to read the myth of Adonis and Myrrha as anything but a myth about seduction. The two episodes involve a double seduction — that of the mother as well as that of the son. In the first part of the myth which centres on Myrrha, the seduction is set squarely within the context of marriage. Myrrha is a young woman who refuses the status of marriage[26] and sets any such tie 'aside'. She refuses to choose a husband from amongst the suitors available. Because Myrrha rejects marriage and refuses the lot of Aphrodite that is an integral part of her condition as a woman[27], the goddess condemns her to desire to make love with her father; she is impelled to seduce the only man whom she may not normally and legitimately desire.[28] Marriage thus appears as an intermediate term between the two statuses of Myrrha. She is first a virgin appalled by her suitors and, later, a woman in the grip of a passionate desire for sexual union with her own father. In this story of a daughter who seduces her father, the myth appears to be illustrating the most exaggerated form seduction can take, — seduction that unites two beings whose apparent but deceptive closeness hides the fact that, in reality, they of all couples are held strictly apart by the social order.

In the second part of the myth, which is devoted to Adonis, what is portrayed is seduction pure and simple. No sooner is he born from the myrrh tree whose form his mother has taken than Adonis arouses, first in Aphrodite and then in Persephone, the possessive and exclusive desire that a mistress feels for her lover. 'For the sake of his beauty' the myth runs, 'while he was still an infant, Aphrodite hid [him] in a chest unknown to the gods and entrusted [him] to Persephone. But when Persephone beheld him she would not give him back'.[29] Adonis is he who is loved as much on earth as on the shores of the Acheron: that is how Theocritus[30] describes him, indicating how, following Zeus' arbitration between the two over-possessive mistresses, Adonis was to be, turn and turn about, first Aphrodite's and then Persephone's lover. As in the story of Myrrha, seduction makes it possible to bring together terms that are usually held apart: a mortal seduces two immortals; a single lover belongs, successively, to a mistress from Above, Aphrodite, and to a mistress from Below, Persephone. That it is correct to interpret the myth in these spatial terms seems to be borne out by a reference to the animal kingdom. In his *History of Animals*, Aelian[31] describes the peculiar habits of a fish which customarily sleeps on the rocks and thus divides its existence between the sea and the land, and points out that this kind of mullet is known by the name Adonis, an allusion to the double way of life of the son of Myrrha, who divided his time between two mistresses, 'now above the earth and now beneath it'.[32]

Spices appear to be just as intimately connected with seduction in the ritual of the Adonia, as celebrated in Athens at the end of the

fifth century, as they do in the myth. The Adonia, an exotic festival
tolerated by the Athenian city on the periphery of the official cults
and public ceremonies, were a private affair.[33] This was so in two
respects, first in that they took place in the house of a private
individual and not in a sanctuary or other public place, and
secondly in that those who took part, whether men or women, were
lovers, courtesans and those who frequented them. In a letter
attributed to a *hetaira* believed to have lived at Athens at the
beginning of the fourth century, Alciphron[34], the sophist who
was a contemporary of Lucian, gives us some important
information about the devotees of Adonis. A certain Megara,
writing to her friend Bacchis, scolds her for not having gone to a
party which was the occasion for an exceptionally good feast:

'Even Philomena who has only just got married and who is very
carefully watched by her husband, managed to join us late at
night when her husband was fast asleep. You are the only one
who thinks of nothing but your Adonis and are scared stiff that
he will be taken from you by Aphrodite or Persephone'.

Then follows a detailed invitation:

'We are going to arrange a banquet to celebrate the [Adonia][35]
at the house of Thessala's lover. It is she who is going to be
responsible for providing "Aphrodite's lover". Remember to
bring a little garden and a statuette with you. And also bring
along your Adonis whom you smother with kisses. We will get
drunk with all our lovers.'

The authenticity of this description, traced back to the second
century A.D. is guaranteed by a series of testimonies in various
works of Attic comedy on the Adonia of the fourth century; and it
was precisely in Attic comedy that Alciphron found most of his
information when editing his *Letters*. Two examples taken from the
work of Diphilus will be enough to prove the point. In a play
entitled *The Painter*[36], one of the characters who is telling
another how to set about choosing a patron, ends his speech by
confiding: 'The place I am taking you to now is a real brothel
(*porneîon*). A *hetaira* is busy celebrating the Adonia, with no
expense spared, along with other *hetairai*. You'll be able to stuff
yourself to the gills and carry something away with you in the folds
of your tunic'. In another comedy[37], the same poet presents three
courtesans from Samos, gaily celebrating the Adonia, drinking
many a toast and asking each other smutty riddles such as 'Who is
the strongest?' 'Iron is,' says the first; 'the blacksmith', says the
second. 'No, it's a penis as stiff as a rod', shrieks the third: 'That's

what makes the blacksmith groan.' The libertine nature of the
ritual was recently confirmed by the discovery of a work of
Menander, published in 1969. In *The Woman of Samos*, the hero,
Moschion, seduces a young girl in the course of a festival held in
honour of Adonis, given in the house by his father's concubine, a
former courtesan, among friends and neighbours.[38]

Since the festivals of Adonis were characterised by the
abandoned enjoyment of lovers, the drunkenness of courtesans,
recherché meals and *risqué* talk, it is easy to understand that in the
eyes of the citizens of Athens, at the end of the fifth century, they
were considered as the very spectacles of feminine licence, the very
image of disorder and of the *truphé*[39] that women, left to
themselves, inevitably produce. But at the same time these features,
which are confirmed throughout the tradition, suggest that the
unbridled behaviour of the devotees of Adonis carried a
quasi-ritual significance as did the burning of spices which also
took place on these occasions in the honour of the lover of
Aphrodite. Bedecked and perfumed[40], the women celebrating the
Adonia met their lovers all the more freely because, on a mythical
level but within a ritual framework, the couple formed by Adonis
and Aphrodite epitomised the type of relations that exist between a
lover and his mistress.

The study of the sociological code of the myth of Adonis
demands consideration of a number of other myths which must be
considered consecutively. But before we pursue these problems we
must first proceed analytically both to confirm the significance of
myrrh and to take further our deciphering of the vegetable code
whose richness and importance must by now be quite apparent.
The existence of Adonis is punctuated by a violent opposition
between life and death: Myrrha's son dies tragically, in the full
bloom of his youth and beauty. According to the best known
version of the myth[41], he is fatally gored by a boar in the course
of a hunt. In Greco-Roman art this episode is depicted on many
sarcophagae and, regardless of whether he is killed or emerges
victorious, the *virtus* of the hunting hero is always emphasised.[42]
In mythical tradition, however, Adonis is the antithesis of the
heroic hunter. In that he is overcome by a boar he is marked out as
possessing qualities the opposite of the aggressive warrior's
strength and virility that this animal embodies. Like the lion which
it resembles the boar[43] is, for the Greeks, a terrifying and
monstrous animal which symbolises warlike frenzy and power.
When Tydeus[44], the wild warrior of the Theban epic, presents

himself to Adrastus to offer him his services, he is clad in a boar's skin. The fact is that victory over this wild beast confers on young men the status of warrior. By vanquishing such an adversary hunters demonstrate that they themselves possess the audacity and courage of a ferocious boar.

Adonis the seducer, who is attracted to the world of women and pleasure and attached to his mistresses by the exaggeraged bonds of a 'shameless passion'[45], is excluded from the world of war and of hunting. To the Greeks he is the perfect antithesis of a warrior hero such as Heracles.[46] In this hunting episode in which the boar takes the role of the hunter, Adonis is nothing more than a victim as weak as he is pitiable. There are other versions of his end which stress this aspect even more strongly. For instance, in the second book of his *Glossary*, the Alexandrian poet, Nicander of Colophon[47], writing about the name given by the Cypriots to a particular kind of lettuce, reveals that Adonis was killed by a boar while hiding in a bed of lettuce. A version by Callimachus seems equally shaming for the lover of Aphrodite: here, Adonis's mistress hides him in a lettuce[48], no doubt to save him from the attack of the boar. But the interest of these traditions concerning the end of Adonis lies not only in their showing that he is a coward and the opposite of a hunter and a warrior; but also in that they introduce a new vegetable term in this myth about spices: namely, the lettuce. Whether Adonis takes refuge or is hidden by his mistress, it is always in a bed of lettuce, sometimes wild and sometimes cultivated.[49] At the beginning of the fourth century this mythical feature was an integral part of the story of Adonis, as is confirmed by a character from a comedy by Euboulos who remarks that 'according to legend the body of Adonis was laid out in a lettuce bed by Aphrodite'.[50]

In the same way that myrrh stands for the youth and vigour of Adonis, the lettuce is closely associated with his death. Another remark made by the same character in Euboulos's comedy throws some light upon the meaning of this relationship: 'Lettuce is a food for corpses (*nekúōn brôma*)', he says.[51] The significance of the remark is clarified by the title of the comedy and the immediate context of this remark. In this play entitled *The Impotents* (*Ástutoi*), the reference to Adonis is occasioned by the appearance of a dish of lettuce on the table of a man dining. The man protests, saying to his wife: Ah! Don't put lettuce on the table or if you do you have only yourself to blame'.[52] There are two essential features, both of them connected with Adonis, which throw some

light on the mythical significance of the lettuce: sexual impotence
and a lack of vital force. The evidence of the botanists bears out
that of the doctors: for Dioscorides as for Oribasius, the lettuce is a
plant whose nature is cold and wet, *hugròn kaì psukhrón.* It is a
cold plant, Oribasius explains[53], but not cold to the ultimate
degree, just as cold as the water from springs. The importance of
this remark will become apparent later.[54] In every type of Greek
writing, from botany to comedy, the lettuce suffers from the same
unfortunate reputation as does bromide among the soldiers of
today: 'Its juice is of use to those who have wet dreams and it
distracts a man from the subject of love-making'. This apparently
scientific pronouncement made by Dioscorides in the *Materia
Medica*[55] tallies with the bawdy jokes of the comic poets on the
disadvantages of the lettuce: 'Two cheers for the lettuces, a plague
on them. If a man, even of less than sixty years, eats them and then
takes a woman to him he will toss and turn all night long without
managing to do what he wants to, even with a helping hand to rub
the offending part'.[56] The belief that this vegetable hindered the
pleasures of love was so strong, that in the chapter entitled 'Lettuce'
of his culinary encyclopaedia, Athanaeus refers, as if to
incontrovertible evidence, to the fact that in poetic language the
image of Adonis hiding in the lettuces is an allegorical way of
referring to the impotence occasioned by the continual use of this
vegetable.[57]

There are two senses in which the lettuce is 'food for corpses',
and both obtain in the myth of Adonis. In the first place it is a cold,
wet plant and this aligns it with that which is bound to die and rot;
and secondly, it puts a stop to men's sexual powers. For
Aphrodite's lover, death and impotence coincide. There is a radical
opposition between myrrh and lettuce, the two plants which
encompass the career of Adonis the seducer. Myrrh has the power
to arouse the desires of an old man while lettuce can extinguish the
ardour of young lovers; myrrh confers extraordinary sexual and
vital powers while lettuce brings impotence, which is equivalent to
death.

There is another account which also demonstrates how lettuce
inverts the powers of myrrh. It is the story of Phaon, the ferryman,
and this myth presents the same structure and incorporates the
same codes as the story of Adonis. Moreover, the similarities
between Adonis and Phaon are so striking that, some years ago,
C.M. Bowra suggested that these two lovers of Aphrodite were, in
fact, one and the same mythical figure.[58] We must consider three

different versions of the myth.[59] The first is told by Palaiphatos in the *Incredibilia*[60]:

'Phaon was a boatman; he spent his life at sea. The sea where he worked was a straits. No one had anything against him as he was a reasonable man and only asked those who could afford it to pay. This was a source of amazement to the people of Lesbos. But his behaviour won the approval of the goddess. She was, it seems, Aphrodite. She took on the form of an old woman and asked Phaon to ferry her across which he did, immediately, without asking for any payment. So what did the goddess do then? She apparently transformed the old man into a handsome youth ...'.[61]

In his *Historia Varia*[62] Aelian gives a second version of this myth:

'Phaon was a ferryman; that was his profession. One day Aphrodite paid him a visit, wanting to be taken across. Phaon received her kindly; he did not know who she really was and very politely offered to take her wherever she wished to go. As a reward to his kindness Aphrodite made him a present of an *alabastron*. This vase contained a perfume which made Phaon the most attractive of men and all the women of Myteline fell in love with him. In the end he died a violent death, being surprised in the act of adultery.'

The last version, which is substantially the same, only differs from these first two in certain stylistic variations, the most important of which concerns the perfume:

'In return for having, for nothing, ferried across the goddess disguised as an old woman, Phaon received a vase of ointment. As he rubbed himself with this every day, he attracted women who all fell in love with him ....'[63]

In all three versions of the story of Phaon it is immediately clear that the myth concerns seduction and spices. Through the favour of Aphrodite who possesses all the charms of love the ferryman Phaon is changed into a seducer. The goddess of love reacts with excessive generosity to the graciousness, the *charis*, of the ferryman: she gives Phaon dazzling beauty, a *charis* which attracts all women and irresistibly prompts them to offer themselves to him. It is thus a *charis* which takes on one of its most ancient meanings.[64] The attraction of Phaon is the result of *charis* which it, in turn, promotes. It represents the extreme form of a particular type of social relationship lying outside the normal framework. The exceptional and unusual nature of this relationship is conveyed both by the metamorphosis of Phaon and by the effects of the perfume Aphrodite gives him. In the one case an old man is transformed into a handsome youth; in the other a common boatman is given a magical substance which makes him the most attractive of men. By his dazzling beauty or by the power of the perfume which attracts and seduces, Phaon draws to him all the women of the district. Phaon the seducer is both perfume and lover, just like the beautiful Adonis, and he meets the same sad fate as the son of Myrrha. Only one of the three versions apparently tells the end of the story: Phaon is killed by a deceived husband. However, in this same account by Aelian, just before the last episode there is a clear allusion to another ending: 'Phaon was the most beautiful of men but Aphrodite hid him among the lettuces'.[65] Inspired by this second version, the poet Cratinos, in a comedy devoted to Phaon[66], presented to his audience of fourth century Athenians an Aphrodite madly in love with her new protégé whom she hides, as she did his predecessor, in a bed of lettuces. There can be no doubt then that Phaon suffered the same fate as Adonis: since his mistress, in her anxiety, had consigned him to the lettuces, he was inevitably condemned to impotence. The two versions of the death of Phaon seem a perfect parallel to the double tradition concerning the death of Adonis. In each case the seducer is dispossessed of his powers of seduction, whether through the effects of the lettuces or through a violent death. The identical fate shared by Phaon and Adonis makes it possible categorically to refute the conclusion reached by one philological analysis, — namely that the suggestion that Phaon is consigned to the lettuces is the gratuitous invention of some comic poet.[67] If lettuce reappears in the story of Phaon, it is because its presence is demanded by the mythical significance of perfume. In both these myths the same plant effects an inversion of perfume and seduction. The two seducers follow the same path, leading from super-virility to impotence or — to put it another way — from spices to lettuce.

The two myths share a common framework and common codes and the slight differences between them simply emphasise their common basic structures. For instance, the different versions of the myth of Phaon are all variations on the theme that it is implicit in the story of Adonis, of the equivalence between perfume, spices and seduction. And similarly, the career of Phaon, in the first version of the myth, simply gives clearer expression to the opposition between youth and old age: the life cycle of Adonis that passes from precocious boyhood to premature old age is repeated and reversed in Phaon's case, with Phaon passing from old age to youth and then back again in the opposite direction, from youth to old age denoted by impotence. Even the vegetable code which is common to both myths is confirmed by one aberrant version in particular of the adventures of Phaon. In this version his powers of seduction are attributed to the effects of the Hundred-headed Eryngium. In a passage[68] devoted to this thorny plant which is reputed to be an effective antidote to poisonous snakes and animals, the Elder Pliny writes that amazing claims are made for the properties of this plant:

> 'that its root grows into the likeness of the organs of one sex or the other; it is rarely so found but should the male form come into the possession of men, they become loveable in the eyes of women. This, it is said, is how Phaon of Lesbos too won the love of Sappho.'[69]

Although the root in question, which confers powers of seduction, is not as has sometimes been thought[70] that of the Mandragora but belongs to the Eryngium family, a cultivated variety of this plant shows swellings, excrescences and ring-shaped scars and lumps whose strange shapes could well evoke the male and female sexual organs.[71] In this case the lettuce is diametrically opposed not by the perfume of spices but by the root of a plant whose aphrodisiac properties are the result of the resemblance it bears to the human genital organs. Despite its apparent difference the reference to the Eryngium simply confirms the significance of spices in that it emphasises, in the figure of Phaon, one essential feature of man's powers of seduction: sexual super-virility.

IV
The Misfortunes
of Mint

Although it becomes easier to interpret the myth of Adonis when it is compared with the story of Phaon, its full significance is not revealed by this comparison alone. In order to decipher the different episodes in the myth in which the lover of Aphrodite is shown to be inseparable from Myrrha, these episodes must be set in the context of the models provided by other myths, some closely connected, others less so. It is through them that we may discover the sociological and astronomical codes which are as essential as the botanical code to an understanding of these Greek myths about spices.

The adventures of Mintha, or Mint, can immediately be seen to have a connection with the myth of Adonis by virtue of the role Persephone plays in both stories. We have seen Persephone, seduced by Adonis, become his passionate mistress. In the story of Mintha, by contrast, Demeter's daughter appears as a legitimate wife thwarting the ambitions of a concubine. According to the myth[1] the nymph Mintha used to live in the underworld kingdom of Hades who was her lover. When the king of the underworld brought home Persephone, to make her his lawful wife, his abandoned mistress uttered terrible cries and threats which provoked the anger either of Demeter or of Persephone herself. Mint declared that she was more beautiful than her rival and that she would win back her lover and chase Persephone from the palace of Hades.[2] Mintha had no time to put her threats into action. According to one version. Persephone tore her limb from limb (*diespáraxen*), while Hades granted that she should become a fragrant plant called *minthē* or *hēdúosmos*, 'the sweet-smelling', that is should be transformed into 'garden mint'.[3] In another

Mosaic of the
Phoenix
(Daphne)
Louvre Museum

Iunx Torquilla
or Wryneck
(from *Riverside
National History of
Birds*, fig. 217,
reproduced in *AJA*
vol. XLIV 1940,
p.445 fig. 2).

Iunx (from A.S.F. Gow, *JHS*, vol. LIV, 1934, p.6, fig. 5).

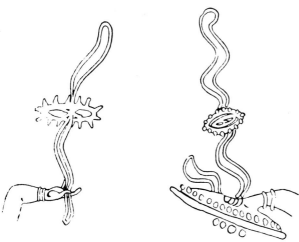

Iunx depicted on Apulian vases (from A.S.F. Gow, *JHS*, vol. LIV, 1934, p.6, fig. 4).

Hyfria from Populanis (detail): "the Meidias painter".
Archaeological Museum. Florence.

Lecythus of aryballos type
from Ruvo.
(Badisches Landesmuseum
de Karlsruhe).

Lecythus of aryballos
type from Apollonia
in Thrace.
(Staatliche Museen
de Berlin).

version it is an enraged Demeter who tramples her underfoot, reducing her to dust. And Mintha rises again from the earth in the guise of 'the insignificant grass' which henceforth bears her name.[4] There seems to be yet a third version of the misfortunes of Mint: one day a mourning Demeter noticed the wild mint plant and was filled with hatred for it. She condemned it to sterility, no longer to bear any fruit.[5] The evidence for this mythical relationships between Mintha, Hades and Demeter is incomplete and fragmentary but it is corroborated by certain religious links suggested by topographical features of South Eastern Elis: in Triphylia there is a Mount Mintha, named after mint, on which is situated one of the extremely rare *témenos* to Hades, and this is flanked by a wood consecrated to Demeter.[6]

Like the myths of Adonis and Phaon that we have already considered, the story of Mint has a tragic ending. But whereas the two lovers of Aphrodite are successful seducers whose unhappy end must be seen simply as the counterpart to seduction, Mintha is an unfortunate mistress whose downfall, provoked by the concerted attack of Persephone and Demeter, cannot be taken out of the context of the sociological factors which affect relationships based on seduction. In this new myth about seduction the sociological and vegetable codes are, in fact, closely interconnected. Mintha is both a demanding mistress and at the same time a fragrant plant, while Demeter combines the qualities of the Power of cereal plants and those of a mother jealously attached to her daughter.

	MINTHA	PERSEPHONE (+ DEMETER)
Sociological code	concubine	legitimate wife (daughter + mother)
Vegetable code	mint	cereal plants

Mint and her rival

Just as Adonis' seductive powers refer back to his vegetable status as the fruit of the myrrh tree, Mintha's story only becomes meaningful when it is placed in the ethnographical context of the plant whose name she bears. Mintha, the concubine and mistress of Hades, lets it be known that she has the means to win her former

lover back and separate him from his new wife. And in doing so she
is, no doubt, alluding to the procedures of love magic covered by
the Greek idea of the *iunx* (whose connection with Mintha we shall
later be demonstrating).[7] But the seductive powers of mint lie
first and foremost in the pleasant smell of the plant which 'sweetens
the breath'. Peppermint, which is an aromatic species of the *Labies*
family[8], has an ambiguous status in ancient botany. Because it is
a highly appreciated condiment which brings out the flavour of
many foods[9], mint is considered as one of the spices.
Dioscorides[10] notes that, being of a 'heating' and exciting nature,
it incites men to the pleasures of love. But this aphrodisiac also
serves to procure abortions. Mint is believed to make women
sterile; if applied before sexual intercourse it prevents women from
conceiving, discouraging generation by preventing the sperm from
coagulating.[11] While it excites sexual desire, mint prevents that
desire from being productive. When taken in larger quantities it is
believed to melt the sperm and cause such serious losses of semen
that an erection is made impossible and the body is weakened.[12]
These different properties of mint suffice to explain why this
aromatic plant is sometimes seen as a chthonic species, a plant of
the underworld, connected with death. 'Do not eat mint' is one of
the prohibitions in the *Treatise on the sacred disease* just as is that
against wearing a black cloak.[13] Similarly, when the author of
the Aristotelian *Problemata* comes across the proverb, 'Neither eat
nor grow mint during wartime'[14] he suggests that this plant has a
destructive effect on seminal secretion and that it is opposed to
courage and virility. Mint cools the body; it is simply one more raw
herb amongst the other 'cold and wet' plants. It seems likely that it
is in this semantic context that we should understand the links
established by Greek lexicographers between the name of the plant
mintha and the word *minthos* which is its synonym[15] but which
also denotes goat's dung[16], human excrement[17] and other
equally foul-smelling substances.[18]

Since it oscillates between the spices and the cold, wet grasses,
the botanical status of mint corresponds to the double status of
Mintha who is now transformed by metamorphosis into a fragrant
plant[19] and now changed into an 'insignificant grass'.[20]

These botanical details are echoed in the third version of the
myth of Mint whose theme is a double opposition: between with
and without fruit, and fertile and sterile. Demeter's hatred is vented
this time not upon the aromatic species of mint but upon
calamint[21], a species of wild mint which gives off a strong,

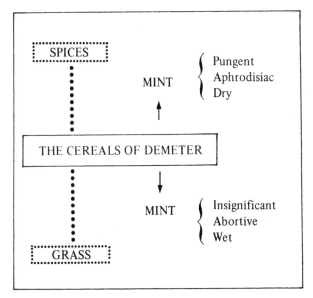

The position of Mintha

unpleasant smell[22] reputed to put snakes to flight[23] and which, when replanted the wrong way up, with its head down, loses its wild character and becomes cultivatable.[24] As mint really is a sterile plant or one that bears only atrophied fruit[25], the 'sterility' inflicted upon it by Demeter might well appear to be simply a reflection of the botanical facts. However, on the mythical level on which the episode is set, the Greek concept of *ákarpos*, 'sterile', combines two meanings the second of which is expressed in a line of Orphic poetry on the subject of wild mint: 'In former times it used to be a large tree, laden with fruit, *pherékarpos*'.[26] Once a fruit-bearing tree but now transformed into a small chthonic plant, the 'fruitless' calamint is, equally, a vegetable species afflicted with sterility or *akarpía*. It is thus doubly set in opposition to Demeter, the goddess of the fruitful earth and protectress of fruits — of the 'dry fruits' of the cereals as well as of some of the fruits from trees. In this third version, which complements the other two, spices — in this case represented by mint — are defined, through their opposition to Demeter, as being both below and above cereals and fruits. Both the lower and the higher position are characterised by a sterility that is both vegetable and sexual, as is proved by the fact that mint not only has stimulating qualities but also procures abortions. Seen in relation to Demeter, the distance between the aromatic plant and the insignificant grass, in the myth of Mint, corresponds to the difference that emerges between myrrh and lettuce in the myths of Phaon and Adonis.

But Mintha's disappointments are not played out in the vegetable domain alone. The misfortunes of the mistress of Hades are also set within a sociological context and a study of this will enable us to distinguish a new code, one which is fundamental to the entire corpus of myths about seduction. Mint, the concubine of the ruler of Hades, comes into conflict not only with the rival who presents herself as the legitimate wife, namely Persephone, but also with Demeter. In one version it is the daughter who attacks Mintha so violently, in the other two it is the mother who demonstrates her hatred of the concubine. Is this simply a story-telling motif in which a mother flies to the assistance of a daughter whose prerogatives as a legitimate wife are threatened? The couple formed by Persephone and Demeter together is too important, in the context of marriage, for their hostility towards Mintha not to take on a greater significance in a myth revolving round the subject of seduction. There is a detail in one version of the myth of Adonis which we have left to one side up till now and should now return to and examine. In the *Metamorphoses*, Ovid's account of the tale of Myrrha, while incorporating the traditional episodes also includes several new ones which relate to other aspects of the story. The pathetic note that they introduce and their rather baroque character might well lead one to conclude that Ovid added them, himself. Take, for example, the description of the circumstances in which Adonis' mother commits incest. Myrrha's union with her father takes place not just during an ordinary absence of his legitimate wife, but

> 'at the time when married women were celebrating that annual festival of Ceres at which, with snowy bodies closely robed, they bring garlands of wheaten ears as the first offerings of their fruits and for nine nights they count love and the touch of man among things forbidden'.[28]

These details given in the *Metamorphoses* may seem gratuitous but they are nevertheless of great value in defining one aspect of the cult of Ceres, namely the different phases in the ceremony known as the *Sacrum Anniversarium Cereris* which constituted the most important ritual in the hellenised cult devoted to Ceres-Demeter which was introduced in Rome in the second half of the third century B.C. and became an integral part of the most ancient worship of the Roman Ceres.[29] Now, this moveable feast, celebrated each year when the wheat was ripe, was focussed both on the cycle of growth of edible plants and also on the relation between Demeter-Ceres and her daughter. The *Sacrum Anniversarium Cereris* was divided into two stages. In the first, the *Castus Cereris*, the matrons associated themselves with Demeter's mourning. For nine days they abstained from bread and from wine and also from all sexual relations with their husbands.[30] In the second part, Demeter found Persephone again and the matrons participated in her joy by offering up to mother and daughter, now reunited, the first fruits of the cereal harvest.[31] A final essential feature of this ritual addressed to Ceres-Demeter must be mentioned: men were strictly excluded from the festival which, like the Thesmophoria, was reserved for married women.[32] This exclusion of men was even consecrated by a linguistic taboo which persisted through the duration of the festival: the words *pater* and *filia* were strictly forbidden.[33] In a ritual which served to emphasise the intimacy between Demeter and Persephone, the privileged nature of the relations between mother and daughter were strengthened by the censure directed against all links between father and daughter.

Once the sociological character of this ritual timed to coincide with the period during which Myrrha becomes her father's mistress is understood it seems most unlikely that the description of the festival of Ceres in Ovid's *Metamorphoses* should be merely gratuitous. The reference to the *Sacrum Anniversarium Cereris* simply accentuates an opposition already suggested in Panyassis' version — the opposition between the two social statuses of Myrrha: not only is she the daughter of a legitimately married woman but, when she becomes her own father's mistress, she is also this woman's rival. In Ovid's version this double status is given all the emphasis conferred by the significance of the ritual he refers to: the lovers commit incest in the conjugal bed of Thoas or Kinras at the very moment when all the married women are gathered together in honour of Ceres-Demeter, celebrating a festival that lays emphasis on the closeness of relations between mother and daughter at the same time ruling out any complicity between father and daughter. In other words, the union between Myrrha and her father is consummated at the very point in time when the distance between them is being confirmed in the most formal manner conceivable, in the ritual terms of a linguistic taboo.

The question of whether this detail in the myth was invented by

Ovid or whether he borrowed it from some model that he used in his *Metamorphoses* could no doubt be expertly discussed in a philological analysis. However, for our type of study it is sufficient that this 'Demetrian' episode not only illustrates the sociological framework in which the seduction is set but also the importance of the opposition between the world of Demeter and that of the lovers. In this way it proves that the open hostility between Mintha and the couple formed by Demeter and Persephone is an essential element of the myth of Mint. The ritualistic details given in Ovid's version make it immediately possible to distinguish a number of oppositions between the sphere of Demeter and the sphere of seduction. As has already been noted[34], although the *Sacrum Anniversarium Cereris* does not exactly correspond to any Greek festival, it nevertheless strikingly resembles the most important ritual devoted to Demeter in the Greek world, namely the Thesmophoria.[35] The Thesmophoria were a festival of sowing celebrated in the autumn whereas the ritual of Ceres-Demeter was connected with the harvest and occurred at the height of summer. However, if this difference is set aside the Greek festival and the Hellenised Roman one have a number of features in common that establish a ritual model which is the perfect antithesis of the Adonia.

Whereas the festivals of Adonis, dominated by courtesans, were the very image of female licence, the ritual devoted to Ceres-Demeter and the Thesmophoria were held in an atmosphere of grave, almost harsh solemnity. In Greece, only married women, the legitimate wives of citizens, could take part. In late fifth century Athens, participation in the Thesmophoria even amounted to legally valid proof that a woman had contracted a legitimate union with an Athenian who enjoyed full political rights.[36] The fact is that slaves[37], the wives of metics and foreigners and, of course, concubines and courtesans were all excluded from the Thesmophoria. One of the speeches written by Isaeus is explicit evidence that the 'scandalous' behaviour of a woman was incompatible with her presence at the festival of Demeter.[38] This evidence is confirmed and expanded by Lysias. His speech 'On the murder of Eratosthenes' is devoted to justifying a husband's killing a lover caught in the act, and to convincing the judges that this punishment was richly deserved. Lysias claims that the adulterous wife took advantage of the Thesmophoria to organise — with the help of her lover's mother — nocturnal meetings in the house of her husband who had retired to the country for the duration of the festival.[39]

Lysias' aim is, in fact, identical to that which we have already indicated in Ovid's version of the myth of Myrrha: the seduction is made to seem all the more shameful in that it takes place at a moment when married women are separated from their husbands for the express purpose of associating with Demeter *Thesmophore* and being solemnly confirmed in their double status of mother and of legitimate wife.

It is in their sexual behaviour that the women celebrating the Thesmophoria present the greatest contrast to the devotees of Adonis. In the Adonia, men are welcomed by women — lovers by their mistresses and libertines by the courtesans; in the festival of Demeter, in contrast, men are kept strictly away from the ceremonies and separated from their wives. In the Roman version of the festival referred to in the *Metamorphoses* 'married women ... count love and the touch of man among things forbidden'.[40] whilst in Greece, sexual abstinence is the rule prevailing throughout the three days duration of the festival.[41] The sexual liberty encouraged by the Adonia contrasts with the enforced continence of the Thesmophoria. Furthermore, this prohibition of sexual relations is even guaranteed by the use of a species of plant which, in this ritual context, assumes in a diluted form, the same significance as that held, in myth, by lettuce. The plant in question is commonly known as the 'chaste tree', the *vitex agnus castus*, a member of the *verbenacaea* family which grows in humid areas of the Mediterranean coast and which smells rather like pepper.[42] It is from branches of this shrub that the women make themselves litters on which to rest during the Thesmophoria.[43] The Greeks derived their name for this plant, *ágnos*, from the word meaning 'that which is chaste and pure' (*h*)*agnós*[44] and had no difficulty in believing that it encouraged chastity[45] and that 'mixed in a drink, this plant calms the sexual appetite'.[46] And modern botanical studies confirm the plant's reputation, recognising that its components, vitexine or vitexinine, do have sedative, soporific or stupefying effects.[47] Once reset in the context of the vegetable code obtaining in the myths already considered, this anti-aphrodisiac *agnus castus*[48], used in the Thesmophoria, can be seen to be both analogous to Adonis' lettuce and opposed to the myrrh and spices whose perfume pervades the entire Adonia festival. So far as perfumes are concerned, the difference between the two types of women involved respectively in the two rituals is expressed in an explicit contrast. The married women who take part in the Thesmophoria are given the ritual title of *Mélissai*, the Bees of Demeter[50] and this insect — which, on an animal level symbolises the wife, the epitomy of domestic virtues — has one striking characteristic: it has an absolute horror of perfumes and an uncontrollable aversion to seduction and debauchery.[51]

On this level of perfumes the opposition between the women of Adonis and the matrons of Demeter can be made still clearer. The contrast between the Thesmophoria and the Adonia is like that between Lent and Shrove Tuesday. Whereas the Adonia are an occasion for feasting, drinking and gaiety, the ritual addressed to Demeter Thesmophore is characterised by a Fast which lasts the whole of one of the three days of the festival.[52] Instead of drinking and dancing on the rooftops the women are 'seated on the ground'[53] in the same prostrate position as that adopted by Demeter when Persephone was separated from her. The noisy revelry of the girls of Adonis is opposed to the sadness and grief of these mothers who remain motionless in their posture of mourning and death, neither eating nor drinking.[54] In the myth it was thus that Demeter, covered with a dark veil, without smiling and tasting neither food nor drink, remained seated and was consumed with longing for her daughter.'[55] The entire atmosphere of the Thesmophoria is pervaded with this grief and fasting to such a degree that, when the gods in Aristophanes' *Birds* complain that they can no longer smell the aroma from the sacrifices, they declare 'It is the Thesmophoria'.[56] At the Thesmophoria there is a 'smell of fasting' in the air, a nauseous odour which one of the Aristotelian *Problemata*, devoted to the expression *nēsteías ózein* (to give off a smell of fasting), ascribes to the putrefaction of breath and excretions of phlegm.[57] The matrons of the Thesmophoria are not women covered in spices nor perfumed wives: they give off a slightly rotten smell which is, as it were, the sign denoting the distance set between man and wife, but may also be a way of ensuring that they indeed remain separated for a while, for the smell of fasting fulfills the same role here as does the smell of the garlic that women eat during the festival of the Skirophoria so that, as Philichorus of Athens put it, their breath should not smell sweet and that they may thus abstain from the pleasures of love.[58]

This set of antitheses between the Adonia and the Thesmophoria would be incomplete without our returning to consider the sociological situations which are expressed in their respective myths and which further distinguish the two festivals. In relation to Aphrodite and Adonis whose love-affair stands for seduction,

Demeter Thesmophore represents a particular image of marriage and legitimate union. The epithet Thesmophore may refer to the rightful laws (*thesmoi*) of the life of society which, like marriage, are the product of Demeter's instruction[59]; or it may come from the precepts (*thesmoi*) relating to the sexual life and fertility of women, for there are several features of the Thesmophoria which clearly indicate the importance of these.[60] Whatever the case may be, the women-bees, the *Mélissai*, are not only chaste wives faithful to their husbands but also — and above all — fertile mothers of legitimate children. The ritual evidence coincides with the mythical representations. The women of the Thesmophoria are spouses taken right out of the context of their conjugal life (in the strictest sense) and they model their behaviour on the Demeter who is both mother and nurse whose image emerges clearly from the Homeric Hymn consecrated to her: a woman 'whose great age deprives her of the gifts of Aphrodite'[61] and who devotes her energies to rearing (*tréphein*) a child of the hearth.[62] Purified of any seductive powers as she is, the Demeter of the Thesmophoria appears as a mother concerned exclusively with her daughter.

The sociological model for the myth of Myrrha emerges as a contrast to this couple formed by the mother and the daughter both in the Thesmophoria and in the story of Mintha. As a daughter seducing her father, Adonis' mother is the very epitomy of seduction. This is because, in the first place, the situation emphasises the tension between proximity and remoteness: a seductive relationship is set up between the two terms, father and daughter, which despite their apparent proximity are in reality strictly separated and held at a distance from each other. Secondly, the figure in the myth of the father's daughter-mistress makes it possible to mediate between what is near and what is far away and to unite those terms which are most strictly set apart. The story of Myrrha makes explicit the double movement of separation and union which is expressed in the seductive power exerted by a daughter who becomes her own father's mistress: at the very moment when the most widely separated of terms ritually speaking (father and daughter), are closely united the terms that are closest to each other in ritual (mother and daughter) are set decisively apart. There is one further reason why Myrrha can be taken as the culmination of seductiveness: she presents the best example of how seduction affects social relationships. When Myrrha commits incest

	ADONIA	THESMOPHORIA
Divine Powers	Adonis and his mistress, Aphrodite	Demeter Thesmophore and her daughter, Persephone
Social status of the women	Courtesans and concubines	Lawful wives
Status of the men	Invited by the women	All excluded, even the husbands
Sexual behaviour	Seduction	Continence
Botanical code	Frankincense and myrrh	agnus castis
Smells	excessive use of perfumes	slight smell of fasting The Melissais detestation of perfumes
Food	Feasting	Fasting

The Adonia and the Thesmophoria

with her father the seduction short-circuits and destroys a triple relationship between husband and wife, mother and daughter, and daughter and father.

The far-reaching sociological implications revealed by the myth of Mint are not limited to the types of relationship which are embodied in the pair Demeter-Persephone. In order to complete this analysis of the sociological code for seduction, we must examine another couple of divine powers. This pair is complementary to the first, and its connection with the story of Mint reveals a new aspect of Mintha, more directly connected with the methods and means of seduction. We may recall that, confronted with the threat of Persephone whom Hades had brought to his subterranean home, Mintha's first response was to proclaim her own power over

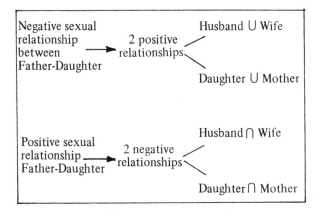

Myrrha, the mistress of her father

her lover and her superiority over a rival whose only trump card appeared to be her status of lawful wife.[63] Although the ending of the story might seem to suggest that these claims are no more than the boasts of a lover at her wits' end, there is other evidence in the myth that proves them to be well-founded. According to Zenodotus of Ephesus — who was the first librarian for the Museum of Alexandria — some people knew Mintha by the name of *Iunx*.[64] Now *Iunx*, which is both a proper name and a common noun, has three meanings in Greek: it is a species of bird; also an instrument used in love magic; and, finally, a sorceress who is an expert on love philtres. The bird known as the *Iunx* is the Wryneck, the *Iunx torquilla L.*[65], which the Greeks seem to have classified as one of the woodpecker family, although it is not really a climber and is incapable of drilling wood. The Wryneck, which is slightly larger than a finch, has a series of characteristics that are listed in Aristotle's *Historia Animalium*.[66] It is a many-coloured bird, *poikílos*, with a shot plumage[67] and it has three distinguishing morphological characteristics: unlike most birds which have three claws pointing forwards and one backwards, the Wryneck has two forwards and two backwards[68]; secondly, it can, as snakes do, turn its head right round, keeping the rest of its body still[69]; and, finally, it can extend its tongue for a distance the length of four fingers and then roll it up again.[70] Pointing in both directions, both above and below, afflicted with head, tongue and tail (*seisopugis*) in constant movement that is emphasised by the shimmering of its feathers and the stridency of its cry which is often likened to the sound of the transverse flute[71], the *Iunx* is the very incarnation of movement in a bird.

It is by fixing the Wryneck firmly to a wheel that Aphrodite fashions an all-powerful charm to seduce Medea and draw her close to Jason.[72] The Wryneck with its four limbs attached to a circle that revolves unceasingly is 'the bird of frenzy'.[73] In women's hands it becomes an instrument of seduction to be used in love magic. The evidence of several decorated pots has enabled the English philologist, A.S.F. Gow[74] to give a detailed description to the technical aspects of this object which the procuresses of ancient Greece used to manipulate in secret so that the desires of their clients should be fulfilled. The *iunx* takes the form of a wheel pierced by two holes, one on either side of its centre; this wheel is held by a cord passed through first one and then the other hole with quite a long piece left over at either end.[75] The wheel is set in motion by pulling on both ends of the cord and, as it turns, it makes a strange whirring noise or whistling sound. This *iunx*, which is as mobile as the bird of seduction, is an instrument whose many sounds correspond to the movements it performs. One detail in the myth can clarify this reference to the sphere of sounds: *Iunx* is the daughter sometimes of *Peithō*, the power of Persuasion and sometimes of the nymph Echo[76], described in an epigram attributed to Lucian as 'the sonorous reflection of all kinds of voices'.[77] When sorceresses manipulate a *iunx* it emits deep notes which provoke the same fascination as the movements of the 'bird of frenzy'.

As a wheel or as a bird, the *iunx* has but one function: to reunite a lover with his mistress or a mistress with her lover. In Theocritus' poem entitled *The Sorceresses*, the nine incantatory couplets pronounced by a woman separated from her lover, as Mintha is from hers, are punctuated by one line which is repeated nine times: '*Iunx*, draw to my dwelling this man, my lover'.[78] This erotic function of the *iunx* is further confirmed by the equivalence that some lexicographers see between this magic instrument and the term *kinaidion* which in Greek denotes debauchery and an obsessive quest for sensual pleasure.[79] Finally, the third form that the *iunx* can take is that of a sorceress, the daughter either of Echo or of *Peithō*, whose spells are strong enough either to make the king of the gods unite with her or to inspire Zeus with the desire to possess the young Io.[80] There are two versions of how Zeus' lawful wife takes her revenge: either Hera changes *Iunx* into the bird of the same name, to be used to further love affairs[81] or she changes her rival into a block of stone.[82] The two versions are complementary, the one corroborating the connection between the sorceress and the instrument used in erotic magic and the other expressing the inversion of the ever-mobile *iunx* into its extreme opposite: a lump of unhewn stone devoid of movement or life.

All these different meanings of *iunx* are illustrated on the beautiful *hydria* of Populonia on which 'the painter of Meidias' [83] depicts Adonis and Aphrodite, side by side. Aphrodite is wearing a gold necklace and magnificent bracelets and has placed her hands on Adonis' shoulders while he, sitting below her, is leaning backwards against the knees of his mistress in a pose of amorous ecstasy. Two figures opposite them spell out the meaning of this scene which the principal characters themselves make immediately understandable. The two secondary figures are *Hímeros*, Desire, who is holding in his hand a *iunx* which he is vibrating, while a young woman — probably *Peithō* or Persuasion — carries perched on her forefinger a bird which appears to be a wryneck. The perfumed lovers are surrounded by the bird, the magic wheel and the powers of seduction. But, just as the tale of Mintha's love brings us back to the figure of Adonis the seducer, one at least of the semantic overtones of *iunx* refers us directly to the seductive powers of spices. Aelian's *Treatise on Animals* enables us to amplify the several meanings of the term already discussed by indicating certain other significances that it has in erotic terminology. The word *iunx* is sometimes used to mean the love call of the male during the mating season. It can, for instance refer to the call of the toad[84] or equally well to the fascination exerted on the female tortoise by a particular kind of grass which the male carries, sticking out like an ornament at either side of his mouth.[85] But this same word can also be used to refer to the powers of seduction peculiar to the panther[86], the carnivorous cat which was believed in Greece to emit a magical fragrance and to exploit this to catch the animals it liked to eat, without exerting itself. Overcome by the enchantment of its exquisite smell[87], fawns, gazelles and wild goats would come and offer themselves to their enemy. Such are the powers of attraction of perfume, here transposed into a hunting technique but exactly equivalent to the allure projected by a mistress or courtesan covered in spices, to attract a lover.

These different aspects of the *iunx* all help to illuminate the seductive nature of Mint. However, it is the woman called *Iunx*, the sorceress expert in love philtres, who most closely resembles the mistress of Hades. As in the case of Mintha, Iunx's story is that of a failure, and the reason for her failure is identical. In the same way as Hades' concubine is confronted by the couple formed by Demeter and Persephone, the daughter of Peitho provokes another couple which proves to be a no less formidable obstacle to her plans for seduction. To establish this new sociological context for seduction we must extend the story of *Iunx* and introduce another myth in which the principal figure, named Ixion[88], is doubly connected with the meanings of the *iunx* — first through his attempts at seduction presided over by *Peithō* and secondly through the punishment which changes him into a kind of *iunx*, with his four limbs fixed to a wheel whirling forever between heaven and earth.

In all three episodes of his story Ixion emerges as a destroyer of the social order through his systematic negation of marriage, his excessive practice of seduction and his denial of *charis* which goes along with his abuse of *peithō*. The first episode takes place in the world of men. Ixion, who is the son either of Ares or of Phlegyas, asks for the hand in marriage of Dia, the daughter of Hesioneus (or Eioneus), promising his father-in-law many presents in exchange. But it does not cross the son-in-law's mind to keep his promises and his incensed father-in-law seizes as surety a herd of mares belonging to Ixion. Ixion then makes what appears to be a gesture of reconciliation: he sends an invitation to Hesioneus, swearing to make rightful amends. So the father-in-law sets out for the banquet of his son-in-law who has prepared a *bóthros* for him in the middle of the road, a hole filled with glowing embers but covered over with brushwood mixed with fine ashes. It is not clear whether Hesioneus falls in by accident or is pushed by Ixion; but at all events he is burned alive.[89] It is the first time in human history that a man sheds the blood of a relative.[90] The second episode takes place among the gods. The murder of a father-in-law by his son-in-law seems so monstrous that no god dares accept Ixion to purify him. Only the king of the gods is prepared to welcome him at his table as his guest. However, Ixion is already plotting another crime, even more heinous than the first. He covets the wife who belongs to Zeus alone and makes his way right into the bed-chamber of Hera. There he tries to seduce and even attempts to rape her.[91] The final episode, concerned with his punishment, takes place in what is already the world of illusion in which Ixion is to exist once he has been changed into a *iunx*. He thinks he is holding Zeus' lawful wife in his arms but is really embracing nothing but a cloud. He is thus united with *Nephélē* who looks to him as if she is Hera. The seducer's first punishment is to fall into the trap Zeus sets for him in the form of the illusion of a Cloud that he desires. The fruit of this union devoid of *charis*[92], love or any exchange is a monstrous being, *Kéntauros* who is held in horror by gods and men alike. He is the ancestor of the Centaurs, the half-human and half-animal powers who live in the undergrowth, eating raw meat and behaving like brutes, always ready to violate the social pact offered them by mankind. The second punishment meted out to Ixion is to be changed, like the sorceress *Iunx*, into an instrument of magic seduction. His arms and legs are fixed to a wheel whirling in the air, half way between men and gods, and the Olympians condemn him, ironically, forever to repeat to mortal beings the following precept: 'Show gratitude to your benefactor by offering him in return a gift that will bring joy'.[93] Once Ixion has become a love-charm whose sole function is to strengthen the powers of seduction in dealings between the sexes, this man of *peithó* is forced to bear witness that the social order rests on the principle of *charis* which he has always contravened.

In effect, the entire myth of Ixion rests on the opposition between the concepts of *charis* and *peithó* and it is on this that the structure of each separate episode depends. But the contrast between these two powers, both divine, only emerges clearly once their role in the domain of erotic relationships has been recognised. *Charis* is a complex and variable thing[94]: it covers the flashing light of the eyes, the shining beauty of a body and the allure emanating from a desirable being, as well as a woman giving herself in response to a man's desire, in the context of marriage. However, this gift of the visibly desirable being in an erotic relationship is never quite free from some trace of *peithó*. Aphrodite's *charis*[95] is accompanied by not only *Póthos* and *Hímeros* — Desire for the being who is absent and Desire for the being who is present — but also a third power, *Peithō* or Persuasion 'who has never been refused'.[96] 'Tenderness, gentleness and sweet pleasure', promised by the loved one are never given without the 'beguiling words and seductive deceits'[98] which underlie the smiles and sweet nothings of erotic relationships. *Peithō* is fundamentally ambivalent, being both good and evil, and in a love relationship it defines the scope of illusion which makes it possible to captivate another person and draw him to one by a kind of surreptitious compulsion. When Hera wants to arouse the erotic desire of Zeus, her brilliant *charis* is reinforced by a magic *peithō*.[99] In order to make her body, which already possesses all the forces of life, irresistible, Hera obtains from Aphrodite an all-powerful 'charm' which will enable her to seduce her own husband. In order to captivate the desired being who is always separated or at a distance from the seducer the latter has to resort to any means possible to attract him and, in may instances, distract him from some other erotic relationship: the seducer must reverse feelings, upset hearts, change minds and exert his own fascination by bringing into play a complex web of illusion affecting the senses of sight, sound and smell. When the balance between *charis* and *peithō* tips over on the side of *peithō* conjugal relationships give way to those of seduction.

The first words spoken by Ixion are deceits intended to pervert the effects of *charis* in marriage and indeed in social life as a whole. By promising wedding gifts (*hédna*)[100] to his father-in-law and subsequently refusing to hand them over Ixion upsets the functioning of marriage which is an essential component of the social system. In archaic Greece, as in other societies of the same type, the circulation of women cannot be dissociated from exchange and the circulation of goods. At every level of social life the binding rule of gift and counter-gift applies, not only between men and gods, and between men and nature, but also between different groups of men. To thwart *charis* at any of these levels is to upset the entire system of exchange and presentation and to carry corruption to the very heart of the social order. In this respect there is a kind of causal chain at work in the myth of Ixion, leading on from one crime to another. Instead of responding to the *charis* of his father-in-law, Ixion makes him false promises which lure him into a fatal trap: his denial of *charis* and his desire to deceive lead him to the murder of a relative. When the heinousness of his crime excludes him from human society, Ixion who now eats at the table of the gods aims his *peithō* at a higher mark. He takes on the divine couple whose sacred marriage is the foundation and guarantee of the order of the cosmos. His seductive propositions to Hera[101] are followed by the amorous caresses he lavishes on her double, and by the marriage *devoid of charis* with the deceptive Cloud. After this episode the failure of the seducer[102] is made public in an inverted *iunx*: the whirling wheel to which Ixion is chained[103] like a wryneck, emits, as it turns a voice which, far from announcing the power of seduction, proclaims the power of *charis* in the world of men.

This new myth of the *iunx* thus makes it possible to compare the mistress of the world Below who tries to short-circuit the marital relations of Hades and Persephone with a seducer who, like the sorceress *Iunx*, sets about disuniting the Hera-Zeus couple in the world Above. The Mother-Daughter couple which stands in the way of Mintha's attempt at seduction is replaced, in the myths of Ixion and *Iunx*, by a Husband-Wife couple which completes the representation of marriage outlined in the first myth. Just as Demeter is no ordinary mother outraged in the person of her daughter, Zeus is no ordinary husband affronted in his legitimate rights. For an entire religious tradition the marriage of Hera and Zeus constituted the mythical and ritual model of monogamous marital relationships. The sacred marriage between Zeus and Hera was celebrated each year in various cities of the Greek world.[104] In Attica the Theogamia took place on the 27th of Gamelion[105] during a winter month (January-February) that was consecrated to Hera, at the height of the season which the Greeks considered to be the most propitious for marriage.[106] Hera *Teleía*, 'the guardian of the Keys of Marriage'[107], and Zeus *Téleios*, the master of the hearth[108], are the two divine protectors of marriage: preliminary sacrifices are offered up to them[109] and it is from their solemn guarantee that the nuptial rites derive their force and efficacy.[110] Thus, on the religious and mythical level the Zeus-Hera couple represents marriage as a ritual contract binding together a man and a woman. Where the Demeter-Persephone couple lays emphasis upon the fruit of marriage and the relations between the mother and her legitimate child, the Zeus-Hera couple stresses the ritual consecration that sanctions the union of husband and wife. Just as Mintha's seduction cannot prevail against the former couple similarly Ixion's *peithō* proves powerless when faced with the latter. But conversely, if these two divine couples together constitute the religious model of monogamous marriage the seduction undertaken by Myrrha is revealed as all the more excessive in that, by being aimed at a father who is 'ritually' forbidden, it short-circuits not only the Demeter-Persephone relationship but also the Zeus-Hera one.

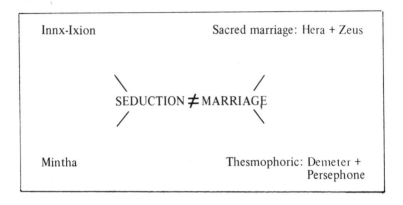

From the story of Mintha to that of Ixion our paradigmatic analysis has revealed an increasingly rich and complex sociological code underlying the myths about perfumes. One final myth with a similar framework will help us to understand the astronomical code which is parallel to the two codes already considered. And, as we thus extend our analysis, this new myth will enable us to decipher the central ritual of the Adonia whose understanding is necessary if we are to complete our interpretation of the myth of Adonis.

By projecting the same appeal as perfume which unites lovers, the *iunx*, which cannot be dissociated from Mintha, represents a situation which is diametrically opposed to the state of the women taking part in the Thesmophoria, separated from their husbands and characterised as they are by their slightly nauseous smell. This close correlation between these two aspects — separation and an unpleasant smell — is emphatically established by the myth of the Lemnian women who are from the outset both women who smell unpleasant and wives who have been abandoned.[111] The myth of the Lemnian women is composed of two episodes the second of which is an inversion of the first. Like the myth of Myrrha it starts off with Aphrodite being forgotten, neglected or even resented. [112] Whereas, with Myrrha, the injury done to Aphrodite leads to an excessive union presided over by fragrant perfumes, the same mistake on the part of the Lemnian women results in an extreme separation characterised by their foul smell.

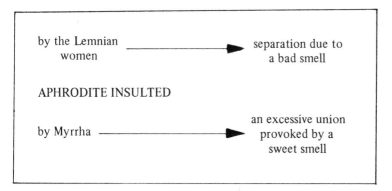

by the Lemnian women ────────▶ separation due to a bad smell

APHRODITE INSULTED

by Myrrha ────────▶ an excessive union provoked by a sweet smell

Aphrodite and smells

Being afflicted with a repellent stench, the women of Lemnos are no longer found desirable by their husbands who, in their stead, take as concubines Thracian slaves captured during their warring forays. The theme of separation is already suggested by the distance the unpleasant smell imposes between the husbands and their wives. It now finds brutal consummation in the action of the neglected wives who, in a single night, massacre every single male — their husbands and every male child too. The evil-smelling women reveal themselves as frenzied warriors.

The second episode opens with the Lemnian women appearing before the Argonauts when the latter come within sight of the island. These women bearing their arms and filled with warlike frenzy seem as terrifying as the Thyiades who 'devour raw flesh'.[113] However, in an episode that is the converse of the first part of the myth, the Lemnian women, whose alienation is emphasised by features as violent as their cannibalism, are about to resume their wifely role. There are two stages to their conversion. First the viragos accede to the request made by a herald sent in by the Argonauts[114]: they agree to send wine and food to the strangers, hailed at first as enemies, on condition that they do not approach the city. The second stage is the women's decision to receive the Argonauts as their guests. They proceed down to the shore where they place their *xeinēia*[115], the gifts of hospitality which are to bind the foreign sailors to them. And now the cycle of exchanges is resumed and the power of *charis* is restored by the collective marriage which unites the Argonauts with the women of Lemnos, following games and competitions for which the prizes are garments woven by the women.[116] The ceremony is the occasion for a festival in which the finest of sacrifices are offered up in honour of Hephaistos of Lemnos and his wife, Aphrodite.[117] In his version of the myth, Apollonius Rhodius stresses two further details which emphasise the reversal that takes place from one episode to the other. First he makes the point that the marriages of the Lemnian women to the Argonauts are brought about by Aphrodite herself, for the purpose of the propagation of the human race on the island of Lemnos; these marriages are blessed with offspring.[118] Secondly, when the city is full of dancing and feasting, the whole of Lemnos gives off a delicious fragrance in which the aroma from the sacrificial meats mingles with the perfume from the spices burned in honour of Aphrodite.[119] Not only is communication between the land of Lemnos and the gods re-established but also the stench of the women is definitively eliminated by the perfumed fragrance occasioned by the reacquired favour of the Power of erotic desire.

In Aeschylus' version, the same reversal is marked in a scene which even more clearly demonstrates the ambivalence of the Lemnian women. When the Argonauts arrive at Lemnos, to winter there, the armed women advance to meet them and prevent them from landing until they have sworn to marry them.[120] Marriage and war are two terms between which a choice must be made which lie at the very heart of the myth of the Lemnian women. In a society in which marriage is for a girl what war is for a boy and in which these two institutions signify for a boy and girl 'the fulfillment of their respective natures as they emerge from a state in which each shares something of the other's character'[121], if a girl should refuse marriage, thus rejecting her female condition, she finds herself to some extent faced with the alternative of war. The warrior status of the Lemnian women is thus an indication of the state of anti-marriage of these women who have spurned Aphrodite. In the same myth, however, the negation of marriage is also expressed by another feature that is more relevant to our discussion: this is the women's stench which has no reference to an inversion of the female role into a male one but is connected with the question of separation and disunion.

The *dysomie* of the Lemnian women, their revolting smell, emanates according to one version[122] from their mouths, and according to another from their sexual organs.[123] There is, however, a third version in which it comes from their armpits[124], the part of the body whose unpleasant smell is explained by the author of the Aristotelian *Problemata* by the absence of air circulating there, which has the effect of producing in this intimate part of the body what is, in effect, a putrefaction (*sêpsis*)[125]. Simple-minded as it is, this is a repetition of the same author's explanation for the expression 'smell of fasting' which we have already mentioned above[126] as applying perfectly to the women of the Thesmophoria when they are separated from their husbands and compelled to abstain from food and sexual intercourse. This is enough to suggest a similarity between the women of Lemnos and the women of the Thesmophoria, the latter being characterised by a slightly unpleasant smell associated with their temporary separation from their husbands, and the former by a stench which is part of a more radical separation. The comparison is all the more convincing in that it finds strong confirmation in a mythical tradition that is peripheral to the *dysosmie* of the Lemnian women. In the first book of his work on Lesbos, Myrsilos of Methymna tells how, when the sorceress Medea was sailing past Lemnos with Jason, at some distance out to sea, she threw *phármaka* (drugs or poisons which are supposed to have afflicted the women with their repellent smell) in the direction of the island.[127] Now there is an anonymous gloss[128] to Myrsilos' account which gives the name of the plant used by Medea in her *phármaka* as rue or *péganon*. This belongs to the Rutaceae family; its medical properties are remarkable and it gives off a strong, unpleasant smell which is why it is known as 'stinking rue' but which did not prevent it from being a highly appreciated condiment, in Rome at least, for in cooking the harmful effects of this plant are eliminated.[129] In that it is an evil-smelling poison possessing the reverse qualities of a condiment, rue seems particularly suitable for Medea's wicked schemes.[130] But it also has other qualities to justify its choice. Although it has a bitter taste[131] and its effects are heating and drying, it also has well established anti-aphrodisiac qualities. Not only is it an abortive agent for pregnant women[132] but it is also believed to coagulate sperm, dampen desire and aid continence[133] to such a degree that — as one scholiast dryly remarks — 'those who are initiated use it for this purpose'.[134] It is clear from this list that the 'stinking' rue of the myth of the Lemnian women has the same properties as the *agnus castus* used by the women in the rite of the Thesmophoria. To put it another way, the unpleasant smelling plant of Medea's choice could be seen as a foul-smelling *agnus castus*, an extreme form of which could be represented by the 'food for corpses' which cuts Adonis so radically off from Aphrodite. Lovers' myrrh is thus opposed not only by the *agnus castus* and the lettuce but also by the 'stinking' rue whose unpleasant smell sets husband and wife apart just as surely as the smell of spices brings them together.

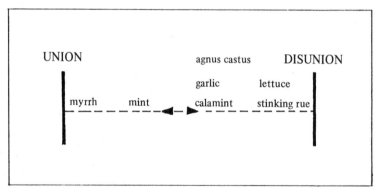

Comparison between the various plants capable of
bringing about union or disunion

The ritual of the Lemnian festival that corresponds to the myth of the Lemnian women provides indisputable confirmation that in this myth there is a close correlation between the rupture of marital relations and the women being afflicted with putrefaction. The fact is that each year, on account of their unpleasant smell, the women of Lemnos were separated from the men and boys.[135] According to Myrsilos of Methymna this separation lasted one day, but according to Antigonus of Carystus it went on for several days.[136] Whether the *dysosmie* of the women is caused by their chewing cloves of garlic, as in the Skirophoria[137] or whether it is simply a fiction imposed by the festival, the ritual distancing of women from men was part of a wider ceremony in the course of which all the fires of Lemnos were extinguished for several days. Here, the evidence of Philostratus' *Heroicos*[138] is of capital importance:

'In memory of the crime committed by the Lemnian women against their husbands at the instigation of Aphrodite, the land of Lemnos is purified at one period of the year.[139] All the fires there are extinguished for nine days. A boat is sent, according to ritual, to Delos to fetch fire. If it returns before the purifications are completed it does not come to land at any point on the island but remains waiting out by the rocks until it is allowed to approach the shore. Calling upon the chthonic gods and those whose names it is not permitted to mention, the *theores* keep the fire, out at sea. When they disembark and share the fire out for all the needs of life and for the artisans' forges, then, they say, "a new life commences"'.

We are bound to draw a parallel between this ritual of the extinguishing and relighting of the fires and the myth of the Lemnian women, and are indeed prompted to do so by the fact that Philostratus points out that the ceremony commemorates the story of the Lemnian women. There are two episodes to the myth: the first consists of the foul-smelling women being separated from their husbands, a separation which leads to the murder of all creatures of the male sex; the second, of the renewal of life through the collective marriage between the Argonauts and the women of Lemnos who have become desirable again. These two episodes correspond to the two parts of the ritual. Here, in the first phase, when fire, heat, cooking and sacrifices disappear all normal life is abolished; in the second, the introduction of a pure fire heralds the beginning of a new life for Lemnos. There is every indication that it is in the first part of the festival that the separation of the men from their foul-smelling wives takes place. For nine days, Lemnos is a land without fire of any kind — whether for cooking, for sacrifice or for metal work — and this cold land is inhabited principally by women separated from their husbands and characterised by the smell of putrefaction emanating from their sexual organs, mouths or arm-pits. Lemnos could thus be seen as a 'rotten' world in which, according to a model evolved by Claude Lévi-Strauss[140], mediation between Earth and Sun is no longer assured by the cooking fire which, in Greece, is seen first and foremost as a sacrificial fire. The disunion between men and women, indicated by the smell of putrefaction, could thus be seen to correspond to another disunion, a cosmic one this time, between Sun and Earth.

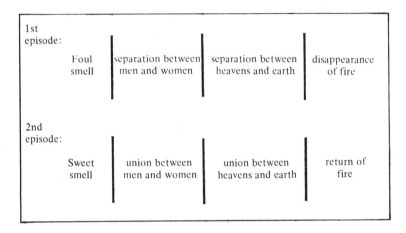

1st episode:

| Foul smell | separation between men and women | separation between heavens and earth | disappearance of fire |

2nd episode:

| Sweet smell | union between men and women | union between heavens and earth | return of fire |

There is one detail of the Lemnian ritual which would seem to authorise our establishing a correlation between the sociological and astronomical levels. The fire which brings life back to the island permeated by the smell of death is no earthly fire. It is not produced by striking as is the fire which makes it possible for Philoctetes to survive in the wild desert of Lemnos when he is abandoned there by the Greeks who are disgusted by the stench of his wound.[141] Nor is it a fire produced by rubbing two sticks together, one male and the other female, as for the first sacrificial fire lit by Hermes.[142] This new fire in Lemnos comes from Delos which, in the Greek world, shared with Delphi the privilege of nurturing an 'immortal and ever pure' fire which the other cities came to supply themselves with when they needed to relight their own perpetual hearths, as happened after the invasion of the Persians who defiled all the public fires.[143] There is only one reason to account for the exceptional purity of the fires of Delphi and Delos: the solar origin of the flame that feeds them. Plutarch, who was a priest of the Pythian Apollo, tells us that when the

Delphic fire happens to go out: 'they say it must not be kindled again from another fire but made fresh and new by lighting a pure and unpolluted flame from the rays of the sun'.[144] To do this the Greeks used

'metallic mirrors the concavity of which is made to follow the sides of an isosceles rectangular triangle and which converge from their circumference to a single point in the centre. When, therefore, these are placed opposite the sun so that its rays, as they fall upon them from all sides, are collected and concentrated at the centre, the air itself is rarefied there and very light and dry substances placed there quickly blaze up from its resistence, the sun's rays now acquiring the substance and force of fire.'[145]

The fire which the people of Lemnos went to fetch from Delos was a fire from Above of this same type and by going there they avoided having to use a technique which was as uncommon as it was hazardous.[146] The hazard lay in that it truly did bring about a real union between Earth and Sun. Such a union could result in spices being magically produced but its dangerous nature is clearly illustrated in the misfortune of Phaeton who, by driving the chariot of the Sun too close to the Earth, nearly destroyed the latter in a huge fire. It is also an uncommon technique[147] for the Greeks only have recourse to it in cases of extreme urgency, when some unforeseen cataclysm destroys the fire of solar origin, normally kept alight by the ministrations of women abstaining from all sexual relations.[148]

The 'new life' in Lemnos cannot begin until this mediation by the fire brought from Delos intervenes to abolish the disunion between the Sun and the island by encouraging a return to the civilised life that results from the combined presence of fire for technology and fire for cooking. Henceforward sexual relationships between the couples are reestablished and the women are delivered from the putrefaction with which they were afflicted. However, this reference to a state of normality which can be restored by the reintroduction of fire for cooking and by marriage may understandably seem an inadequate foundation for affirming the equivalence, in myth, of three terms, namely the stench of putrefaction = disunion between couples = separation without mediation between Earth and Sun. In order to establish this equivalence we must do more than merely discuss the lightly perfumed women who are matched by the slightly foul-smelling wives. We must contrast the Lemnian women with the mythical image of women who are diametrically opposed to stench and separation. Such an image, the symmetrical converse to that of the Lemnian women as defined can only be revealed through studying the ritual behaviour of the devotees celebrating the festival of Adonis. Thus, through the stench of the Lemnian women, we are brought back to the myth of perfume which was our original point of departure and whose essential elements reappear — although in different combinations — in the structure of the two separate parts of the ritual of the Adonia.

	Lemnian women	Thesmophoria	Adonia
Olfactory code	Stench	Slight smell of fasting Moderate use of spices	Perfumes
Sociological code	excessive disunion between men and women	Husbands held at a fair distance	Excessive union between the sexes
Cosmo-logical code	Earth disunited from sun	Sun + Seasons	Earth united with Sun

From the Lemnian women to the Adonia

V

The Seed
of Adonis

Faced with the coup brought off by Lysistrata and her accomplices when they decided to occupy the Acropolis, summarily hustling out the city elders, the stalwart 'officer of the people' who arrived upon the scene at the head of a squad of Scythian archers, initially sought reassurance by identifying the incident as some 'festival of Adonis':

'Has then the women's wantonness blazed out,
Their constant timbrels and Sabaziuses
And that Adonis feast upon the roof
Which once I heard in full Assembly time?
'Twas when Demostratus (beshrew him!) moved
To sail to Sicily: and from the roof
A woman, dancing, shrieked "Woe, woe, Adonis!"
And *he* proposed to enrol Zacynthian hoplites;
And *she* upon the roof, the drunken woman,
Cried "Wail Adonis!" yet he forced it through,
That god-detested, vile, ill-tempered man.
Such are the wanton follies of the sex.'[1]

The interest of this episode in the *Lysistrata* of Aristophanes does not solely lie in its amusing depiction of the short-sightedness of a political official incapable of coming to terms with a new situation without first identifying it with some other which is familiar and reassuring. It lies first and foremost in the picture that it gives of the Adonia, a picture that was probably widely accepted by the Athenians: we are told of a noisy festival of ill-repute in which the indecent behaviour of the women[2] at their antics on the rooftops scandalises many citizens although the city does not allow the agitation of a handful of private individuals of the female sex who do not, after all, enjoy any political rights, to distract it from carrying on public life. A further interest in the episode lies in the fact that it suggests the date for the celebration of the Adonia by indicating that — as is confirmed by Plutarch[3] — the festival was taking place at the same time as the tragic expedition to Sicily which Thucydides tells us was undertaken 'at a time when the summer was already half-over (thérous mesoûntos ếdē)'.[4]

The summer was, in fact, the time for the Adonia. The famous gardens were sown 'in the summer' and this information, given by Plato in the *Phaedrus*[5], is made even more specific by Theophrastus' remark that this type of cultivation is undertaken 'when the sun is at its most powerful'.[6] However, recent research on the chronological system used by Thucydides makes it possible to date the festival of the Adonia even more precisely.[7] On the basis of the astronomical tables constructed by his contemporaries, in particular Eucktemon, Thucydides divides the year into two seasons, the good and the bad, summer (*théros* in the wide sense) and winter (*kheimốn*). Summer is devoted to military activities and to farming, extending from sowing to harvest, that is a period of eight months from March 6th (the evening rising of Arcturus) to November 8th (the morning setting of the Pleiades). This period is further subdivided into three parts: the spring (*éar*), from March 6th to May 13th; the summer (*théros* in its more limited sense), from May 13th to September 14th; and the autumn (*metópōron*), from September 14th to November 8th. In view of this, Thucydides' information regarding the date of the Sicilian expedition — and, by extension, that of the Adonia — should not be understood to mean 'the middle of the good season', that is the beginning of July, but rather the middle of summer in its narrower sense, that is mid-July[8] which coincides perfectly with the period mentioned by Theophrastus as the time for cultivating the gardens of Adonis: 'when the sun is at its most powerful'.

Various data which stress the close correlation between Adonis and Sirius make it possible to establish that the festival celebrated over several days in honour of Myrrha's son took place during the very hottest period, the dog-days. The start of this period is marked by the heliacal rising of the constellation of the Dog, which is dated to July 20th by the Athenian astronomer, Meton,[9] but to July 23rd or 27th by the astronomical tables of his contemporaries depending upon whether they refer to the real or the apparent rise of Sirius.[10] On the basis of the evidence in the *Acts of the Saints Justus and Rufinus*, Franz Cumont was able to establish that during the Roman Empire the Adonia were celebrated on July 19th which, in the Julian calendar, is the date of the morning rising of the Dog star and the beginning of the Canicular or Sothic year.[11] Moreover, our entire enquiry on the subject of spices has indicated the importance of Theophrastus' evidence that the harvesting of myrrh and frankincense takes place at the rising of the Dog star, 'during the hottest days of the year'[12], that is to say at the very same time as he tells us that the gardens of Adonis are cultivated. Consequently, it is surely because the canicular period is the most propitious both for harvesting myrrh and for the cultivation of Adonis' gardens that it represents the appropriate astronomical framework for a ritual whose two essential phases involve, as we shall see, on the one hand the cultivation of the gardens and, on the other, a kind of collection of spices.

One of the best known features of this festival celebrated by women in honour of the lover of Aphrodite is the growing of cereals and vegetables, within a few days, in small pots of earth set out in the open. Despite the clear and unambiguous ancient evidence on the technical methods used, the subject of the gardens of the Adonia has given rise to all sorts of misunderstandings in one school of historians of religion. It is on the interpretation of these ritual gardens that the two most widely accepted theories of the myth of Adonis are based. The disagreement between them arises from the apparent ambiguity of this type of gardening in which plants emerge from the ground within only two or three days, only to wither away immediately in the very heat which made their rapid growth possible. According to one interpretation, the gardens were intended to be a reminder of the death of the god of spring vegetation which is burned up by the great heat of the summer.[13] According to the other, the gardening represents an agricultural rite intended to herald and encourage the resurgence of the dessicated vegetation.[14] Both theories are so strongly tied to the Frazerian ideology involving a god Adonis who alternately dies and is reborn that they are not only interchangeable but can, without difficulty, be combined together, as can be seen in the interpretation put forward by the most positivist of the historians of Greek religion, M.P. Nilsson, who writes on the subject of the gardens of Adonis:

'cet usage confirme ce qui est si evident qu'on ne l'a jamais mis en doute: Adonis est un dieu de la végétation qui incarne la croissance et le dépérissement des plantes, et leur mort dans la chaleur de l'été' ('This custom confirms what is so obvious that it has never been questioned: Adonis is a god of vegetation who embodies the growth and withering of plants and their death in the heat of the summer'.)[15]

We can counter this purely ideological 'evidence' with other data to be found in the entire ancient tradition relating to the Gardens of Adonis, from Plato down to Simplicius: it shows that the plants in these gardens bore no fruits and were fundamentally sterile.[16] This is borne out, in the first place, by a number of proverbs commented on by the Greek paroemiographers and which indicate the semantic framework for this type of gardening. *'You are more sterile (akarpóteros) than the gardens of Adonis'* is a proverb used in connection with people who are incapable of producing anything worthwhile (*mēdèn gennaîon tekeîn*).[17] The gardens of Adonis is a proverbial expression used to refer to whatever is lightweight (*koûphos*) and superficial (*epipólaios*)[18]; it is also used to describe anything that is immature (*áōros*) or what has no roots (*mè errhizōménos*). In effect Adonis, the object of Aphrodite's passion, died before coming of age (*proēbḗs*) and this is why his followers who cultivated in clay pots these gardens which, being rootless, soon withered away (*takhéōs maraínesthai*), called them by the name of Adonis.[19] Elsewhere too, the meaning of the same proverb — used to refer to anything lacking maturity, anything ephemeral (*oligokhrónios*) or lacking virility (*ánandros*), sterile, or to that which dies prematurely (*ōkúmeros*) — is connected with the figure of Adonis. In one instance he appears as a young, handsome man who does not make the most of his beauty, like the owner of a garden of stone (*kēpos líthinos*) who can derive no profit from it.[20] In another he is compared to a young man whose premature death is reminiscent of those plants 'which grow rapidly in a pot of earth, a basket or some kind of wicker receptacle, and are then immediately cast into the sea where they soon disappear.'[21] "Fruitless, lacking maturity, without roots ...", none of these qualities connected with the gardening practised under the sign of Adonis are particularly suggestive of magic to 'promote the growth of vegetation, especially of the crops ...'[22]; nor do they prompt us to see here a substitute for authentic cultivation which might have withered away under the sun's brilliance.[23] On the contrary, the negative character of all these epithets indicates that the gardening of Adonis stood for a negation of the true cultivation of plants and was an inverted form of the growing of cereals as represented, in a religious context, by the principal power responsible for cultivated plants, namely Demeter. Underlying the proverbs which all provide variations on the theme, the opposition between Adonis and Demeter — the importance of which has been demonstrated by the myth about Mint — becomes explicit in the most ancient description we know of the ritual of the Adonia, Plato's *Phaedrus*. In the course of Plato's trial of writing, and of the confrontation between the spoken and the written word, Adonis and his gardens are evoked in a long comparison whose purpose is to show that the written word is no more than the shadow and imitation of animated, living speech.[24]

'And now, tell me this: if a sensible farmer had some seeds to look after and wanted them to bear fruit (*énkarpa*), would he with serious intent plant them during the summer (*théros*) in a garden of Adonis and enjoy (*khaírein*) watching them grow up into fine plants within eight days? If he did so at all, wouldn't it be in a holiday spirit (*heortḗ*), just by way of pastime (*paidiá*)? For serious purposes, wouldn't he behave like a scientific farmer (*geōrgikē tékhnē*), sow his seeds when it is suitable (*eis tò prosēkon*) and be well content if they come to maturity (*télos*) within eight months?'

The oppositions indicated in the *Phaedrus* between the cultivation of cereals and the gardening of Adonis are expressed in terms of the polar opposition between, on the one hand, what is serious — purposeful activity (*spoudḗ*) — and, on the other, frivolity — the holiday spirit and amusement (*paidiá*). The contrast between these two types of behaviour is reflected in a series of oppositions between the types of seeds used, the respective fruits and the time involved in each type of cultivation. The strong, fertile seeds used in true cultivation are opposed to the weak, quickly exhausted seeds used in the festival gardening and, similarly, the lasting and nourishing fruits of the former are contrasted with the fruits of the latter which soon wither away and are not suitable for eating. Cereal cultivation takes a long time, the whole of the eight months that are necessary for the seeds to reach their fruition, their *télos*; to cultivate Adonis' gardens, on the other hand, takes hardly any time, just the eight days which are sufficient for the growth of shoots which never do reach their maturity or *télos*. And these oppositions are repeated throughout an entire body of evidence which, emphasising now one aspect and now another, makes free use of this antithesis between the two spheres of Adonis and of Demeter.

Plato contrasts the solemn, patient toil of the farmer of Demeter with the pleasure (*khaírein*) and the amusement of the gardener of Adonis. Whereas serious agriculture sets out to 'educate' the plants and attempts to be a *paideía*, the gardening of Adonis is no more than a game, a kind of *paidiá*.[25] This contrast is echoed by several other writers who also stress the frivolous and illusory aspect of the festival gardening. One, paraphrasing the *Phaedrus*, condemns the 'ephemeral charis' of these gardens which wither away in no time at all: their brilliance is fleeting and the pleasure that they provide is shortlived.[26] On a deeper level, Simplicius sees them as a form of illusion: 'These are gardens which appear to the eyes of fools to be in full flower, but only a few days later they are completed ruined'.[27] Their green, flourishing appearance conceals nothing but death and desolation: they are gardens of stone.[28] And, Plutarch remarks, the women who exert themselves with all the 'cares of a nurse' in order to cultivate little gardens which wither away as soon as they have grown, resemble a frivolous (*kenóspoudos*) god who might amuse himself by making ephemeral souls grow in bodies which are too delicate (*trupherós*) for life ever to become rooted there.[29]

But one of the differences most strongly stressed in the *Phaedrus* concerns the period of time involved in the two different types of cultivation: eight days in one case and eight months in the other. In the Attic calendar eight months is approximately the length of time between *Pyanopsion* (October) and *Thargélion* (May), that is the period between the sowing, before the winter rains, and the festival of the Thargelia which heralds the impending harvesting of the cereals of Demeter. In the Adonia the long period of time necessary for nature, *phúsis*, to produce barley and corn shrinks and is contracted to eight days in which the whole natural process from the sowing to an ephemeral and illusory harvest is condensed. The shortened, restricted time of this ritual gardening can therefore be seen as a kind of violence done to nature. And indeed, Aristotle and Simplicius describe the Gardens in these very terms. In the fifth book of the *Physics*, where he is analysing the two concepts of 'in conformity with' and 'contrary to' nature (*kata phúsin* and *para phúsin*), Aristotle gives a number of examples of growing and withering away which are 'violent and not in conformity with nature' in which he includes the 'precocious flowering of the sensual adolescent and the accelerated growth of corn which has not even been firmly bedded in the ground'.[30] In his commentary on these lines, Simplicius explicitly confirms that this is an allusion to Adonis and the cultivation of his gardens and he goes on to say that in this type of cultivation, 'the corn grows quickly on account of the great heat (*thérmē*)[31] and shoots up before it has firmly thrust its roots into the earth'.[32] The difference between eight day shoots and eight month cereals is that which separates 'what has matured in conformity with nature from what is subjected to violence'[33], to use the expression of Epictetus.

This 'violence' which is such a feature of the gardening of Adonis appears not only in the diminished time span involved but also — as Theophrastus points out — in the timing of the gardening, in the obvious untimeliness of sowing seeds in high summer, scorning the season which is 'suitable'[34] for each type of plant cultivated in these little gardens. It is, however, in the special techniques used in this festival gardening that the systematic violation of the rules for correct agriculture appears most clearly. The plants of Adonis do not grow in land suited to the sowing of seed or in land suited to planting[35]; they germinate in pots, in bowls (*khútrai*), in clay vases (*aggeîa keramiká*), in shards (*óstraka*), on in baskets (*árrhikhoi*) and wicker receptacles (*kóphinoi*)[36], all of which are filled with earth — no doubt enriched earth, some kind of compost (*gê lakhaniá*) — but earth which is no more than a derisory reflection of the real earth which nourishes men and is a secure foundation for them. The situation is all the more acutely derisory in that these little receptacles cultivated by women (whereas farming in Greece is specifically work for men)[38], are carried about, moved from place to place and ultimately suspended between heaven and earth: the women finally deposit their little gardens, which truly become gardens 'in the air' (*metéōroi*), on the rooftops where the festival is celebrated, carrying them up there by means of a ladder, as is depicted on certain fourth century vases.[39]

Although the techniques it employed revealed this roof-top

gardening to be spurious, it would seem that trouble was taken to present it in the guise of the very system of which it was, in reality, an inverted travesty. Almost as soon as the seeds were sown the shards and baskets were filled with green shoots whose freshness could compete with the luxuriance of the corn-fields at the beginning of the month of Thargelion when the Athenians made sacrifices to 'luxuriant' Demeter, known as *Khlóē*, so as to place the new corn under her protection and that of her associate, Mother Earth (*Gê Kourotróphos*).[40] However, in contrast to the greenness of Demeter which heralds an abundance of the earth's fruits, the greenness of Adonis guaranteed no harvest at all. Its illusory vigour revealed only its impotence, its inability to produce fruit, and its brilliance was all the more of a deception in that its excessive violence brought about its total exhaustion; no sooner green than dessicated. There can be no doubt about the evidence: the plants of Adonis 'only grow until they are green' (*ákhri chlóēs mónēs*); 'hardly have they started to become green (*khlōrḗsanta*) than they wither away.'[41]

The transformation from green to dessicated is promoted not only by the techniques employed in this sort of gardening but also by the meteorological conditions selected for the planting of these gardens. The violent heat of the Dog days is responsible both for making the plants grow within a few days and for destroying them equally rapidly. The stifling heat of Sirius is necessary for the rapid germination of these gardens and it is also the burning heat of the mid-point of the solar year that dries up the plants on the stems that have only just shot up. The gardening of the Adonia only assumes its full significance in the context of the Canicular period and within the framework of this astronomical situation in which the power of the sun threatens to burn up the earth. In this connection, the ladder which is a central feature in the vase paintings illustrating the Adonia is not only the instrument which is indispensible to cultivate the little gardens by putting them out 'closer' to the sun; it is also, in the pictorial terminology of the vases, the symbol of an exceptional linking of the Earth Below and the Sun Above.

The unusual transition in these Gardens from green to dessicated is confirmed by the nature of the plants from which they are composed. The seeds planted in the clay pots and bowls belong to

	THE SOWING OF SIRIUS	THE SOWING OF DEMETER
Type of cultivation	Amusement, distraction. *Hēdonē*	Serious farming *pónos*
Timing	8 days: canicular period An inopportune time	8 months: from the Thesmophoria to the Thargelia A suitable time
Medium	Baskets, jars, shards, bowls	Mother Earth
Agents	Women	Men
Vegetable products	No fruits False *Khloē* No *Télos*	Fruits *Khloē* *Télos*
Metaphorical products	An ephemeral *charis* *Mēdēn gennaîon* *Aōros* Superficial, lightweight No roots	Charites *Gómmos* *Hōraîos* Serious, solemn Rooted

The sowing of seeds: from Sirius to Demeter

four distinct species: wheat, barley, lettuce and fennel.[42] The presence of the first three is easily explained by reference to the botanical code that we have distinguished at work in the myths about spices: wheat and barley, both cereals, are the foods of Demeter just as lettuce, a garden plant, is the vegetable symbol of the death and impotence which assail the master of these gardens. As for fennel, *márathon* (*Foeniculum vulgare Gaertn.*), its various qualities fit it for the role still vacant in this vegetable micro-system. The fennel known to the Greeks is a plant used both as a condiment and as a spice in a large range of seasonings: as a spice, since its smell and taste are close to those of aniseed; and as a condiment since the Greeks were no doubt not familiar with the cultivated species of fennel, known as sweet fennel, which provides the well-known vegetable.[43] But for the ancient botanists this pungent condiment also possessed properties which set it in clear opposition to the lettuce. Not only does fennel heat and have a drying effect,[44] but it is 'excellent for the genital organs' and provokes an abundance of sperm.[45] Although the aphrodisiac and drying properties of fennel do seem to oppose it to a cold and sterile-making plant such as lettuce, there is one characteristic peculiar to certain species of fennel which suggests that we should not identify this plant with spices too categorically. Dioscorides and Pliny the Elder both point out that, in Eastern Spain, fennel produces a sap similar to gum which is collected by two different methods. In the first the stem is cut half-way down when the plant flowers and is placed near a fire so that the heat makes it sweat and secrete the gum; by the second method the sap is collected when the stem begins to bud and is put to dry in the sun, later to be used with honey as a lineament.[46] Both these techniques emphasise the ambiguity of a plant which can secrete a type of gum, like certain oleoresinous species, although this gum is insufficiently concocted since it must be further subjected either to the heat of the fire before it can be collected, or else to the sun in order for it to form a concretion. We must add to this first ambiguity the fact that this plant with aromatic qualities which is nevertheless distinct from the spices as such is also a seed or fruit-bearing species[47] which is sometimes cultivated in gardens and sometimes grows in a wild state.[48] It then becomes even more clear that, in the cultivation of the gardens of Adonis, fennel possesses all the qualities necessary to represent the significance of the spices[49] within the framework of a cultivated garden — a framework that does not include the majority of perfumed substances in Greece, these being accepted to be products of nature in the wild.

In consequence, the four species cultivated by gardeners during the Adonia can be classified on two levels, first in relation to cereals which belong to Demeter, and secondly in relation to garden plants which are intimately linked with Adonis whose two essential sides they represent. The two pairs of terms involved (fennel and lettuce on the one hand, wheat and barley on the other) can be positioned on intersecting axes. It is the axis composed by the pair lettuce and fennel that represents the gardening of Adonis, a misleading imitation of the agriculture of Demeter, oscillating between the two extreme states of greeness and dessication.[50] Under the blaze of Sirius the garden plants of Adonis are subjected to an intensive roasting; they undergo a treatment which we know to be perfectly suitable for spices but so bad for garden and cereal plants such as wheat, barley and lettuce that to force these plants to undergo the same conditions as fennel is to commit them to an imminent and complete dessication. This, in a way only apparently paradoxical, condemns the whole group to the state of lettuce. What, in effect, is the fate of these green shoots once the Dog star has baked and withered them? They are cast into springs or into the sea.[51] Frazer and his followers only paid attention to the first of these alternatives, seeing it as proof of the connection between this ritual of the Adonia and fertility magic — for the water of springs must surely be interpreted as being fertile.[52] However, we are bound to dismiss such an interpretation which perpetuates a totally false understanding of the gardening of Adonis, especially since it not only ignores the casting of the plants into the sea but also takes no account of a botanical factor whose importance we have already briefly indicated. This is the connection between spring water and lettuce mentioned by Oribasius, who was a doctor living at the time of the Emperor Julian. He calls the lettuce 'this cold, wet plant' and goes on to say that 'although it does not reach the highest degree of wetness, it is as wet as spring water'.[53] Whether they are cast into the sea whose saltiness withers and burns the plants or thrown into springs, here the symbol of death and sterility in the same way as lettuce, the garden plants of the Adonia, spurious spices that they are, all come down on the side of the plant which stands for the impotence and tragic death of the lover of Aphrodite.

This tension between fennel on the one hand and lettuce on the other establishes the framework for the dual movement passing from green to dry and from dry to dessicated or, to be more exact, from a deceptive greenness to a false dryness which is really only dessication and, as such, committed to rapid putrefaction. As a result of their having been treated as spices the wheat and barley of Demeter are transformed into the lettuces of Adonis. The whole of this first period of the ritual of the Adonia provides, so to speak, an almost experimental proof that the seeds of Adonis are afflicted with sterility and impotence and that this frivolous type of gardening has the effect of corrupting the fruit-bearing seeds and cereals of Demeter, the provider of food.[54]

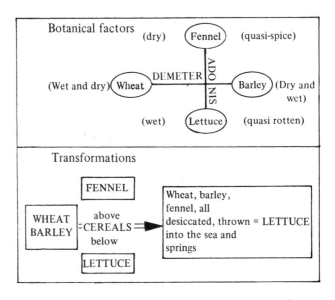

The path taken by the gardens of Adonis

This account of the various oppositions between the sphere of Adonis and that of Demeter would be incomplete if we did not mention a final contrast, this time of a culinary nature, which defines more closely the idea of roasting which has already figured in our account, and throws more light on the astronomical features of the two spheres. If, for Plato in the *Phaedrus*, the distance between *Pyanopsion*, (October) and *Thargélion* (May) represents the time necessary for cereal plants to come to maturity, the converse period, from *Thargélion* (May) to *Pyanopsion* (October) appears, in the Athenian calendar, to be connected with a particular image of the cultivated earth. The five months from *Thargélion* to *Pyanopsion* do not correspond either to summer in the strict sense (4 months) or to summer in the wider sense (8 months), as defined by the fifth century astronomers.[55] But they represent a slice of time which is characterised by the close collaboration between the Sun (*Hélios*) and the Seasons (*Hôraí*), the deities to whom the Athenians made joint sacrifices to mark the two festivals named after the respective months in which they took place, namely the *Thargélia* with which this period of the year opened and the *Pyanopsia* which brought it to a close.[56] The Sun, the power which gives life and makes young shoots (*phútios*) grow[57], is associated with *Thalló*, 'the Power of the Branches', *Auxó*, 'the Power of Growth' and *Carpó*, 'the Power of the Fruits'. These are the three 'Seasons', the three Athenian *Hôrai* which make the branches grow and ripen the fruits of the earth. The activities of these powers of nature are best described in a passage from the Atthidographer, Philichorus. This describes the type of sacrifice which the people of Athens reserve for the 'Seasons':

'When they sacrifice to the *Hôrai* their custom is to boil the meats instead of roasting them. For they ask these powers to set aside the excessive heat (*periskelê kaumata*) and the drought (*ankhmoús*) and to bring the fruits of the earth (*ekteleîn tà phuómena*) to maturity, by dispensing a moderate heat and regular rains. The Athenians in effect believe that roasting (*óptēsis*) is a procedure inferior to cooking by boiling (*hépēsis*) which not only removes the rawness from the meats but can also soften the tough parts (*tà sklērà maláttein*) and cook the rest to a turn (*pepaínein*).[58]

As we have already mentioned, the Greeks' sacrificial practice corresponded to their methods of preparing meat. Roasting and boiling were neither completely interchangeable nor mutually exclusive cooking methods. In the *thusía* type of sacrifice of animal victims, which was practised from Homeric times down to the end of the Classical period, there was a place for both roasting and boiling. True, in certain circumstances all meats might be roasted (as they are in Menander's *Dýskolos* by sacrificers who have forgotten to bring the cooking pot indispensable for boiling)[59], or, equally, they could all be cooked in the pot (as is done by the people of Aigialos when they sacrifice a ram in honour of a young man who has been made a hero.[60] However, as a rule roasting and boiling are used alternately in the course of the same sacrifice. The 'noble' entrails from the victim are roasted on a spit while the pieces of meat for the sacrificial banquet are set to boil in a stewing pot. A careful distinction is made between the two operations both in a relevant piece of written evidence and also in a ceramic painting of the subject. The ritual rules of the 'Singers', the *Molpoi* of Miltus, mention, among other privileges of the *Onitades* 'the grilling of the entrails' (*óptēsis splágkhnōn*) and the 'cooking by boiling of the meats' (*kreôn hépsēsis*).[61[This evidence is matched by the great sacrificial scene on the Ionian *hydria* from Caera which has a succession of representations illustrating first grilling, with the meat threaded onto spits turned by three young men, and then the huge pot from which another acolyte, wielding a meat-hook, has just taken a piece of meat to test whether it is cooked.[62] In this painting, which faithfully depicts the organisation of an ordinary sacrifice, the boiling comes after the roasting. Indeed the entrails were normally eaten before the remaining parts of the victim which constituted the true sacrificial meal. Thus, when the man-eating Cyclops decides to devour the Greeks he has discovered in his cave, the meal, which is described as some monstrous and horrible sacrifice, is divided into two parts. The giant starts off with the pieces of flesh 'still burning as they come from the fire' and follows this up with the remaining parts which are 'softened by being cooked in a pot'.[63] The roasted meat is followed by the boiled. The custom seems to be so binding that a ritual in which this order is reversed appears as a kind of anti-sacrifice. Such is the cannibal sacrifice to the young Dionysus, the 'consumer of raw flesh'[64] which is carried out by the Titans, the ancestors of the earliest men: they first boil the flesh, limb by limb, and then roast this boiled meat on spits over the fire.[65] It is such an unusual cooking procedure that it is the subject of one of the Aristotelian *Problemata* where the roasting of the boiled meat is denounced as a veritable retrogression: just as roasted meats were considered more raw and more dry than boiled meats, so cooking on the spit preceded the use of cooking pots in the history of mankind.[66]

But the difference between boiling and roasting is not simply a difference between two methods of which the former is more refined and less violent than the latter. It is also a matter of balance. The Athenians boil their meats at the Thargelia and the Pyanopsia just as, during these festivals, they simmer over a gentle heat (*en glukeî*) all kinds of seeds mixed together (*panspermía*).[67] The reason for their doing this is that, in the sphere of cooking, this method midway between the raw and the burned effects the balance between the dry and the wet which is produced in nature during the period lasting from *Thargélion* to *Pyanopsion*, by the harmonious combination of moderate heat and regular rainfall and this equilibrium creates the conditions that are most favourable for the gradual ripening of the fruits of the earth.[68] There is a perfect analogy between cooking by boiling which eliminates the rawness of the meat, softens the tough parts and cooks the rest to a turn (*pepaínein*)[69] and the ripening (*pépansis*)[70] of the fruits of

	THARGELIA AND PYANOPSIA	ADONIA
Astronomical code	Sun and the *Hōrai*	Sirius: the canicular period
• meteorological	Balance between the Dry and the Wet	Imbalance between the Dry and the Wet
• culinary	Boiling	Roasting
• vegetable	Ripening ⟶ Fruits of Demeter	Immaturity ⟶ Sterile Desiccation ⟶ gardens
• ritual	*Panspermía* Sacrifice of boiled meats	The gathering and burning of spices

Thargelia, Pyanopsia and Adonia

cultivated plants under the protection of the *Hôrai*,' sheltered from dryness and from excessive heat'.

This reference to the canicular period is explicit enough to prompt us to analyse the model which is the reverse of that on which the Athenian ritual of the 'Seasons' is based, namely the violent, harsh roasting undergone by the gardens of Adonis which are subjected to the excessive heat of the canicular sun.

The appearance in the sky of the 'dessicating' star marks the beginning of the period of imbalance between the dry and the wet the disastrous consequences of which are evident at every level: animals and men are affected just as violently as cultivated plants. In a whole body of evidence the disaster is of cosmic proportions: Sirius makes the fields sterile, deprives the seeds buried in the earth of nourishment, burns plants and afflicts the flocks with sickness. Parched men and beasts are struck down by fever, *puretós*, a fire which burns them up and kills them.[71] One phenomenon in particular illustrates the harmful effects of this star with its all-devouring, killing heat (*purphóros astér*); it is the heat-stroke — the sun-stroke (*seiriasis*) which afflicts the human race[72] and the sideration or blasting (*sideratio, astroblēsía*) of plants and crops.[73] 'Siriasis' finds its victims among the young children, the least robust of the human seedlings. Similarly, 'sideration' — mentioned by Theophrastus as one of the most common diseases of cultivated plants — mostly strikes down the young shrubs and plants whose roots are not strong enough to stretch deep down into the earth for the moisture which they need.[74]

However, this imbalance between the dry and the wet that is brought about by the appearance of Sirius at the height of summer is not only the determining factor in the fate of the gardens cultivated during the Adonia but also creates the conditions most favourable to the operation which appears to constitute the second phase in the ritual celebrated by women in honour of Myrrha's son. For many years now archaeologists have recognised the existence, alongside the series of vases depicting women carrying their gardens up ladders, of another group of paintings (on three *lecythoi* and one *hydria*) which are clearly shown to be part of the Adonis cycle by the central presence in each one of them of a ladder. [75] This time the ladder has nothing to do with gardening. A woman or an Eros descending the rungs, not climbing them, is placing in a bowl held by a young woman an object which is not immediately identifiable in any of the paintings but whose significance is betrayed in one of them which is slightly different from the others (*Lecythus E 721 in the British Museum*).[76] This shows an Eros holding out a perfume-burner (or *thymiatērion*) to his partner. Given that two of the other paintings in this series depict large incense-burners placed prominently at the foot of a similar ladder, most archaeologists, from A. Furtwängler to H. Metzger, have correctly deduced that the mysterious objects placed in the bowl are the grains of frankincense or loaves made of myrrh intended to be burned in honour of Adonis and his mistress, Aphrodite.

That the paintings indeed show a kind of harvesting of spices[77] was recognised at the beginning of this century by A. Furtwängler. It is proved in the first place by the relationship depicted on the different vases between the three principal figures in the scene. One is bringing the spices back from Above, the second is receiving them and the third is feeding the incense-burner. Secondly, it is borne out by the close ties connecting spices with Adonis and making them an inseparable element of the canicular period, the time most suitable for the harvesting of myrrh and frankincense. It is, to be sure, a fictional harvesting but it is nevertheless fully adequate from the point of view of the myth for, although the ladder is clearly not actually used to gather the 'fruits' of the myrrh tree as if they were those of any common-or-garden apple tree[78], in all these paintings, as in the depiction of the Gardens, it is invariably the symbol of a positive coming-together of the Earth Below and the Sun Above. Furthermore, it is in relation to this theme of the ladder which is so important for the Adonia that the two separate phases of the festival are organised.[79] During the first phase the women climb up it in order to set out their gardens in a position exposed to the burning Sun; during the second they climb down its rungs, bringing with them the fruits of Sirius, the spices which the Dog days have brought to maturity and whose purpose is two-fold — to feed the incense-burners in honour of Aphrodite and her lover, and to provide the devotees of Adonis with the perfumes and ointments of seduction.

Both phases of the festival occur at the mid-point of the solar year, the period which submits the gardens to this devastating scorching while at the same time providing the dryness necessary for the production of dessicated substances such as myrrh and frankincense; and the two phases correspond to each other, being two antithetical aspects of the Adonia, two forms of anti-cultivation standing in opposition to Demeter, the one falling short of cultivated plants and the other reaching beyond. The first is negative, being no more than a systematic negation of cereal foods; the second positive, being a manifestation of the all-powerful nature of frankincense and myrrh. Thus the same contrasting terms are repeated in myth and ritual alike. The opposition presented in the myth between myrrh and lettuce is matched in the ritual by the antithesis between the harvesting of the spices and the failure of this type of gardening condemned to the fate of the lettuce. However, the order of the terms becomes reversed: while the myth moves from myrrh to lettuce the ritual leads from lettuce to myrrh just as if the ruination of the cultivated plants was deliberate and essential for the now uninhibited enjoyment of the spices of Adonis.

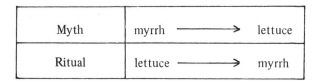

Myth	myrrh ⟶ lettuce
Ritual	lettuce ⟶ myrrh

Adonis: Myth and ritual

The festival and the story of Adonis correspond too exactly for them not to be reflected on the sociological level which our earlier analyses have shown to be invariably parallel to the botanical. Given the double meaning of the word 'seed' (*spérma*) in Greek thought and language, it is natural to seek to define more closely the various form of imbalance represented by Adonis when he stands in contrast to Demeter who is the power of marriage as well as that of cultivated plants. However, before outlining the sexual significance of Myrrha's son and before indicating where his abnormality lies, we should provide a closer definition of the normality in which, under the sign of Demeter, marriage turns out to be inseparable from the life of cultivated plants. It is not merely the case that, in accordance with archaic representations, Athenian ritual identifies the woman with a field which the husband ploughs and sows when he produces legitimate children.[80] In three separate but interconnected ways it also recalls the fact that marriage accompanies the introduction of cultivated life. It does so, firstly, through the obligation imposed upon young Athenian girls to carry, on the day of their marriage, a pan for roasting barley (*phrúgetron*)[81]; secondly, through the custom of hanging a pestle (*húperon*) outside the marriage bed-chamber, a pestle that is matched by the sieve (*kóskinon*) that is carried by a young child taking part in the procession[82]; and finally through the formula, 'I have fled from evil and found what is best', uttered on the wedding day by a child wearing on its head a crown of thorny plants entwined with acorns and offering bread from a winnowing basket (*líknon*)[83] to all the guests. Greek tradition interprets this last custom as a reminder of the decisive transition from the thorny life (*bíos akanthṓdēs*) to the cultivated life (*bíos hḗmeros*), from the wild life (*bíos ágrios*) to the life of milled corn (*bíos alēlesménos*). [84] Set in such a context, the various culinary instruments paraded on the wedding day — the pan for roasting barley, the sieve and the pestle — can be seen as mediators between the two extreme terms reconciled in the figure of the child who is both crowned with thorny plants and loaded with bread. At one extreme we have the wild fruits and plants which represent the food of an age that preceded the cultivation of cereals; at the other, the loaves of bread ready to be eaten as a pledge for the newly married couple's impending participation in the life of milled corn.

The gardening of Adonis is so blatant a perversion of the cereals of Demeter that the seed of Aphrodite's lover must also symbolise the corruption of the fertile seed that is a feature of marriage and conjugal life. The Hippocratic *Treatise on Dreams* already suggests in general terms that trees without fruit (*akarpíē déndrōn*) symbolise the corruption of human seed.[85] On several occasions the ambiguous images chosen to describe the Gardens reveal aspects of the anti-marriage that Adonis, the seducer, represents. Thus, the term *aóros* suggests the immaturity of the plants but also the state of someone who has not yet reached a marriageable age: a boy or a girl is 'too green' (*áōros*) when they have not yet reached an age suitable for marrying.[86] The epithet *atelḗs*, without maturity, has the same double meaning, as is illustrated by a passage in Epictetus' *Conversations*, where the example of the Gardens of Adonis prompts the philosopher to explain to his disciples that philosophy cannot be acquired as quickly as the short cloak or long hair sported by the Cynics. In order for the fruit to

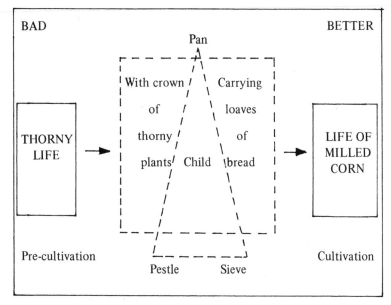

Marriage and cultivated life

develop, says Epictetus,

'the seed (*spérma*) has to be buried and hidden for a season and
be grown by slow degrees (*katà mikrón*) in order that it may
come to perfection (*telesphoreîn*). But if it heads out while it still
has a stem without nodes (*gónu*), it never reaches maturity
(*atelēs*), it is from a Garden of Adonis'.[87]

The ambivalence of the word 'maturity' is suggested here by the use
of the word *gónu*, meaning the node in a stem but also the knee,
which was considered the seat of vigour and sexual power.[88] To
lack *télos* is not only to be seen to be immature and sterile but also
to fail to reach *télos* in the sense of fulfillment when one of the
major forms of this was, for the Greeks, marriage, represented on
the religious level by *Héra Teleía*.[89] Whether the seed of Adonis
be vegetable or sexual, it is characterised by sterility and
immaturity, standing in radical contrast not only to Demeter but
also to Hera, the divine power who presided over the initiation that
marriage represented.

Other aspects of the gardening of the Adonia also present
obvious allusions to the sexual activity of Adonis. Gardens which
produce 'nothing of good stock' (*médén gennaîon*) immediately

suggest sexual relations which do not produce legitimate offspring (*gnēsios*), whether because, as the Lawgiver in the *Laws* writes, it is a matter of 'sowing unholy and bastard seed (*áthuta ... kaì nótha*), with concubines or sowing unnatural and barren seed (*ágona*) with males, contrary to nature'.[90] It is no doubt no accident that the same work by Plato adds to these two forms of sexual abnormality a third, which can be seen as resembling the stoney ground of the garden of Adonis since it involves quite simply the perversion of 'sowing seed on rocks and stones where it can never take root and have fruitful increase'.[91] Since it is doomed to fall on stoney ground, the seed of Adonis can never become a root, a *rhíza*, as good, legitimate seed can.[92] Instead, it is destined to produce only deceiving products, false likenesses (*eídōla kaì pseúdē*)[93] like the bastards or rejected new-born infants whose resemblance to the plants of Adonis is further stressed by the way that they are exposed in pots (*khútrai*)[94] in wild, uncultivated places.

The lack of maturity, sexual union before coming of age, and the sowing of sterile seed are features which all combine to create an image which is the negative of marriage and fertile sexual union and which stress the impotence and sterility of Adonis. However, as the myth itself indicates, what falls short of marriage is simply the other side to what exceeds it. The other side to the sterile sowing of seed is an excessive sexual potency. Adonis is also the precocious adolescent. Aristotle rightly compares him to forced corn which shoots up all at once without having been properly embedded in the earth. It is a comparison which is repeated and developed by Simplicius in such a way as to shed further light on the theme of precocity.[95] Just as a great heat (*thérmē*) hastens the germination of corn, sensuality and the quest for erotic pleasure (*truphē̃*) provoke a more rapid growth.[96] Adonis is still very young when he seduces Aphrodite and Persephone simultaneously and he thus indulges in what medical writers were even then solemnly describing as 'a premature and excessive use of sexual relations'. [97] But this too spectacular seducer is like the 'stem without nodes' mentioned by Epictetus: because there are no solid foundations his sexual potency is doomed to ruination. Violent waxing and violent waning are inseparable terms: sexual excess (*aklosía*) brings in its wake a premature old age, the inevitable consequence of a precocious adolescence. To Simplicius' mind the two phenomena can be similarly explained in terms of the 'physics' of the elements: in both cases there is an imbalance between the hot and the cold, 'the one becoming hotter, the other colder, sooner than is suitable'. And medical diagnosis confirms this theory: 'Those who constantly indulge in sexual union reap the harvest of a seed that is raw and green (*ōmà kaì áōra ... spérmata*)'.[98] Instead of possessing the warmth and consistency of fertile sperm, which has undergone a complete concoction, sterile seed is 'wet and cold (*hugròs kaì psukhrós*)'[99], in other words it possesses the same qualities as the vegetable that symbolises the death and impotence of Aphrodite's lover. Thus the fate of the sensual youth is, as it were, forecast in the gardening of the Adonia: no sooner 'green' than already dessicated and withered. Just like the forced plants which fade as soon as their stem has shot up, the precocious and sensual youth is plunged, in no time, into a premature old age. The brief life which is the lot of the seducer, be he Adonis or Phaon, is simply the temporal expression of this fundamental transition from one extreme to another.

The internal imbalance peculiar to the sexuality of Adonis can be seen to be analogous to the external imbalance characteristic of Sirius. But this is not sufficient proof, in itself, that the 'erotic frenzy and madness'[100] shown by the seducer of Aphrodite and Persephone are particularly provoked by the astronomical position of Sirius which we have seen to be a determining factor in the ritual and also the foundation of the power of spices. However, there is proof to show that, in Greek thought, the canicular period is considered to be more conducive to sexual excess than any other time. Cultivated plants are not alone in being threatened with heat-stroke at the Heliacal rising of the constellation of the Dog; the human race is exposed to the same danger. In Hesiod's calendar the danger is said to exist between the harvest and the treading-out of the grain, 'when the thistle flowers and the chirping grasshopper sits in a tree and pours down his shrill song continually from under his wings, in the season of wearisome summer'.[101] Everything is parched under the burning heat of Sirius: it is the time to stay in the shade of a rock with a well-risen griddle cake and the tasty meat of a heffer pastured in the woods and to stretch out in the cool, drinking the dark wine of Byblos.[102] But the danger of the canicular period is not really drunkeness, particularly as Hesiod takes care to tell his farmer to take three parts of water with every one part of pure wine. The real danger during these wearisome days of summer is that the burning heat of Sirius might produce an imbalance within the couple formed by man and woman: 'Women are then most wanton (*makhlótatai*) and men are feeblest because Sirius parches head and knees and the skin is dry through heat'.[103] Not content to fan the desire of women, Sirius encourages them to seek excessive sensual pleasure. The Greek word '*makhlosúnē*' describes the immodest conduct of a woman and the lasciviousness of courtesans.[104] Under the effect of the Dog star wives become 'most perverse' (*miarótatai*)[105], and this at the very time when their husbands, with their burned heads and knees, appear to be sapped of their strength, 'light' (*leptoí*) as Alcaeus puts it.[106].

What occasions this imbalance? Why does the impact of the devastating heat of Sirius arouse in the woman a sexual appetite that it appears to extinguish in the man? These are more or less the terms in which the question is put in the Aristotelian *Problemata*: 'Why is it that in summer men are less capable of sexual intercourse and women more so?' The answer is such as Hesiod himself might have given if directly asked the question: given that the man is naturally dry and hot the superabundance of heat in the summer weakens by excess whilst it has the effect of balancing the wet cold nature of females.[107] Just when the man's power is on the wane the vigour of the woman is in full flower. But this excess of female sexuality, under blazing Sirius, is not, to Hesiod's way of thinking merely accidental or without importance. The 'lasciviousness' of the woman is a feature of the mythical representations developed in the *Works and Days*.[108] By allowing the Powers of the Night to be dispersed all over the earth Pandora, the original woman, brings men not only Deceit and Hunger but also the progressive dessication that comes with old age: 'However vigorous her husband may be' an evil wife 'burns him without any torch and delivers him to a premature old age while still green with youth (*omós*)'.[109] Woman was sent to men by the Sovereign of the gods as the counterpart to the fire [110] that Prometheus stole and, like an inextinguishable fire[111], she dries up (*maraínein*) her companion and changes his youth into a premature old age.[112] Such is the disturbing image of woman devouring man of which the canicular period each year is a reminder: impelled by her lasciviousness which is fuelled by the burning heat of Sirius, the wife bids fair to transform her husband from 'green' to 'dessicated'. So far as the married couple is concerned, her amorous desire has the effect of reinforcing the devastating brilliance of a star which is already beating harshly upon the head and knees of beings who are 'hot and dry'.

As with Adonis, this is a form of excessive sexual potency and in this instance it is explicitly linked with the period when the fire of the sun is exceptionally close to the earth. No doubt the objection could be made that in the transition from Adonis to the woman in Hesiod the person whom Sirius possesses has changed sex; in terms of the principles of the 'physics of the elements' referred to earlier, the lover of Aphrodite ought, on the day of his festival, to be just as feeble and impotent as the unfortunate husband dessicated by Sirius. However, this would be to forget that in the myth and for the Greeks Adonis is not a husband or even a man: he is simply a lover, and an effeminate one. He symbolises all that is not virile[113] and, as Plutarch notes, his following consists entirely of women or bisexuals.[114] The youth with such abundant seed[115] and the sensual woman of the Dog Days stand for the same thing: they both present an image of seduction.

Sirius, which is so favourable for spices, equally encourages erotic madness to break out. The contemporaries of Aristophanes were not mistaken: licence and shamelessness lie at the very heart of the Adonia. It is the moment when lovers triumph and women behave as demanding mistresses.[116] The following conclusion may be drawn: the position of the devotees of Adonis is the polar opposite of that of the foul-smelling Lemnian women, separated from their husbands at the time when Earth and Sun are set furthest apart; and the combination of the fragrance of spices, seductive relations and the extreme closeness of Earth to the solar Fire is the mark of the time for general seduction.

VI
The Lettuce
of Pythagoras

The thesis that the culminating point of summer constituted a threat to sexual life and marital relations can be established by the further evidence provided by the Pythagoreans. Their evidence is all the more telling in that the dual character of their movement led them to consider the status and behaviour of women with attention, even anxiety. Whether committed to the reorganisation of the city or to a path of renunciation, the disciples of Pythagoras displayed the same distrust where the female sex was concerned. For them not only was woman synonymous with pleasure, sensuality and softness (*truphḗ*), a symbol of all that is diametrically opposed to ascetic endeavour (*pónos*)[1] and to the Pythagorean desire to purify the soul, but furthermore the powers of disorder seated within her rendered her, in their view, largely responsible for the political crisis which the city of Croton underwent at the end of the sixth century. At the time when Pythagoras came and settled there the city was a prey to licence, to *truphḗ*, the economic and social evil which can take the form of an invasion of oriental luxury goods — such as perfumes, clothes, precious objects — as well as that of an imbalance created by inequality between citizens. In Pythagorean thought this evil was simply an extension to the entire social body of the disorder and debauchery, the *truphḗ*, which originates in woman.[2] If the city was to be reformed it was the behaviour of the women which had to be controlled. On this point the Pythagoreans were at one with Plato. To abandon to disorder and licence that part of the human species which is already inclined, through its natural weakness, towards plotting and deceit, is not merely to neglect half the city, as one might think; for, as Plato writes, 'Insofar as females are inferior in excellence to males, just so far do they count for more than half of our task'.[3] Consequently, the reasons for the Pythagoreans taking great account of women within the framework of their reorganisation of the city were the very same that led them to frown on pleasure and condemn the female sex.

A whole area of their political activity was aimed at establishing a particular image of the married woman: when she is led by the right hand to the hearth of her husband, the wife deserves the same respect as the suppliant who has come to place herself under the protection of Hestia. She is good and chaste, modest and reserved and her duty is to give birth to legitimate children, to renounce any form of abortion and, when she is united to her husband, never to wear the jewelry which is the mark of a courtesan.[4] The statement made by a Pythagorean woman who was, for centuries, much admired by the Fathers of the Church, epitomises the praise due to the virtuous wife. Asked how soon a woman who had just had sexual relations with a man could take part in the Thesmophoria, Theano is said to have replied: If this man was her husband she may take part forthwith; if it was a lover, never again.[5] The Pythagorean model of female virtue is normally set within the mythical and ritual framework of the Thesmophoria, the great festival to which the city gave an exclusive right of attendance to the 'legitimate' wives of the citizens.

However, this model would be incomplete without its negative counterpart represented by the different forms of perversion of marriage and sexuality. It is here that the Pythagoreans betray their anxiety when faced with women and sex. Courtesans and concubines are the first example of this. They were the first targets for condemnation when Pythagoras arrived from Samos and his admiring disciples credit him with having, once and for all, eradicated in Croton the practice of illegitimate (*anégguoi*) sexual relations with women.[6] Seed should not be used for pleasure, it is reserved for the reproduction of the species. Similarly, all precocity in the sexual domain was severely criticised. Since neither precocious animals nor forced plants bear good fruit and since a certain time must elapse before a fully grown body is capable of bearing seeds and fruit, the moralists of the sect recommended that young men be kept in ignorance of the pleasures of love until they reached the age of twenty. At this stage they might taste these pleasures but only with moderation, never to excess.[7] Precocity and sensuality were not the only dangers to guard against where sexuality was concerned. Sexual activity, even at the appropriate time and within the bounds of married life, was considered by the Pythagoreans to be a source of debilitation[8], the degree of which varied according to season: lower during the winter which, in Greece, was traditionally the season for marriage, and greater during the autumn and spring. In the summer, however, it became so extreme that the Pythagoreans had no hesitation, on this score alone, in forbidding all sexual activity during the hot season. They thus extended their anxiety to include both a period before and one after the Heliacal rising of Sirius on which Hesiod's concern had been focussed.[9]

It is no doubt no mere chance that this rejection of all sexual relations during the season of the frenzy of the Dog star should find expression in this particular group of people whom we have already seen to be the most tenacious users of spices for exclusively religious purposes. This becomes all the more evident in view of the fact that the various pathological features of sexuality seized upon by the Pythagoreans — namely, sensuality, seduction, precocious sexual relations, coitus during the heat of summer — together compose a veritable reflection of what we might term the sexuality of Sirius. One detail in the Pythagorean diet demonstrates that the reference to Sirius at this point is a pertinent one. According to a certain Lycon[10], the author of a work about the type of life led by the sect, the Pythagoreans gave the name of 'eunuch' to a species of lettuce with wide, spreading leaves and no stem 'because it encourages serous secretions and lessens the desire for the pleasures of love'. It is not only by virtue of its 'refreshing qualities' that this vegetable, particularly appreciated (according to the elder Pliny [11]) during the summer, is considered, as Lycon puts it, 'the best to eat'. The Pythagoreans expected more than purely gastronomic satisfaction from a lettuce known by the name of 'eunuch'. It is only included in the diet of the sect because it makes it possible to avoid the perils of summer and triumph over the erotic temptations prompted by the Canicular period. The impotence the Greeks believed it brought about seemed to the Pythagoreans to offer the best means of neutralising the excess of female sensuality.

By returning to this marginal group through which we have

already been able to identify one fundamental aspect of spices, we find confirmation of the close relationship between the time of Sirius and a particular state of sexuality. But this is not all. The Pythagoreans also provide proof that the lettuce and spices are terms that are necessarily linked in the complex of myths and religious representations centred on perfumes. But when we turn from considering the schema of Adonis and Phaon to that of Pythagoreanism, the relationship between the two terms necessarily undergoes a change in significance. The lettuce of the Pythagoreans is no longer simply the negative term corresponding to the sexual potency spices confer upon the seducers of myth. On the contrary, an apropriate use of this vegetable supports the religious power of the spices for the impotence imparted by this 'cold and wet' plant thereafter guarantees the omnipotence of perfumes in bringing together gods and men. The lettuce of Pythagoras, being invested with a function which equates it with some kind of super-*agnus castus*, definitively strips the spices of the ambivalence which made it possible for these products of nature in the wild to attract two sexual partners to each other as well as to link together the heaven of the Olympians and the earth of men.

The particular interest of the case of the Pythagoreans is that it emphasises the difference, in Greek thought, between these two ends. As expressed through the myths and rituals, the difference takes the form of a clear-cut opposition between a good, and a bad, use of spices. The one leads, ultimately, to a form of commensality with the gods; the other is connected with impotence, sterility and a shortened life. All the Greek myths about spices are organised around the destiny that leads Adonis from myrrh to the lettuce. It is a path which is inverted on the ritual level but this inversion does nothing to alter its significance — a significance which is confirmed by the parallel destinies of Phaon and Mintha and which is, furthermore, fundamentally rooted in a representation of Sirius which is of major importance. Of the three codes, — botanical, sociological and astronomical — that are parallel keys to this body of myth there can be no doubt that the third dominates the other two. It does so not only by virtue of Sirius being so closely related to the collection of spices and the gardening of the Adonia but also because of the strategic position of this constellation whose appearance in the sky marks the beginning of a period of imbalance that favours the switching between two opposite extremes. Not only are spices the sign of this period of imbalance, they are also its fruit. To collect them, men must wait until this climactic point situated outside the seasons, when the balance between the dry and the wet guaranteed by the collaboration between the Sun and the *Hôrai* is upset. On the other hand, these same spices, the products of a disordered situation, in their turn cause a disturbance in cultivated life on the two levels implied by the ambivalence of the word *spérma*, that is the levels of fruit-bearing, and of human, seed.

Both where marriage and where cultivation are concerned spices introduce perversion. Aromatic substances by-pass marital relations either by emitting the irresistible appeal of perfume which brings together the most distant of beings or else by provoking precocity in the sensual adolescent, or extreme sexual potency in the seducer or hyper-sexuality in women — all of which are forms of excess bound to undergo more or less explicit inversion into their opposite, namely impotence which is inseparable from sterility. Analogously, on the botanical level, aromatic substances by-pass the order of cereal-producing plants for, on the one hand, the heat-wave of the Dog days, so necessary for producing frankincense and myrrh, roasts the feeble plants and burns up the tender shoots, and on the other, even though they represent what is beyond the cereal plants, spices are also, so to speak, close to the plant that represents what is below them, namely the lettuce, which is simply the converse to myrrh. But it is perhaps possible to analyse more closely why the particular role spices seem to have in Greece is to denote the perversion of marriage and cultivated life. The fact is that, although spices stand in diametrical opposition to cereals and the way of life represented by Demeter, they are not necessarily — and essentially — excluded from the sphere of that goddess. There is within marriage a definite, albeit moderate, place for the use of spices and perfumed ointments; and similarly sacrifice, which is an integral part of cultivated life, traditionally calls for the burning of pungent substances which have the recognised virtue of summoning the gods to the sacrifice being offered to them. This is the good use of spices and it is thus that they become integrated, as it were, in cultivated life. Hence, as soon as perfumes are principally, even if not exclusively, devoted to erotic ends they are, as it were, diverted from their ritual and religious purpose; they are withdrawn from their correct role which

is to return to the gods the substances with which these have
particular affinities. So it is on the level of ritual sacrifice that the
line between a good and a bad use of spices would appear to be
drawn. An excessive use of perfumes in sexual relations necessarily
entails neglecting the relations that sacrifice establishes between
gods and men and thus perverts this entire cultivated way of life in
which blood sacrifice is just as important an element as
monogamous marriage. So if there is a meaning to the Greek myths
about spices centred on Adonis, if the common codes to these
different but interconnected myths are really intended to transmit
any message in particular, it is perhaps this: any form of seduction
harbours within it the principle of a threat of corruption.

The dominant position held by Adonis in this mythical material
which seems to be particularly concerned with the pathology of
marriage probably has something to do with his oriental origins. It
is not that Eshmun or Tammuz, who have sometimes been
suggested as the near-Eastern models for Adonis, can in any way
explain the destiny of this figure in the religious and social life of
the Greeks. Neither the Phoenician Eshmun nor the Syrian
Tammuz, nor — *a fortiori* — the Sumerian Dumazi, are clearly
enough drawn in the oriental traditions for them to throw any light
at all on the characteristics conferred by Greek mythology upon the
child born from the myrrh tree.[12] Nor is it reasonable to believe
that further acquaintance with these near-Eastern deities would
give us any direct help in understanding the Greek Adonis any
better. For although the foreign origins of Adonis are indisputable
— his very name is evidence of his Semitic connections — his
Oriental qualities appear to be more affected by the way in which
the Greeks represented the East, that was at once so close to them
and yet so far away; this was a world where the refinements of
civilisation and the enjoyment of the most dissolute pleasures
favoured a way of life characterised by softness and sensuality. To
fill the role of the seducer and effeminate lover and embody the
persona of the young boy condemned, through his pursuit of
pleasure, to a premature old age, it was necessary to find a deity
whose features were sufficiently indistinct for them to merge in
with the image the Greeks had created for themselves of the lands
of the East. Besides, only a foreign god could so openly stand,
within a Greek system, for the Other; only an oriental power could
thus stand for the radical negation of the religious and political

values represented by Demeter.

The opposition we have seen to exist between the Adonia and the Thesmophoria is too marked for it not to represent an essential element in Greek social and religious thought: Adonis' excessive seductive prowess only takes on its full significance when contrasted with marriage as symbolised in the Thesmophoria and as defined by Demeter. And the two terms appear so closely interconnected that we must surely take them to be elements of the same system. Moreover, this system would appear to date back to the archaic age since the Thesmophoria are both one of the most commonly celebrated festivals in the Greek world and also one of the major rituals through which Greek society attempts to express the fundamental social relationship represented by monogamous marriage. It is, in this connection, remarkable that in terms of the institutions of the city marriage appears to have had no very definite status, certainly no truly legal one. There was no clear distinction between the 'legal' wife and the concubine. And concubines, in their turn, appear to have varied between, on the one hand, the status of a courtesan — a woman for the pleasures of the bed and, on the other, that of a companion. In the latter case she could, in certain circumstances, assume the role of a wife who bears children to her husband. This institutional omission is perhaps not unconnected with the development of a body of mythology based upon the radical opposition between marriage and seduction. It is as if religious thought took it upon itself to make a distinction between two positions which social thought persisted in confusing together. Thus the distinction between the concubine and the married wife was made all the more sharply by religious thought because, socially, in day-to-day life, it was so difficult to tell them apart.[13]

However, it is not simply this opposition of Adonis to Demeter which gives the mythology of spices an important place in Greek history. Most of our evidence — whether from written texts or in the form of vase paintings — comes from fifth or fourth century Athens. This was the period when Adonis enoyed a vogue in which one essential aspect of his persona in particular was stressed, the very one which can account for the popularity he enjoyed in Attica and possibly throughout the Greek world. In contrast to a festival such as the Thesmophoria which was celebrated in public and in a very official manner, the Adonia took place in private, in some private house where women would meet together, each the confidant of the other's secret love affairs, for a fleeting moment rejecting, in this way, a social order noted for its public and masculine character.[14] Now, at the end of the Peloponnesian War, at the beginning of the fourth century, the crisis in the city is expressed in particular in an explosive expansion of the private sector which had hitherto been confined to the extreme periphery of political life. As a bourgeoisie developed within the city, each citizen took on another, private role.[15] This individual with a private persona first makes his appearance in the works of the authors of 'middle' and 'new' comedy, plays which are a veritable vehicle of propaganda for women, for the devotees of Adonis (*Adōniázousai*) at the same time as they draw attention to the emotional complications for which the Adonia are both opportunity and pretext.[16] The political crisis which developed in the fourth century thus provides a historical context for the myth and ritual of Adonis — a context in which the tension within a more ancient pattern of behaviour comes to the fore.

Finally, the history of these Greek myths about spices raises the more general problem of the level of thought that they represent. In order to identify the various layers of meaning which give form and content to the story of Adonis and the other stories, we had first to refer the mythical material to its ethnographical context. This was not to discover the underlying technological or sociological situation which these stories might reflect on their own imaginary level but in order to trace the roots of the oppositions at work in them in the system of thought and customs of the society which produced these myths and adopted rituals to correspond with them. Now, one of the characteristic features of the Greek world is that its ethnographical context is not simply composed of economic, technical or religious facts but is to a great extent shaped by different branches of knowledge — botany, medicine, the study of religious festivals and so on. In the fifth and fourth centuries, these branches of knowledge took shape in a number of works ranging from the Hippocratic *Corpus* to Theophrastus' *History of Plants* and including the treatises of Philichorus of Athens devoted to religious festivals and sacrificial practices. In the case of all our sources of information — whether they be doctors, botanists, zoologists or liturgists — the evidence does more than simply reveal the background against which the most secret details of the mythology of spices are projected. Whether it be Theophrastus' description of spices or Philichorus' explanation of the significance of what was burned at sacrifices or of the symbolism of the ritual held in honour of the Seasons and the Sun, the information that is yielded is essential to an understanding of the mythical material as a whole. We have, in this way, found ourselves in a position to recognise the remarkable parallelism between the categories operative in the rational thought of the fifth and fourth centuries on the one hand and the principal concepts underlying the mythical material on the other. It is as if secular knowledge, in its various branches, had undertaken to spell out in a decoded form the major types of opposition on which the myths hinge. It is a decoding that is, no doubt, much facilitated by the transparently obvious nature of the basic framework of most of the myths in this group: they are told in a style so sober and apparently unadorned as to express only what is essential. In other words, the paradoxical situation is that, in Greece, in this particular sector, the structural analysis applied from the outside turns out to be in agreement with the analysis which the Greeks who were contemporary with these myths elaborated from within. Neither Theophrastus nor Philichorus of Athens, any more than Hesiod, would have felt themselves on unfamiliar ground confronted with an interpretation in which our only innovation has been to co-ordinate that decoding which the Greeks themselves had already initiated in works that were parallel and, in many cases, complementary to most of the myths themselves.

Notes to the Text

NOTES TO FOREWORD

1 J.G. Frazer, Preface to *Adonis. Etude de religions orientales comparées* (translated by Lady Frazer), Paris, Geuthner, 1921 pp.v-vii.

2 A. Lang, *Custom and Myth*, London 1904, p.63.

3 J.G. Frazer, *Adonis, Attis, Osiris. Studies in the history of Oriental religion*, London, Macmillan & Co. 1907, p. 183.

4 W.Atallah, *Adonis dans la Littérature et l'art grec*, Paris (*Collection Etudes et Commentaires*, LXII) 1966: this thesis ends up with the conclusion that Adonis is a spirit of vegetation associated first with the tree of myrrh and later with ripe fruits (pp.320-7). Right at the end of his enquiry the author, having collected some very useful evidence, began to sense the importance of myrrh in this complicated mythical system, but he failed to draw the necessary conclusions.

5 Cf. G.L. Huxley, *Greek Epic Poetry*, London 1969, p.177 ff., in particular, pp.186-7.

6 Panyassis, F. 25 Kinkel, ap. [Apollodorus], *Library*, III, 14.4.

7 Kinras of Cyprus replaces Theias of Assyria; Cyprus and Pheonicia replace Syria. In Hygienus, *Fab.* 58, the anger of Aphrodite is provoked by the insolence of Smyrna's mother who prefers the beauty of her daughter to that of Aphrodite. In Antoninus Liberalis' version (*Metamorphoses*, 34), and in Ovid's (*Metamorphoses*, X, 315-7), Myrrha rejects all her suitors and falls passionately in love with her father, no doubt for having too much neglected the power or the worship of Aphrodite. For these variants relating to the genealogy and death of Adonis, cf. W. Atallah, *op.cit.*, pp. 23-62.

8 J.G. Frazer, *op.cit.* pp.185-7.

9 This entire method of interpreting the mythology of spices derives from that applied by Cl. Lévi-Strauss in his *Mythologiques*, and defined by him especially in his contribution to the collective volume entitled *Problèmes et méthodes d'histoire des religions*, Paris 1968, p.5 ff.

10 Cf. P. Vidal-Naquet, Athènes au IVe siècle: fin d'une démocratie ou crise de la Cité?' *Annales E.S.C.*, 1963, p.348.

11 The analysis of these myths is the result of a series of seminars

(1968-69) at the Ecole des Hautes Etudes (Social and Economic Sciences). Among the participants who were so kind as to discuss the different problems as each arose, I should particularly like to thank J.-P. Darmon, St. Georgoudi, Cl. Gaignebet, V. Regnot and M. Tardieu. Most of all, however, I am indebted to J.-P. Vernant: not only was he generous enough to find time to attend the seminars, but on more than one occasion his remarks and questions on important points gave a new direction to the enquiry and modified the interpretation of the material. Finally, I should like to thank Alain Schnapp who helped me to design the schemata and diagrams. The symbols used in the diagrams are adopted from *Mythologiques* (I, p.348). The abbreviations are taken from *L'Année philologique*.

NOTES TO CHAPTER ONE

1 F.102 Wyss.

2 *Metamorphoses*, X, 476-481.

3 M. Mayer, *s.v. Hyperboreer, Roscher's Lexicon* (1886-1890), c.2805-2841; Daebritz, *s.v. Hyperboreer*, R.-E. (1914), c.258-279; H. Gallet de Santerre, *Délos primitive et archaïque*, Paris 1958, p.165 ff; J.D.P. Bolton, *Aristeas of Proconnesus*, Oxford 1962, *passim*.

4 III, 106-7.

5 *Hist. Pl.* IX, 4, 2. Saba, Hadramaout, Qatabân and Maʿîn are four states in *'Arabia Felix'* where inscriptions have revealed the importance of offerings of spices in cult practices (G. Ryckmans, *Les Religions arabes préislamiques*, Louvain 1951, p.32). But Theophrastus only knows of three of these four States, and he believes them to be towns. In fact Mamali is probably simply a corrupted form of Mainaia of the Land of the Minaeans (cf. *Grohmann, s.v. Mamali, R.-E.* (1928), c.948-949; D.H. Müller, *s.v. Arabia, R.-E.* (1895), c.344-359; *s.v. Chatramis, R.-E* (1899), c.2197-2198; and above all Tkač, *s.v. Saba, R.-E.* (1920, c. 1299-1314).

6 Cf. the information provided by the botanist, P. Fournier in his commentary to Pliny's *Natural History*, XII, ed. A. Ernout, pp.85 and 87, and by Steier, *s.v. Myrrha, R.-E.* (1933), c. 1134-1146, and in particular that given by J. Innes Miller, *The Spice Trade of the Roman Empire*, Oxford 1969, pp.102-5. For the botanical, geographical and commercial facts relating to frankincense and myrrh, cf. G. Van Beek, 'Frankincense and Myrrh in Ancient South Arabia', *JAOS*, vol.78, 1958, pp.141-52; J. Ryckmans, 'Petits Royaumes sud-arabes d'après les auteurs classiques', *Le Muséon*, vol. LXX, 1957, pp.75-96 (which demonstrates, in particular, that the land routes remained the only access to the spices of Southern Arabia right up till the time

of Pliny; Richard LeBaron, Bowen Jr and Frank P. Albright, *Archaeological Discoveries in South Arabia*, Baltimore 1958, pp.35, 41, 61-62, 84-84, etc. (who undertook a comparison on the spot between the archaeological discoveries and the writings of the ancient authors).

7 Theophrastus, *H.Pl.*, IX, 4, 2; Pliny, *H.N.* XII, 66.

8 Pliny, *H.N.*, XII, 67.

9 *Id.ibid.* 32 and 58. Cf. Theoph. *H. Pl.* IX, 4, 4.

10 Pliny, *H.N.*, XII, 32.

11 35.

12 Theoph. *H.Pl.*, IX, 4, 6, Cf. Pliny, *H.N.*, XII, 63-4; *Peripl. Mar. Erythr.*, 27.

13 Theoph. *H. Pl.*, IX, 5, 2.

14 Pliny, *H.N.*, XII, 90.

15 Two other details noted by Pliny may reflect the same belief. At XII, 93 of the *H.N.* he suggests that sometimes cinnamon forests catch fire when the burning south winds start to blow (cf. [Arist.], *Problemata*, XXVI, 12, 941b). At XII, 98, on the subject of a kind of cassia which might be cultivated even on the frontiers of the Empire 'on the lands washed by the Rhine', he noted that this kind does not have 'that burned colour that the sun gives'.

16 Theoph. *H. Pl.*, IX, 1, 6.

17 Pliny, *H.N.*, XII, 58 and 60.

18 *Id.Ibid.*, 68.

19 The time of the harvest is determined by when *incisions* are made in the trunk and branches.

20 Cf. P. Fournier in his commentary on Pliny, *H.N.*, XII, 58, ed. A. Ernout, p.85, and H. Bretzl, *Botanische Forschungen des Alexanderzuges*, Leipzig 1903, pp. 282-4.

21 July 23 or 27, depending on whether it is a matter of the true or the apparent rising of Sirius: Gundel, *s.v. Sirius, R.-E.* (1927), c.340.

22 Theoph. *H.Pl.*, IX, 1, 6, and IX, 6, 2. In the latter passage, Theophrastus uses the expression: *hótan pnige osi*. The advent of stifling heat, *pnigos*, is the sign that the tables of Euktemon mention to specify the heliacal rising of the constellation of the Dog star (Geminos, *Elementa astronomiae*, ed. K. Manitius (1898), p.212, 1.17).

23 Aristophanes, *Thesmophoriazusae*, 1050, and the remarks of A. Willems, 'Notes sur les Thesmophories d'Aristophane', *Bull.Acad. Royale Belg., Cl. Lettres Sc. Mor.*, 1908, pp.668-74.

24 Pliny, *H.N.*, II, 107. He adds 'This is the constellation which has the most widespread effects on earth. At its rise the seas are rough, wine in the cellars bubbles, marshes are stirred'. In his *Hist. Anim.* (600 a3ff) Aristotle makes similar remarks: this is a period of great

upheavel when the sea is extremely rough and amazing catches are made, when the fish and mud rise to the surface.

25 *Iliad*, V, 4-8; XI, 62.

26 Hesiod, *Works and Days*, 414-417; *Schol.vet.in. Hes. Op.* 417a and 588-590 ed. Pertusi; Suda, *s.v.Seirion*; Archilochus, F.85 Lasserr-Bonnard ap. Plutarch, *Quaest. conviv.*, III, 10, 1, p.658 B; Hesychius, *s.v.Seirios*; Aratos, *Phainom.* 331-332 and *Schol. in Arat. Phain.*, 330, p.408, 1 ff. Maass.

27 Virgil, *Aeneid*, III, 140 ff. and Apollonius Rhodius *Argonautica*, III 959.

28 Pliny, *H.N.*, XVII, 222; Theoph. *H.Pl.*, IV, 14, 2; *C.Pl.*, V, 9, 1; Aratis, *Phainom.*, 331-7.

29 *Il.* XXII, 31. In particular, Sirius provokes *siriasis*, a type of meningitis that principally attacks young children: Oribasius, V. p.207; Hesychius., *s.v. astrobolethenai.*

30 Hesiod., *Works*, 582-7; Alcaeus, F. 347 Lobel and Page.

31 Pliny, *H.N.*, II, 107: VII, 152; *Schol.in. Arat. Phain.* 27, p.345, 7-8 ed. Maass; Timotheus of Gaza, *Perì Zōiōn*, 26, p.16, 24 and 31 ff. ed. Haupt (*Hermes*, III, 1869). Cf. Celsus, *De Medicina*, V, 27, 2, ed. Daremberg.

32 Euripides, *Hecuba*, 1001; Coins from Ceos (fourth century BC): J.N. Svoronos, 'Sternbilder als Münztypen', *Zeitschrift für Numismatik*, vol. XVI, 1888, tabl. X, nos. 18-21; 'Calendar of Hagios Eleutherios at Athens: no. 34 of pl. 39 in L. Deubner, *Attische Feste*, Berlin 1932, [description p. 253]: Illuminations from the manuscripts of Aratos: G. Thiele, *Antike Himmelsbilder*, Berlin 1898, p.121, fig.46 [*Cod.Voss.* vol. 69v]

33 Cf. [Arist.], *Problem.*, XXVI, 12, p.941 b with the indispensible correction made by J. Röhr, 'Beiträge zur antiken Astrometerologie Philologus', vol.83, 1928, p.288.

34 Pliny, *H.N.*, XII, 82 and 86-8, is violently opposed to this belief and to the fables purveyed by Herodotus. He argues that cinnamon comes Etheopia where, however, its harvesting seems to be no less mythical than the stories in Herodotus.

35 Herodotus, III, 113; Theoph., *H.Pl.* IX, 7, 1 and 2.

36 Pliny, *H.N.*, XII, 86; Diod., III, 46, 4-5.

37 Plutarch, *Vit. Alexand.*, 4, quoting Aristoxenus, F. 132 Wehrli, and basing his remarks on Theoph., *C.Pl.*, VI, 16, 2 ff.; 18, 3.

38 Plutarch, *Sympos.*, I, 6, 623 E-F.

39 *Problem.*, XIV, 9, 909b 25 ff.

40 *Problem.*, XIII, 4, 907b 35 ff.

41 Xenophon, *Oeconomica*, XVI, 14-15. Cf. Virgil, *Georgics*, II, 260.

42 Cf. Arist. *Meteor.*, IV, 3, 380a 11 ff.

43 [Arist.] *Problem.*, XXII, 8, 930b 20 ff.

44 *Problem.*, XX, 12, 924a 18.
45 *Ibid.*, 924a 20-24.
46 924a 16.
47 924a 17-18.
48 924a 22-23.
49 For Theophrastus, too, (*H.Pl.*, I, 3, 6), the *Capparis spinosa L.* is one of the plants that resists cultivation Cf. also Pliny, *H.N.*, XIX, 163, ed. J. André (*Comment.*, p.161).
50 The same idea is expressed in Xenophon, *OEcon*, XVI, 5: earth which produces wild plants of good quality can, when it is tended, give cultivated products of good quality.
51 [Arist.] *Problem.*, XX, 4, 923a 17-20: Why must some plants be cooked while others can be eaten raw?
52 *Problem.* XX, 6, 923a 25-29 (plants which, in their raw state, have juices which cannot undergo concoction and which undergo no change under the action of fire are not edible).
53 Cf. Cl. Lévi-Strauss, *Du Miel aux cendres*, Paris 1966, p.259.
54 As opposed to *trophe ek ges*, used to refer to cereals, as A.J. Festugière notes in his commentary on *Ancient Medecine*, Paris 1948, p.35, n.(b).
55 [Hipp.] *On Ancient Medicine*, III, Cf. H. Herter, 'Die Kulturhistorische Theorie der hippokrat. Schrift von der alten Medizin', *Maia*, vol. XV, 1963, p.464 ff. In his study 'Valeurs religieuses et mythiques de la terre et du sacrifice dans l'Odyssée', *Annales E.S.C.*, 1970, pp.1281 ff., P. Vidal-Naquet has shown the importance in archaic Greek thought of a series of models illustrating the transition from wild to civilised life.
56 Paus., IX, 28, 2-4. This passage makes the point that the plants that grow on Helicon, in contrast to those that grow on other mountains, cure reptiles of their wildness and render their venom harmless.
57 Aristoxenus, F.113 Wehrli.
58 Plato, *Laws*, 844 d-e. Cf. N. Weill, 'Adoniazousai ou les femmes sur le toit', *BCH*, vol. 90, 1966, pp.678-81.
59 Cf. [Arist.] *Problem.*, XXII, 8, 930b 20 ff.
60 Pliny, *H.N.*, XIII, 47. According to Aristotle's physiology, 'skin is formed as the flesh dries like the film or "skin" on boiled milk'. (*Gen. anim.*, II, 6, 743b 5 ff).
61 Herodotus, III, 110-1.
62 J. Innes Miller, *The Spice Trade of the Roman Empire*, Oxford 1969, pp.42-7 and pp.153-72 ('The Cinnamon Route'). According to R. Hennig, 'Kinnamōmon und kinnamōphoros chōra in der antiken Literatur', *Klio, N.F.* 14, 1939, pp.325-30, Herodotus' cinnamon is not the same as the usual kind but a different plant which it is, however, impossible to identify.

63 D. Bois, *Les plantes alimentaries chez tous les peuples et à travers les âges*, III, Paris 1934, p.55 ff.

64 Pliny, *H.N.*, XII, 85, W.W. How and J. Wells make the same criticism, *A Commentary of Herodotus*, I, Oxford 1912, p.290 (on Herodotus, III, 107).

65 Theoph. *H.Pl.*, IX, 5, 2.

66 Pliny, *H.N.*, XII, 85. Cf. J. Hubaux and M. Leroy, *Le Mythe du Phénix dans les littératures grecque et latine*, Liège-Paris 1939, pp.72-6.

67 Aristotle, *Historia animalium*, IX, 13, 616a 7ff.

68 *Id., Part. anim*, IV, 13, 697b 1-14. Cf. also *Cyranides* II, in *Lapidaires grecs*, ed. Mély and Ruelle, vol. II, 1898, p.68, 1. 20-1, and Mundle, *Fledermaus* in *Reallexicon für Antike und Christentum*, vol. VII (1969), c.1097-1105.

69 In Neo-Platonic symbolism, bats represent the souls of those carried down to the shadows, to the lowest regions. Their wings of skin are the image for the wings of the soul that are made heavy by the flesh and are thick and earthy (Proclus, *In Plat. Republ.*, I, 120, 5-10 Kroll).

70 Pliny, *H.N.*, XII, 85.

71 Hdt., III, 107.

72 *Id.*, II, 76.

73 In his summary of Herodotus' account, Julius Africanus writes of sacrificed animals (J.R. Vieillefond, 'Un fragment inédit de Julius Africanus', *REG,* 1933, p.199).

74 Arist. *H.A.*, IX, 13, 616a 7 ff.

75 Ant. Liberalis, *Metamorphoses*, XII, ed. M. Papthomopoulos.

76 *Id.ibid*, XII, 6.

77 'La chasse rituelle aux aigles', *Annuaire EPHE* (Sciences religieuses), 1959-1960, Paris 1960, pp.38-41; *La Pensée sauvage,*Paris 1962, 68-72; *L'Origine des manières de table*, Paris 1968, pp.242-7.

78 Cl. Lévi-Strauss: *Savage Thought* (*Nature of Human Society Series* translation) p.51.

79 Ant. Liberalis, XII, 6.

80 XII, 5.

81 Cf. D'Arcy W. Thompson, *A Glossary of Greek Birds,*[2] Oxford, 1936, pp.2-16 (eagle); 82-7 (vulture); J. Heurgon, *Voltur, REL*, vol. XIV, 1936 pp.109-18; A. Roes, 'L'Aigle du culte solaire syrien', *Rev. Arch.*, 1950, fasc. 2, pp.129-46; P. Vidal-Naquet, 'Chasse et sacrifice dans l'Orestie d'Eschyle', *La Parola del Passato*, 1969, pp.406-11.

82 Arist. *H.A.*, VI, 5, 563a; Dionys., *Ixeutikón*, I, 5, ed. A. Garzya; Pliny, *H.N.*, X, 19.

83 *F Gr Hist* 31 F 22a and b.

84 Ant. Liberalis, XXI, 5. Agrios, the brutish giant who despises the

gods and devours travelling strangers, is transformed into a vulture described in these terms.

85 *Il.*, XI, 453-4. Cf., IV, 237.

86 Dionys., *Ixeutikón*, I, 3, ed. A. Garzya.

87 Pliny, *H.N.*, X, 19; Philes, *De anim. propr.*, 115-18.

88 Dionys., *Ixeutikón*, I, 5, ed. A. Garzya. Cf. Theophr. C. Pl., VI, 5, 1; Aelian, N.A., III, 7; IV, 18; Philes, *De anim. propriet.*, 118-20; *Geoponica*, XIV, 26.

89 Aesop, *Fab.* 6, ed. E. Chambry.

90 Cf. J. Hubaux and M. Leroy, *Le Mythe du Phénix dans les littératures grecque et latine*, Liège-Paris, 1939, pp.140-2, who emphasise that the partial burning of the eagle stands in opposition to the total burning of the Phoenix.

91 Plut., *Sympos.*, V, 7, 680 E; Pliny *H.N.*, X, 15; Aelian, *N.A.*, IX, 2; Philes, *De anim. propr.*, 80.

92 Aelian, *N.A.*, I, 45. The feathers of vultures are also used, in hunting, to terrify the quarry, particularly by their smell (J. Aymard, *Essai sur les chasses romaines*, Paris 1951, p.218 ff.)

93 Arist., *H.A.*, IX, 1, 609 a 4.

94 Pliny, *H.N.*, X, 17.

95 Pliny, *H.N.*, XI, 98.

96 Aristophanes, *Peace*, 150-69. With regard to wild thyme, Pliny, *H.N.*, XX, 245, mentions that, when burned, its smell scares away snakes.

97 Theoph., *C.Pl.*, VI, 5,1; Aelian, *N.A.*, I 38; VI, 46; *Geop.*, XIV, 26; Philes, *De anim.propr.*, 120; 1209-15.

98 Aristoph., *Peace*, 133-4, referring to Aesop, *Fab.*, 4. Cf *Paroemiogr. graeci*, I, p.6, 20-3, *ed. Leutach and Schneidewin.*

99 *Peace*, 199.

100 *Ibid.*, 722-4.

101 Arist., *H.A.*, IX, 32, 618 b 31-619 a 3. Is this the wild vulture (D'Arcy W. Thompson) or the Gypaetus (P. Louis)? It is impossible to say on the basis of Aristotle's description.

102 D'Arcy W. Thompson, *op.cit.*, p.303; J. André, *Les noms d'oiseaux en latin*, Paris 1967, p.115; P. Géroudet, *Les Rapaces diurnes et nocturnes d'Europe*, Neuchâtel 1965, pp.66-75.

103 Cf. J. André, *op.cit.*

104 [Epiphanes], *De XII gemmis*, in Migne, *P.G.*, vol.XLIII, 3, c.338-9. Cf. J. Hubaux and M. Leroy, *op.cit.*, pp.170-7.

105 As J. Hubaux and M. Leroy have convincingly shown, *op.cit.*, p.174.

106 [Epiphanes], *op.cit.* and Pliny, H.N.,X, 12.

107 In their *Le Mythe du Phénix dans les littératures grecque et latine*, J. Hubaux and M. Leroy have made a systematic study of the principal ways in which this bird is represented in a whole series of works dating from the fourth century AD, such as Claudian and

Lactantius. In their study, the myth of the Phoenix resembles a
nebula comprising various themes of different origin which do not
appear to be necessarily connected: for example, the Phoenix as the
king of the birds, the Phoenix and the Sun, the rival or double of the
eagle, and its immortality through fire. What we should like to
point out here is that, in order to understand the story of the
Phoenix as it appears reflected in the different ideologies which
promoted it, it is first necessary to define the 'latent system of
relations' ('le système relationnel latent') by which this myth is
shaped.

108 Cf. *supra* p.29.
109 Hdt., II, 73.
110 Hubaux and Leroy, *op.cit.*, p.14. For the Egyptian 'Phoenix', cf.
R.T. Rundle Clark, 'The Origin of the Phoenix, A study in
Egyptian Religious Symbolism', *University of Birmingham Historical
Journal*, II, 1949, pp.1-29 and 105-40, with the c.r. of J. Zandee,
Bibliotheca Orientalis, X, no.3/4, 1953, pp.108-16. I should like to
thank Jean Lecant for having drawn my attention to these two
studies.
111 A. Rusch, *s.v.Phoenix, R.-E.* (1941), c.414-23. Cf. also C. Sourdille,
Hérodote et la religion de l'Egypts, Paris 1910, p.198.
112 Hdt. II, 73.
113 Cf. L. Gernet, 'Dénomination et perception des couleurs chez les
grecs' in *Problèmes de la couleur* (presented by I. Meyerson),
Bibliothèque générale de l'E.P.H.E., VIe section, Paris 1957,
pp.321-4.
114 Hubaux and Leroy, *op.cit.*, pp.1-20. The reference to the Great
Sothic Year has an Egyptian origin; as Hubaux and Leroy note,
no Greek author appears to have established any synchronism or
association between the Phoenix and the constellation of the Dog.
115 Hdt., II, 73.
116 *Id. ibid.*
117 Aristoph., *Birds*, 1248.
118 Arist., *H.A.*, IX, 34, 629 a 1 ff; Pliny, *H.N.*, X, 10; Aelian,
N.A. II, 26 (similarly, the eagle never suffers from thirst); IX, 3.
Cf. Hubaux and Leroy, pp.132-4.
119 *Mythogr. vaticani*, III, 3, 4, ed. Bode, p.162, 1-3.
120 Claudian, *Phoenix*, 76-82. Cf. Hubaux and Leroy, p.129.
121 *Physiologus* (1st edition) ed. F. Sbordone (1936), p.22, 1-2. Cf.
Hubaux and Leroy, pp.136-9). It should be noted that for a whole
group of Christian writers the Phoenix's immortality through fire is
set in opposition to Christian renewal by baptismal water.
122 Jerome, *Comment. in Isaiam Prophetum* XII, 41 = *P.L.* vol.24,
p.412.)

123 Cf. *Supra.*
124 Claudian, *Phoenix*, 39-40. Cf. Hubaux and Leroy, p.140.
125 Hubaux and Leroy, pp.136 and 16. In the Hesiodic tradition (Hes.F.304 Merkelbach and West) the Phoenix is almost at the top of the scale of *makraiones*, long-lived creatures: the crow lives nine human lives, the stag four times as long as the crow, the raven three times as long as the stag and the Phoenix nine times as long as the raven. Above it are only the Nymphs, half-goddesses half-women, who live ten times as long as the Phoenix.
126 Hubaux and Leroy who mention this difference between the eagle and the Phoenix, minimise its importance on the grounds that there is a description in Psuedo-Baruch (VIII) which alludes to a 'partial combustion' undergone by the Phoenix in the course of its daily attendance upon the sun (p.142). But here it is only a matter of fatigue and exhaustion brought on by the heat of the sun which the Phoenix accompanies on its daily course. In exactly the same way, the sun's corona, which has become tarnished by the dirt of the earth, has to be renewed each day.
127 Hubaux and Leroy, pp.143-6. In other versions the Phoenix sets its pyre of spices alight either by friction (beating its wings and thus heating the wood strewn with perfumes), or by striking it (it strikes the wood with its wings) (pp.158-9).
128 Hubaux and Leroy, pp.78-9 and 144-5. C.M. Edsman, *Ignis divinus*, Lund 1949, pp.178-203.
129 This is the view held by Hubaux and Leroy (p.79).
130 C.M. Edsman realised this, but taking no account of the mythology of spices, he saw it simply as an innovation.
131 Ovid., *Metam.*, XV, 393.
132 Manilius quoted by Pliny, *H.N.*, X, 4.
133 Claudian, *Phoenix*, 13-16.
134 Ovid, *ibid.*, 394.
135 Cf. *infra.*
136 Ps. Baruch, *Apocalypse*, 6.
137 Hubaux and Leroy, pp.103-4.
138 Hdt., I, 193.
139 Manilius quoted by Pliny, *H.N.*, X, 4.
140 Apollonius in J. Lydus, *De Mensibus*, IV, 11.
141 Tzetzes, *Chiliades*, V, 6, 1. 386 ff ed. Kiessling.
142 Lactantius, *Phoenix*, 99-108.
143 *Physiologus of Vienna*, ap.F.Sbordone, 'La fenice nel culto di Helios', *Rivista indo-greco-italica*, vol.XIX, 1935, p.28 ff. and ap. Hubaux and Leroy, XXXV-XXXVI, and 147-8.
144 Clement of Rome, *Epist. I ad Corinth.*, c.25. This may throw some light on Herodotus' account which mentions only burial inside an

egg of myrrh and the transportation of the spices, without any reference to palingenesis or to the death of the Phoenix.

145 Theoph., *H. Pl.* IX, 5, 2.

146 Cf. *supra*.

147 All the rest is ideology. In other words, the different symbolical meanings of the Phoenix — political, religious or mystical — are centred round this core of myth, whether they lay particular emphasis on the eternity of the Roman Empire, the resurrection of Christ or the progression from duality to unity.

NOTES TO CHAPTER TWO

1 The name myrrh (*múrrha*) apparently appears for the first time in Sappho (F. 44, 30 Lobel-Page). Cf. E. Masson, *Recherches sur les plus anciens emprunts sémitiques en grec*, Paris 1967, pp.54-6, and Fr. Pfister *s. v. Rauchopfer R. E.* (1914), c.277-8. But there are many references to perfumes in the Mycenean tablets (*infra*).

2 Seasonings (*artúmata*) and condiments (*hēdúsmata*) held an important place in Greek cooking. Cf. the lists given by Antiphanes (fr. 142 Kock, II, 69) and by Alexis (fr. 127 Kock, II, 343).

3 Myrrh is sometimes a component of certain 'pre-drinks' (*própoma*: pepper, herbs, myrrh, sweet cyperus, Egyptian essence in Athanaeus, II, 68 C-D) or may be used to spice certain beverages (cf. wine spiced with myrrh which is a purger as has been shown by J. André 'Vin myrrhé', *Annales de la Faculté des Lettres d'Aix*, vol XXV, fasc. 1 and 2, 1951, pp.45-62).

4 Ovid, *Metam.*, IV, 190-255. According to Lactantius Placidus the myth originates with Hesiod (fr. 351 ed. West and Merkelbach [*fragmenta dubia*]. Cf. W. Kroll, *s. v. Leukothoe, R. E.* [1925] c. 2306).

5 Ovid, *op. cit.*, 209. Lines 214-15 describe the heavens of the Hesperides beneath which stretch the pastures of ambrosia reserved for the horses of the Sun.

6 *Schol. in Aeschin*, I, *Against Timarchus*, 23, ed. Dindorf, p.13, 9-11. As the scholiast recalls, like is attracted to like.

7 H. von Fritze, *Die Rauchopfer bei den Griechen.* Diss. Berlin 1894; F. Ffister, *s. v. Rauchopfer R.-E.* (1914), c.267-286.

8 Cf. J. Casabona, *Recherches sur le vocabulaire des sacrifices en grec, des origines à la fin de l'époque classique*, Aix-en-Provence 1966, pp.69-125.

9 *Id., op. cit.*, p.110.

10 Theoph., *Perì Eusebeías*, F 2 ed. W. Pötscher (Leiden 1964, pp.146-50).

11 *F Gr Hist* 328 f 194.

12 *Satureia thymbra L.* Cf. Pliny, *H. N.*, XXI, 56, with J. André's
notes (Paris, 1969, p.114) and A. C. Andrews, 'Thyme as a
condiment in the Graeco-Roman Era, *Osiris*, 13, 1958, pp.150-6.

13 Pliny, *H. N.*, XIII, 2: [In the days of the Trojan war], even in
the rites of religion, people only knew the scent of cedar and citrus
wood, trees of their own country, or more truly the reek as it rose
in wreathes of smoke'. An unknown comic writer (fr. 34 Kock, III,
404) uses the expression: *allà thûe toùs kédrous*, where the verb *thûsai*
replaces *thumiâsai* (cf. Phrynichos, *Epitome, s. v. thûsai*, ed. De
Borries, p.74, 3-6).

14 Plut., *De Pyth. oracul.*, 397 A: *dáphnē* and *krĩthinon áleuron.*
According to a *Scholium Q. in Od. XIV*, 429, before the discovery
of frankincense the Greeks used barley meal, *álphita*, to sacrifice,
thumiân.

15 *Thumiân* is also linked with *thúein* by Theophrastus, *Peri Eusebeias*,
F. 8 ed. W. Pötscher (p.160).

16 This is a characteristic feature of sacrifice (J. Rudhardt, *Notions
fondamentales de la pensée religieuse et actes constitutifs du
culte en Grèce classique*, Geneva 1958, p.254).

17 Lucian, *Icaromenippus*, 25-6, ed. Jacobitz, vol. II, pp.417-18.

18 *Birds*, 555 ff.

19 *Birds*, 1515 ff. This theme is taken up again by Lucian (*Jupiter
Tragoedus*, III, 18): the gods are threatened with famine if men
cease to offer up sacrifices.

20 *Birds*, 1706-1817.

21 The pages which follow repeat, in a slightly different form, an
analysis presented in the *Archives de Sociologie des Religions*,
29, 1970, pp.141-62, under the title 'La cuisine de Pythagore'.

22 Apart from the fundamental work by W. Burkert, *Weisheit und
Wissenschaft. Studien zu Pythagoras, Philolaos und Platon,*
Nuremberg 1962, (referred to hereafter as W.W.', we need only
mention the articles by K. von Fritz, H. Dörrie, M.B.L. Van der
Waerden, *s. v. Pythagoras, Pythagoreer, Pythagorismus, Pythag-
oreische Wissenschaft, R. E.* (1963) c.171-300, which give a good
general view of Pythagoreanism.

23 The classic works on these taboos are those of C. Hölk, *De
acusmatis sive symbolis Pythagoricis*, Diss. Kiel 1894; Fr. Boehm,
De Symbolis Pythagoreis, Diss, Berlin 1905; A. Delattle, *Etudes sur
la litterature pythagoricienne* Paris 1915, pp.285-94; W. Burkert,
W. W., pp.150-75. As early as the fourth century BC certain historians,
Androcydes and Anaximander for example, proposed allegorical
interpretations for these taboos which are worth considering. A case
in point is the precept attributed to Pythagoras, that what is boiled

must not be roasted: *hepthòn dè paraggéllei me optân* (Iamblichus, *V. P.*, 154, p.87, 6-7 Deubner). In the Aristotelian *Problemata* (III 43, ed. Bussemaker, vol. IV, p.331, 15 ff. Cf. S. Reinach, *Cultes, mythes et religions*, vol. V, Paris 1923, p.62 ff.), this culinary practice which is forbidden in the mysteries would represent a retrogressive step to an inferior stage of civilisation since what is boiled is more 'civilised' than what is roasted (cf. Cl. Lévi-Strauss, *L'Origine des manières de table*, Paris 1968, p.398 ff.) For the Pythagoreans it is not a question of two different degrees of civilised life, but rather two different patterns of moral behaviour. They interpreted the precept as follows: gentleness has no need of anger, *ten praóteta légon me prosdeisthai tes orges*. The opposition between the two methods of cooking is thus transposed into ethical terms. The one is characterised by slow ripening, by a perfect balance between the dry and the wet (*hépsesis*, cooking by boiling, is the culinary equivalent to ripening, *pépansis*, in nature), while the other involves direct exposure to the flames, to the savage attack of the fire.

24 We have proof of this not only in Plutarch's *Quaestiones Conviviales*, VIII, 727 B-730 F, but also in fragments of comedies written in Athens during the second third of the fourth century BC by poets such as Aristophon, Alexis and Antiphanes who create the comic character of the Pythagorean, taking as their models those who survived the political failure of the movement, the disciples of Pythagoras who had taken refuge in Athens (Cf. G. Méutis, *Recherches sur le pythagorisme*, Neuchâtel, 1922, pp. 10-18; W. Burkert, *W. W.*, p.194).

25 L. Robin, 'les débris d'un folklore ou il n'y a rien à comprendre', *La Pensée hellénique des origines à Epicure*, Paris 1942, p.35.

26 A. Delatte has already made an exhaustive study of this question: *La Vie de Pythagore de Diogene Laerce*, Brussels 1922, p.176 ff; p.192 ff.

27 We must draw attention to the link between Diogenes Laertius, VIII, 13 (referred to by the initials D.L.) and Timaeus in *F Gr Hist*, 566 F 147 (cf. the commentary by F. Jacoby, p.592). Cf. I. Lévy, *Recherches sur les sources de la légende de Pythagore*, Paris 1926, p.57.

28 Iamblichus, V.P., 107-8, ed. L. Deubner, p.62, 6-12.

29 D. L., VIII, 22, ed. A. Delatte, p.122, 10-11.

30 Cf. J. Casabona, *Recherches sur le vocabulaire des sacrifices en grec, des origines à la fin de l'époque classique*, Aix-en-Provence 1966, pp.155-96.

31 D. L., VIII, 13, ed. A. Delatte, p.114, 8. Cf. Iambl. *V. P.*, 168-9, ed. Deubner, p.95, 7-12 and 54, p.29, 24-5. Compared with *spházō*, to slaughter, *phoneúō* introduces a definitely pejorative note; it also means 'to assassinate', 'to massacre' (cf. J. Casabona, *op. cit.*

pp. 160-2).

32 Eudoxus of Cnidus, in *Porph.*, *V. P.*, 7. In the bilingual Greek-Aramaic inscription of Asoka, discovered in 1958, near Kandahr in Afghanistan, which states that 'the king abstains from living creatures' (*apékhesthai tôn empsúkhōn*), we are also told that 'all the hunters and fishermen of the king have ceased to hunt' (1. 7-8 of the Greek text published in the 'collective' article by D. Schlumberger, L. Robert, A. Dupont-Sommer and E. Benveniste, 'Une bilingue gréco-araméenne d'Asoka', *Journal Asiatique* 1958, p.3 (for the Greek text); pp.15-16 (for L. Robert's comments on the expression *apékhesthai tôn emsúkhōn*).

33 The three terms *thúein, esthíein* and *phoneúein* seem to be synonymous in this Pythagorean tradition.

34 Plut., *Numa*, VIII, 15.

35 Iambl., *V. P.*, 54, ed. L. Deubner, p.29, 23-4.

36 D. L., VIII, 13, ed. A. Delatte, p.115, 3-5.

37 Cf. the pertinent remarks of P. Boyance, 'Sur la vie pythagoricienne', *REG*, 1939, pp.47-9.

38 Iambl., *V. P.*, 98, ed. L. Deubner, p.57, 8-14. E. Rohde (*Rhein. mus.*, 1872, pp. 35-7,) has shown that these are indeed extracts from Aristoxenus, *Puthagorikai apopháseis*, and many important points in his demonstration have been confirmed by P. Boyance, *REG*, 1939, pp.37-40.

39 J. Casabona, *op. cit.*, p.139.

40 Aristoxenus,   25 Wehrli (Aulus Gellius, *N. A.,* IV, 11, 6). Cf. fr. 28 and 29 a W., and Porph., *V. P.*, 36. 41). *Id.*, fr. 29a W (D.L., VIII, 20, ed. A. Delatte, p.121, 3-6).

41 *Id* fr. 29a W (D.L., VIII, 20, ed. A. Delatte, p.121, 3-6.

42 Arist. fr. 179 Rose (Aulus Gellius, NA, IV, 11, 12).

43 Plut., *Quaest. conviv.*, VIII, 8, 3, p.729 c.Cf. also *ibid.* 728 E; Athanaeus, VII, 308 c; Porph., *De Abstin.*, II, 28.

44 Iambl., *V. P.*, 150, ed. L. Deubner, p.84, 18-21.

45 Faced with this double tradition in the historiography of the Pythagoreans, modern authors have been torn between two attitudes. Some emphasise the contradictory character of our information about Pythagoreanism before the fourth century, claiming this as yet another reason for asserting our radical ignorance concerning the first generation of the Pythagoreans; others disqualify Aristoxenus' version as a rationalisation of an author who sought to present an image of Pythagoras free from all strangeness to his fourth century contemporaries. The latter solution had been widely adopted by authors as diverse as Burnet, I. Lévy and Wiliamovitz. Whatever the solution adopted, however, it would seem that one point has never been called into question: the difference between the two kinds of eating habits within Pythagoreanism is basically an *ideological*

conflict between two opposed views, two different reconstructions by roughly contemporary ancient historians. But this is a preconception which radically falsifies the way of posing and resolving the problem of Pythagorean foods. Did Pythagoras and his disciples eat meat or not? The question does not arise solely because it occurred to the historians of the Pythagorean movement or because it was part of the controversies within fourth century hisoriography. It arises because it is a real problem in Pythagoreanism, a problem generated by the social practice of the Pythagoreans and expressed in the different modes of behaviour of certain members of the sect, particularly the most eminent of them.

46 All the information on Milo of Croton is collected together in A. Olivieri, *Civiltà Greca nell'Italia Meridionale*, Naples, 1931, pp.83-98, and Modrze, *s. v. Milo (II), R. E.* (1932), c.1672-1676.

47 As is borne out by the eagerness of the famous Democedes of Croton to marry the daughter of his fellow-citizen, Milo (Herodotus, III, 137-8).

48 Cf. Philostratus, *Vit. Apoll.*, IV, 28, and the remarks of J. Bayet, *Les Origines de l 'Hercule romain*, Paris 1926, pp.157-9.

49 L. Moretti, *Olympionikai (Atti della Accademia nazionale dei Lincei, Memorie, Scienze morali, storiche e filologiche*, vol. VIII) Rome 1959, pp.72-4.

50 Cf. Iambl., *V. P.*, 267 ed. L. Deubner, p.147, 1, and the observations of A. Olivieri, *op. cit.*, p.89 ff.

51 One of the most important, as Strabo noes, VI, 1, 12.

52 Arist., *Ethic. Nicom.* II, 6, 1106 b 3 and fr. 520 Rose. Cf. also Porph., *De Abstin.*, I, 52.

53 Athenaeus, X, 412 E-F.

54 Cf. M. Detienne, 'Héraclès, héros pythagoricien', RHR, 1960, pp.20-1.

55 G. Giannelli, *Culti e miti della Magna Grecia*[2], Florence 1963, pp.137-8.

56 Diodorus, XII, 9, 2 ff.

57 Cf. Aristoxenus, fr. 18 Wehrli, and the many sources of evidence quoted by A. Olivieri, *op. cit.*, p.85 ff.

58 Cf. 'La cuisine de Pythagore', *Archives de Sociologie des Religions*, 29, 1970, pp.146-7, and my contribution to the fifth *Convegno di Studi sulla Magna Grecia* which has been published in a provisional form in *Filosofia e Scienza in Magna Grecia*, Naples 1966 (1969), pp.149-56.

59 Cf. D. Sabbatucci, *Saggio sul misticismo greco*, Rome 1965, pp. 69-83, who must be given the credit for this discovery. However, in simply reducing Pythagoreanism to a variant of Orphism D. Sabbatucci failed to recognise the uniqueness of a

phenomenon on which his study threw much new light.

60 Hesiod, *Theogony*, 535-60. P. Vidal-Naquet has shown that the same model for sacrifice and eating is also present in the Homeric epic ('Valeurs religieuses et mythiques de la terre et du sacrifice dans l'Odyssée', *Annales E. S. C.*, 1970, pp.1278-97.

61 This is the way of 'rununciation. Cf. L. Dumont, 'Le renoncement dans les religions de l'Inde', *Arch. Soc. Rel.*, 7, 1959, pp.45-69 (*Homo hierarchicus*, Paris 1966, pp.342-50) whose ideas influenced the work of D. Sabbatucci.

62 Aristophon, *The Pythagorean*, in Diels, *FVS*[7], I, p.480, 1. 20-25: in the other world the Pythagoreans alone had the privilege of eating at the table of Pluto.

63 Iambl., *V. P.*, 54: *pópana, psaiatá, kēría, libanōtós; ibid*, 150: *kégkhroi, pópana, kēría, líbanos, smúrna, tà álla thumiámata; *Proph., *V. P.,* 36: *álphita, pópanon, libanōtós, murrhínē.*

64 This is suggested by the model sacrifice made by Pythagoras in honour of Apollo *Genétor* at Delos: barley, wheat and cakes were placed on the altar *áneu purós* (D. L., VIII, 13 ed. A. Delatte, p.115, 3-4). In ordinary sacrificial practice cakes were either burned or else placed on the altar. The Scholiast of Aristophanes' *Plutus*, 661, distinguishes between the *pélanos* which was thrown into the fire and the *pópana* which were placed upon the altar. For the *ápura* as a type of sacrifice, cf. Stengel, *s. v. Apura, R. E.* (1895), c.292-3.

65 D. L. VIII, 13, ed. A. Delatte, p.115, 1-5 (cf. Timaeus ap. *F Gr Hist* 566 F 147); Iambl., *V. P.*, 25, ed. L. Deubner, p.15, 21-4; *ibid.*, 8, p.21, 2-4.

66 Plutarch, *Septem Sapientium convivium* p.158 A, ed. J. Defradas.

67 Plutarch, *De Pythiae Oraculis,* p.402 A.

68 Cf. H. Gallet de Santerre, *Délos primitive et archaique* Paris 1958, pp.176-7.

69 There is a strange contrast in the world of Delos: the two corresponding representations of Apollo are matched by the two opposed altars, each with its own ritual. According to Aristotle, quoted by D. L., VIII, 13, the altar of *Genétōr* was located behind the *keratón* which was consecrated to the Apollo associated with Leto and Artemis and formed, as its name suggests, by the interlocked horns of the victims offered to this god. On the one hand we have vegetable offerings, on the other blood sacrifice.

70 Hyperborean traditions, reflected at Delos in the myth about the Hyperborean Virgins, also help to explain why Pythagorean religious thought was so attracted by the model of the Delian Apollo. Hyperborean elements play a large part in the Apollonian mysticism in Pythagoreanism.

71 In general, see Joseph Murr, *Die Pflanzenwelt in der griechischen*

Mythologie, Innsbruck 1890 (reprinted Groningen 1969). pp.240-3. For further details on the mallow, G. Steier, *s. v. Malve R. E.* (1928), c.922-7, and on the asphodel, J. M. Verpoorten, 'Les noms grecs et latins de l'asphodèle', *L'ant. Classe.*, vol. XXXI, 1962, pp.111-29.

72 Plut., *Septem sapientium convivium*, 157 D. In Plutarch's *Banquet*, Solon steadfastly asserts that Epimenides' diet was inspired by Hesiod's *Works*, 41 ('What great benefit there is in the mallow and the asphodel') as Plato had already noted, *Laws* 677E, quoted by the *Scholia Vetera in Hes. Works*, 41 ed. Pertusi, p.23, where we find a collection of erudite notes on the *álima* and the *ádipsa*.

73 This is the interpretation defended by Periander, also in the *Banquet*, 158 A.

74 Porph. *V. P.*, 35. This tradition appears to be already known in the fifth century, to Herodorus of Heraclea (*F Gr Hist* 31 F 1 with notes by Jacoby).

75 Plut., *op. cit.*, 157 F emphasises that these foods are *drugs: mâllon phármaka é sitîa.*

76 For other traditions regarding these magical foods cf. the information collected in M. Detienne, *La notion de daimon dans le pythagorisme ancien*, Paris 1963, pp. 115-59.

77 Arist., *De Sensu, V*, p.445 a 16.

78 Plut., *De facie in orbe lunae*, 937 D-940 F, ed. H. Cherniss. The absence of excrements goes with oral purity. This is one of the characteristics of those living in the Golden Age according to Dicearchus (in Porph., *De Abstin.*, IV, 2 F. 49 Wehrli) and also in the Pythagorean tradition (M. Detienne, *op. cit.*, pp.143-5).

79 *Ibid.*, 940 B-C.

80 Cf. E. Lohmeyer, 'Vom göttlichen Wohlgeruch', *Sitzungsberichte der Heidelberger Akademie der Wissenschaften, Philos.-histor. Klasse*, Heidelberg 1919, 9 Abh., p.4 ff.; W. Déonna, *Euōdia. Croyances antiques et modernes: l'odeur suave des dieux et des élus*, Geneva, vol. XVII, 1939, pp.167-262; H.-Ch. Puech, *Parfums sacrés, odeurs de sainteté, effluves paradisiaques, L'Amour de l'Art*, 1950, pp.36-40.

81 Cf. C. Smith, 'Harpies in Greek Art', JHS, XIII, 1892, pp.109-14.

82 Apoll. Rh., *Argon.*, II, 272. The Erinnyes give off a pestilential stench (Aeschylus, *Eumenides*, 53). Cf. W. Déonna, *art. cit.*, pp.220-2.

83 Menander, *Dyskolos*, 449-53; F. 117 Körte; Antiphanes, F. 164, Kock, II, 78.-Cf. Theoph., *Perì Eusebeías*, F. 8 ed. W. Pötscher (p.160), and the remarks made by P. Boyancé *Le Culte des Muses chez les Philosophes grecs*, Paris 1936, pp.282-4.

84 The more so in that the inequality of the shares is considered

scandalous: 'Who then is such a fool or shows himself so credulous as to hope that all the gods are pleased by bones stripped of meat and by burnt bile which starving dogs would reject, and to believe that this is the offering due to them?' (Anonymous author quoted by Porphyry, *De Abstinentia*, II, 58, ed. Nauck, p.183, 12-16.

85 All the evidence on the bean in Pythagoreanism has been collected by A. Delatte, in a classic study, *Faba Pythagorae cognota* in *Serta Leodiensia*, Liège-Paris 1930, pp.35-57 (in future referred to as *Faba*).

86 Aristotle in Diogenes Laertius, VIII, 34, ed. A. Delatte, p.131, 5.

87 *Schol. T.* and Eust. *In Il*, XIII, 589. Cf. A. Delatte *Faba*, p.37.

88 Cf. A. Delatte, *Faba*, pp.42-3.

89 *Ibid.*, pp.43-6.

90 Heraclides Ponticus, quoted by J. Lydus, *De Mensibus*, IV, 42, is our first authority.

91 Arist., in D. L., VIII, 34, ed. A. Delatte, p.131, 4.

92 Lucian, *Vitarum auctio*, 6.

93 Antonius Diogenes in Porph., *V.P.*, 44.

94 *Suspeiroménōn kaì sussēpoménōn.*

95 This experiment, reported by Antonius Diogenes is known from two versions: Porphyry, *V. P.*, 44 and Lydus, *De Mens.*, IV, 42. The former refers to *anthrōpeíou gónou*; the latter to *anthrōpeíou phónou*.

96 *Isón toi kuámous te phageîn kephalás te tokéōn.* Here again our first authority is Heraclides Ponticus quoted by J. Lydus, *De Mens.*, IV, 42. For other evidence, cf. A. Delatte, *Faba*, p.36, n.2.

97 On cannibalism, which is a feature both of the world of wild beasts and of barbarians who live like beasts instead of like men grouped into a society (in other words like the Greeks, eating cereals and the cooked meats from domesticated animals), cf. J. Haussleiter, *Der Vegetarismus in der Antike*, Berlin 1935, p.65 ff. and A.J. Festugière, 'A propos des arétalogies d'Isis', *Harvard Theol. Review*, XLII, 1949, p.217 ff.

98 Porph., *V. P.*, 43-4. Porphyry is evidence of the existence of a tradition which justifies Pythagoras' vegetarianism by his intention of dissuading men from practising cannibalism.

99 This interpretation makes it impossible for us to accept the genetic explanation proposed by A. Delatte, (*Faba*, pp.56-7) who sees in the 'flatulant nature' of the bean the origin for the belief that these vegetables must necessarily be related to the souls of the dead.

100 The credit for pointing this out must go to P. Boyance, 'Sur la vie pythagoricienne', *REG*, 1939, pp.40-3.

101 Ovid, *Metamorphoses*, XV, 75-100: 'You have the fruits of the earth
... you have also delicious herbs and vegetables which can be
mellowed and softened by the help of fire ... the earth, prodigal
of her wealth, supplies you her kindly sustenance'. The cooking
fire merely supplements concoction, prolonging the effects of the
cooking process wrought by mother earth.

102 'But after someone, a bad example whoever he was, envied the
food of lions and thrust down flesh as food into his greedy
stomach, he opened the way for crime. It may be that in the
first place the steel was warmed and stained with blood from the
killing of wild beasts. This would have been justified and we admit
that creatures which menace our own lives may be killed without
impiety. But while they might be killed, they should never have been
eaten.' (Ovid, *Metam.* XV, 103-10). The same theory is expressed
in the lines quoted in Plutarch, *De esu carnium*, II, 3-4, 998
A-B, which are believed to be a part of the Pythagorean *Sacred
Speech* reconstructed by A. Delatte, *Etudes sur la littérature
pythagoricienne,* Paris 1915, p.41: here the invention of weapons of
war is inseparable from the death of the working ox.

103 Ovid, *Metam.,* XV, 110-15.

104 *Ibid.,* 116-26. 'Why should we think that we have obligations of
justice towards brutal and coarse men when we do not have them
towards the working ox, the dog which helps us to take the flocks
to pasture and the sheep which give milk and wool to feed and
clothe us?' (Porph. *De Abstin.*, III, 19).

105 Iran and the *Gathas* (*Yasna* 29) come to mind here as we do the
studies of G. Dumézil, *Naissance d'archanges*, Paris 1945, pp.119-24,
and of J. Duchesne-Guillaumin, *Zoroastre*, Paris 1948, pp.193-8,
and *Ormazd et Ahriman*, Paris, 1953, pp.35-8. More recently
G. Dumézil has returned to the meaning of *Yasna* 29, this time to
show it to derive from the 'folklore of herdsmen and farmers':
'A propos de la Plainte de l'âme du boeuf (*Yasna* 29),' *Bull.
de l'Acad. R. de Belg., Classe des Lettres,* LI, 1965, pp.23-51.

106 *Schol. in Arist. Gren.* 338; Servius, in *Verg. Georg.,* II, 380;
Varro, *De re rustica*, II, 4, 9. In Porph., *De Abstin.* II, 9,
it is one Clymenes who kills a pig, by mistake (*akousíoi hamartíai*),
and the oracle at Delphi, when consulted by one Episcopos, declares
that it is permissable to sacrifice a victim which indicates its
consent during the libation. Delphi thus endorsed the full importance
of a sacrificial gesture: when the animal victim was sprinkled
with lustral water it would shake its head in a particular way which
the sacrificer would interpret as a gesture of consent (*kantaneúō*).

107 Varro, *De re rustics*, I, 2, 19; Virg., *Georg.*, II, 380 (and Servius,
in loc.,); Porph., *De Abstin.*, II, 10.

108 Aristoxenus in Iambl., *V.P.*, 99, ed. L. Deubner, p.57, 20-3;
   D. L., VIII, 23, ed. A. Delatte, p.123, 4-5; Porph., *V.P.*, 39.

109 Following J. Haussleiter, *Vegetarismus*, p.112, n. 1, we believe that
   it is very probable that we have here a reference to ancient
   Pythagorean traditions: Plut., *Quaest. conviv.*, VIII, 8, 3, p.729 F ff.

110 At 730 B, the three epithets used to refer to the guilty animals
   are *lēibóteiros*, the harvest-eater; *spermológos*, the seed-eater; and
   trugēphagos, the vine-eater.

111 For arguments to show that the Pythagorean tradition includes a
   representation of the Golden Age, cf. *La Notion de daimôn dans
   le pythagorisme ancien*, Paris 1936, pp.93-117.

112 A 'wild' state in which men behave like wild beasts: cf. A. J.
   Festugière, *art. cit.*, p.217 ff.

113 P. Stengel, *Opferbräuche der Griechen*, Leipzig and Berlin 1910,
   pp.191-6; G. Dumézil, *Tarpeia*, Paris 1947, pp.133-8.

114 Hesiod, *Works*, 405: 2 'First of all get a house [*oîkos*, in the
   sense of habitation], a woman [*gunaîka*: bought, not married, cf.
   line 406] and an ox for the plough [*boûn arotêra*].' For Hesiod,
   the three terms are on the same level. They represent the components
   of the elementary farming unit, the *oîkos* in its widest sense.
   But when Aristotle (*Oecon.*, I, 2, 1343 a 20-1; *Polit.*, I, 2,
   1252 b 11) quotes this line from Hesiod, he makes a remark that
   emphasises the close ties between the peasant and his working beast:'
   For the ox is the poor man's household slave (*oikétēs*).' On this
   subject, cf. the remarks of A. Hoekstra, in *Mnemosyne*, 1950,
   pp.91-8.

115 Among the many studies devoted to this ritual we should like to
   mention P. Stengel, *Buphonien*, 1893 and 1897, reprinted in
   Opferbräuche der Griechen, Leipzig and Berlin 1910, pp.203-21;
   H. Hubert and M. Mauss, *Essai sur la nature et la fonction du
   sacrifice* (1899) reprinted in M. Mauss, *Oeuvres, I: Les fonctions
   sociales du sacré*, Paris 1968, pp.274-83; J. Harrison, *Prolegomena to
   the Study of Greek Religion*, Cambridge 1903, (reprinted N.Y.,
   1955), pp.111-13; *Themis*, Cambridge 1912, pp.142-50; L. Deubner,
   Attische Feste, Berlin 1932, pp.158-73; L. Gernet, 'Sur le symbolisme
   politique: le foyer commun' (1952), reprinted in *Anthropologie de la
   Grèce Ancienne*, Paris 1968, pp.391-2; W. F. Otto, 'Ein griechischer
   Kultmythos vom Ursprung der Pflugkultur' (1950), reprinted in *Das
   Wort der Antike*, Stuttgart 1962, pp.140-61; K. Meuli, 'Griechische
   Opferbräuche', in *Phyllobolia für Peter won der Mühll*, Bâle 1945,
   pp.275-7; U. Pestalozza, 'Le origini delle Buphonia Ateniensi,'
   Rendic. Instit. Lombardo Scien. e Lett., vol. 89-90, I. Milan 1956,
   pp.433-54.

116 Cf. L. Gernet's remarks in his commentary on Book IX of

Plato's *Laws*, Paris 1917, pp.164-7.

117 Two priestly families play an essential role in this political ritual: the Bouzygai and the Eteoboutadai. The first are the official protectors of the working ox. In Athens, it is they who pronounce the speech forbidding that it should be put to death (Aelian, *H. V.*, V, 14; Varro, *De re rustica*, II, 5, 3). It takes the form of curses which are accompanied by a number of other imprecations addressed to those who do not respect the cultivated life for which the Bouzygai, as inventors of ploughing and cultivation of the land, assume responsibility. The Bouzygai, whose duty it is to carry out the sacred ploughing in Attica, guarantee the fertility of the earth and promote the production of food, in close collaboration with the working ox. In contrast, the Eteoboutadai have quite different functions. These are the hereditary priests of Poseidon Erechtheus: they are responsible for the sacrifices of bulls that are made at Athens in honour of that god. They are thus seen as the heirs of *Boutes*, the Cowherd, Erectheus' brother who, at the death of Erichthonios, the true son of the Earth, assumed the religious functions of sovereignty. The Bouzygai and the Eteoboutadai thus fulfill opposed yet complementary functions.

118 The prohibition against killing the working ox appears in a number of texts: *Schol. Arat. Phaen.* 132; Aelian, *H.A.*, 12, 34; *Schol. in Od.*, XII, 353; Nicholas of Damascus, in F Gr Hist, 90 F 103 1 (where to kill a working ox and to steal an agricultural tool are equally criminal actions, both punishable by death); Aelian, *H.V.*, V, 14; Varro, *De re rustica*, II, 5, 4; Columella, VI, *Praef.*; Pliny, *H. N.*, VIII, 180.

119 We cannot tackle this problem within the framework of this work although it is essential to an understanding of the place of the Bouphonia in Greek religious thought.

120 Iambl., *V. P.*, 109, ed. L. Deubner, p.63, 2-5; Porph., *V.P.*, 42-3, ed. Nauck, p.40, 9 ff (Anaximander according to Diels, FVS7, I, p.466, 9-12, and A. Delatte, *Etudes sur la littérature pythagoricienne*, Paris 1915, pp.291-2); Aristotle, fr. 194 Rose. The prohibition against eating the brain has been analysed in depth by Marie Delcourt, 'Tydée et Mélanippe', *Studi e Materiali di Storia delle Religioni*, vol. XXXVII, 1966, pp.169-80.

121 It should be added that these same animals that it was permitted to sacrifice and to eat were excluded by the 'political' Pythagoreans from the list of living creatures in which the human soul could be reincarnated. Cf. Arist., in Iambl., *V. P.*, 85 ed. L. Deubner, p.49, 14-17, and P. Boyance, *REG*, 1939, p.42, n. 2.

122 Porphyry, *V. P.*, 24, and Iambl., *V. P.*, 61, ed. L. Deubner, p.33 ff.

123 *Anthrōpinais trophaîs sitoúmenon*: Iambl., *op. cit.* Instead of eating

raw grass, *botánē ek gês*, the ox has a right to civilised food, *trophê̂ ek gês*. On this distinction cf. A. J. Festugière, *Hippocrate. L'Ancienne Medecine. Introduction, traduction et commentaire*, Paris 1948, p.35 n. (b).

124 The story of the bear of Daunia is constructed on the same model. This concerns a wild beast which eats human flesh and which, thanks to Pythagoras, discovers a diet of barley bread and fruits (Iambl., *V.P.*, 60, ed. L. Deubner, p.33,2-8; Porph., *V. P.*, 23).

125 Athanaeus, I, 3 E.

126 It matters little whether this is the philosopher as A. Rostagni believes (*Il Verbo di Pitagora*, Turin 1924, pp.248-9) or his grandfather, which is the opinion of A. Delatte, (*La Vie de Pythagore de Diogene Laerce*, Brussels 1922, p.174).

127 As a pastry bull, a *psaistón* is made, for many sacrifices, to take the place of a victim that is too costly. Here again the Pythagorean practice is in line with the custom of the city. There was a ritual in fourth century Thera in which the city had to offer up a bull made from one medimne of wheat and two medimnoi of barley (Collitz, *Sammlung griechischer Dialektinschriften*, Göttingen 1884-1915, 4765, 11, 6-15, quoted by J. Casabona, *op. cit.*, p.76). It is an ox of this type, too, that Pythagoras is believed to have offered up to the gods after he had discovered the geometric formula of the square of the hypotenuse (Porph., *V. P.*, 36). 128). As will have been noted,

128 As will have been noted, this expression reflects Cl. Lévi-Strauss's approach to the problem: *L'Origine des manières de table*, Paris 1968, p.411.

NOTES TO CHAPTER THREE

1 V. Chapot, *s. v. Ungunentum, Daremberg-Saglio-Pottier, D. A.*, c.596.

2 Theoph., *De odoribus*, 21-2.

3 *Id. ibid.*, 40-1. Cf. M. Wylock, 'La fabrication des parfums à l'époque mycénienne d'après les tablettes Fr de Pylos', *Studi micenei ed egeo-anatolici*, XI, Rome 1970, pp.116-33.

4 Achaios, *Hephaistos*, F 17 N.[2]: 'What will you do to enchant me (*kēleîn*)?' Hephaistos(?) asks Dionysus(?). And the latter replies: 'I shall anoint your limbs with a fragrant perfume' (*múrōi sè khrísō pámpan euósmōi démas*). For the incident of the return of Hephaistos to Olympus, Cf. M. Delcourt, *Héphaistos ou la légende du magicien*, Paris 1957, pp.84-99.

5 Apuleius, *Metamorphoses*, III, 21.

6 Plato, *Republic*, 398 E; 573 A; *Alc.* I, 122c. In the *Rep.*, 393 A, perfumes (*múra*) and essences for burning (*thumiámata*) are,

together with relishes, part of the refinements of civilised life.

7 Cf. S. Mazzarino, *Fra Oriente e Occidente. Ricerche di storia greca archaica*, Florence 1947, pp.193 ff; 214 ff.

8 Sophocles, F. 334 N[2].

9 Euripides, *Iphigenia at Aulis*, 1301.

10 Archilocus, F. 38, ed. Lasserre and Bonnard.

11 The *Etym. Magnum, s.v. gamelia* refers to a sacrifice offered on the occasion of a marriage to Hera, Aphrodite and the Charites.

12 Aristoph., *Plutus*, 529-30. The vase of perfumes, the *alabástron* is one of the objects carried in the wedding procession: on a tablet at Locri (cf. Quagliati, *Ausonia*, III, 1909, p.220), the last girl to dance up to the young bride is holding a perfume vase identical to the one carried, on another tablet, by a female Eros who is harnessed together with a male Eros holding a dove, to the nuptial chariot of Aphrodite and Hermes (cf. most recently, P. Zancani-Montuoro, *La pariglia di Aphrophide, Mélanges K. Kérényi,* Stockholm 1968, p.16, fig. 1).

13 Oppian, *Cyneget.*, I, 338 ff.

14 Xenophon, *Symposium*, II, 3-4.

15 Plut., *Bruta ratione uti*, 990 B-C.

16 Aristoph., *Lysistrata*, 46-7.

17 *Id. ibid.,* 839 and 844.

18 Cf. G. W. Elderkin, 'Aphrodite and Athena in the *Lysistrata* of Aristophanes', *Classical Philology*, vol. XXXV, 1940, pp.387-96.

19 Aristoph., *Lysistrata*, 938-42. Myrrhina refuses to make love until she has smothered herself in perfume. When Trygaeus, an old grey-beard is about to make love with *Opōra*, the goddess of ripe fruits, the chorus congratulates him 'on having become young again; and having rubbed himself with perfumes' like a young husband (*Peace*, 861-2).

20 Aristoph., *Birds*, 160-1.

21 Rufus of Ephesus, *On the names of the parts of the body* ed. Daremberg and Ruelle, Paris 1879, p.147. For other religious and mythical meanings of this plant, cf. the evidence collected by I. Chirassi, *Elementi di culture precereali nei miti e riti greci,* Rome 1968, pp.17-38.

22 Servius Danielis, *in Verg. Aen.*, V, 72, ed. Harvardiana, III (1965), p.493, 1-20.

23 V, 113, 3. One particularly attractive man is called 'An Adonis triply desirable to courtesans' (Aristenetes, *Love Letters*, 8, 1). Cf. Plautus, *Curculio*, 101; 'Tu crocinum et casia es'. These are the words of love addressed by a hideous old crone to a bottle of old wine, the bouquet of which fills her with passion.

24 *Mythographi vaticani*, I, 200; II, 34; III, 11, 17, ed. Bode.

25 Cf. Bio, *Adonidos Epitaphios*, 77-8: 'Cover him with ointments from Syria, cover him with perfumes. May all the perfumes die. He who used to be your perfume, Adonis, has perished'.

26 Either Myrrha neglects to pay homage to Aphrodite (as in the version given by Panyassis in [Apollodorus], *Bibl.*, III, 14, 4) or her mother provokes the anger of the goddess by claiming that Myrrha's beauty ›s ırpasses the attractions of Aphrodite (Hygienus, *Fab.*, 58).

27 In the version given by Ant. Liberalis, *Metam.*, XXXIV, 1, the rejection of the suitors is said to be occasioned by Myrrha's passion for her father.

28 Cf. Ovid, *Metam.*, X, 337 ff: 'If I were not the daughter of Kinras I could enter his bed but because he already belongs to me he cannot be mine, and all my misfortune comes from the very fact that we are related'.

29 Panyassis in [Apollodorus] *Bibl.*, III, 14, 4.

30 Theocritus, *The Women of Syracuse*, 86.

31 Aelian, *Nat. anim.*, IX, 36. Cf. Clearchus, F.101 Wehrli.

32 From P. Lambrechts ('La "resurrection d'Adonis",' *Mélanges I. Lévy*, Brussels 1953, pp.207-40) to W. Atallah (*op. cit.*, pp.268-301), historians have expressed a series of objections, which we consider to be decisive, against the interpretation which emphasises the 'resurrection' of Adonis and the so-called mysteries of this god.

33 The scholiast glosses on line 389 of Aristophanes' *Lysistrata* make it clear that the city had nothing to do with either the financing or the organisation of the festival.

34 Alciphron, *Letters*, IV, 14. Cf. W. Atallah, *Adonis dans la littérature et l'art grec*, Paris 1966, pp.241-2.

35 [Adōníois] is a correction made by Pierson, replacing the Alóois of the Mss. Its correctness is confirmed by the reference to Adonis two lines further on in the same letter and also by two details of a ritual character; the reference to a little garden (*kēpíon*) and to a figurine (*korállion*). For this meaning of *Korállion*, cf. L. Robert, *Noms indigènes dans l'Asie Mineure,* Paris, I, 1963, p.282, n. 1.

36 Diphilus, F. 43, 39-41, Kock, II, 554.

37 *Id.*, F, 50, Kock, II, 557.

38 Menander, *The Woman of Samos*, 38-47, ed. R. Kasser (*Pap. Bodmer*, vol. XXV, Vandoeuvres, 1969, p.34), together with the remarks of N. Weill, *La fête d'Adonis dans la 'Samienne' de Mánandre*, BCH, 1970, pp.591-3.

39 Aristophanes, *Lysistrata*, 378-98. The licentious nature of the festival is also stressed by the ironic allusion made by Cratinos (F.15, Kock, I, 16) to Adonia being celebrated to the sounds of the passionate and sensual music of his contemporary, Gnisippus.

40 Women celebrating the Adonia wear festive clothes and many jewels, as can be seen from various fourth century vase paintings (*Lécythe aryballisque d'Apollonie de Thrace, au Musée de l'Ermitage 928 et Lécythe du Musée Britannique, E 721* ap. H. Metzger, *Les représentations dans la céramique attique du IVe siècle*, Paris 1951, pp.93-4, nos. 45 and 46). It is no doubt not simply by chance that in drawing up a list of the terminology for female finery, Pollux (V, 100) is led to cite a play entitled *The devotees of Adonis* (Philippides, F. 1, Kock, III, 301) on the subject of a type of bracelet worn on the upper arm (*anamaskhalister*).

41 The version given by Panyassis [Apollodorus] *Bibl.* III, 14, 4) ends with the phrase: 'Later Adonis was killed by a wild boar while hunting'. In other versions (Eur. *Hippolytus*, 1420-1422), it is Artemis who engineers Adonis' death. Before recounting Panyassis' version [Apollodorus] (*Bibl.* III, 14, 4) refers to an account of the death of the lover of Aphrodite in which he is struck down by a boar and thus appears as a victim of Artemis' vengeance. For other versions, such as that of Ptolemy Hephaestion, in which Adonis is murdered by Apollo disguised as a maddened wild boar, cf. W. Atallah, *Adonis*, pp.54-62.

42 Cf. the remarks of R. Turcan, in his review of W. Atallah, *Adonis* in *Rev. Hist. Rel.*, 1968, fasc. 3, p.87.

43 M. Detienne, 'L'Olivier; un mythe politico-religieux', *Rev. Hist. Rel.*, 1970, fasc. 3, pp.18-19.

44 M. Delcourt, 'Tydée et Mélanippe', *Studi e Materiali di Storia delle Religioni*, Vol. XXXVII, 1966, pp.163-5.

45 Philodemes, *Perì Eusebeías*, p.12 Gomperz. Cf. Antimachus(?) F. 102 Wyss.

46 Among the reasons that Aristarchus produces to 'condemn' lines 23-30 of Book XXIV of the *Iliad* — that is to say the allusion to the *Judgement of Paris* — we find the following: 'How could it not be ridiculous to imagine a discussion between Athena whose glance Homer tells us is terrible (I, 200) and Aphrodite whose eyes he describes as magnificent (III, 397)? *You might just as well confront Heracles with Adonis!*' (*Schol. BMV in Il.*, *XXIV, 23 T in Il., XXIV, 31* quoted by A. Severyns, *Le Cycle épique dans l'Ecole d'Aristarque*, Liège-Paris IIII, p.263).

47 Nicander, F. 120 Schneider.

48 Callimachus, F, 478 Pfeiffer. In Hesychius' Lexicon, *adōnéïs* is apparently the name of a particular kind of lettuce (ed. K. Latte, no. 1226).

49 Wild lettuce, it seems, when Adonis hides in it to escape the boar; but possibly cultivated when it serves as a funeral bed for Aphrodite's lover (cf. *infra*). At alle vents, the lettuce is one of the plants

cultivated in the Gardens of Adonis. Whether wild or cultivated, *hēmeros* or *agría*, its qualities remain the same: Dioscorides, *M. M.* II, 136, 1-3 W. In his treatise, *De Alimentorum Facultatibus* Galen points out that his own contemporaries still made a distinction between the wild lettuce (*thridakínē*) and the garden variety (*thrídax*).

50 Euboulos, F. 14, Kock, II, 169.

51 *Id. ibid.*

52 *Id. ibid.*

53 Oribasius, II, 638, Cf. Stadler, *s. v. Lactuca, R-E.* (1924), c.367-369.

54 Cf. p.109.

55 Diosc., *M. M.*, II, 136, 1-3 W; Oribasius, V, 615; VI, 510-11; Rufus, 429; Diphilus ap. Athanaeus, II, 69F.

56 Amphis, F. 20, Kock, II, 241.

57 Athanaeus, II, 69C.

58 C. M. Bowra, *Greek Lyric Poetry*, Oxford 1961, pp.212-4.

59 In a study entitled 'La déese et le passeur d'eau', (*Mélanges O. Navarre*, Toulouse 1935, pp.249-63), Jean Hubaux has attempted to show that the story of Phaon is a repetition of the story of Jason carrying over a river in flood an old woman who is really none other than the goddess Hera. He suggests that this story about Jason is itself simply derived from an Egyptian story, known from the Chester Beatty papyrus: the ferryman Anti carries the goddess Isis, disguised as an old woman, to an island where the gods have taken refuge in order to hide from her. However, this type of analysis — which uses the comparative method only in order to discover an original myth (in this case an Egyptian one) — takes note of the resemblances but not of the differences in these accounts. It thus neglects certain essential elements in the myth of Phaon, such as the seduction, the perfume, the lettuce, and similarly, in the story about Jason factors as important as the ford, the *póros* that the hero makes through the rough waters and the loss of a sandal which makes him a *monokrēpis* when he emerges from the river.

60 Palaiphatos, *Incred.*, XLVIII *Mythographi graeci*, III, 2, ed. Festa, p.69.

61 This version concludes with a reference to Sappho's love for Phaon: 'Sappho often sang of her passion for this Phaon, in her poems.'

62 Aelian, *H. V.*, XII, 18, ed. Hercher, p.127.

63 Servius, *in Verg. Aen.*, III, 279.

64 'The Ancients used to give the name *charis* to a woman's acquiescence to the desires of a man': Plutarch, *Erotikós*, 751 D. Cf.

Il., XI, 227 and 243.

65 Aelian, *ibid.*

66 Cratinos, F. 330, Kock, I, 110. Cratinos' version is matched, in Athanaeus himself (II, 69 D) by the version known to Marsyas (the younger), according to which Phaon is said to have been hidden in 'the greenness of the barley' (*khlóē krithôn*). As is proved by the reference to 'greenness', the substitution of barley for lettuce can only be explained in the context of the gardening of Adonis in which plants only grow until they become green and in which, apart from fennel and wheat, the chosen species are, precisely, barley and lettuce.

67 As J. Carcopino would have it (*De Pythagore aux Apôtres*, Paris 1956, p.52.

68 Pliny, *H. N.*, XXII, 18 ff.

69 This brief passage of Pliny, which was the corner stone of J. Carcopino's *Basilique pythagoricienne* and subsequently essential to the argument of his *De Pythagore aux Apôtres* (pp.14 ff.) has been definitively cleared of the imaginary Pythagorean overtones certain scholars ascribed to it following the discovery, in 1917, of an underground building near the Porta Maggiore, in Rome. The credit for this must go to J. André, 'Pythagorisme et botanique,' *Rev. Philol'*, 1958, pp.218-43.

70 Cf. J. Hubaux and M. Leroy, 'Le Talisman de Phaon', *Mélanges F. Cumont*, II, Brussels 1936, pp.755-63.

71 J. André, *art. cit.*, p.224.

NOTES TO CHAPTER FOUR

1 Mintha is known from a number of sources and they are sufficiently in agreement for it to be possible to establish the essential features of her myth: Oppian, *Hal.*, III, 486-97; Strabo, VIII, 3, 14; *Schol. vet. in Nic. Alex.* 375, ed. Keil, p.97, 42-4; *Etym. Gud.*, 395, 1 ff. O.F. 44 Kern; Photius, *s. v. Mintha*; Aristocles, in *F Gr Hist.* 33 F 2C; *Schol. V in Aristoph. Plut.*, 313; Pollux, VI, 68; Ovid, *Metam.*, X, 728 ff. Cf. Play, *s. v. Minthe, R.-E*, (1932), c.1934-1935, and A. Brelich, 'Offerte e interdizioni alimentari nel culto della Magna Mater a Roma', *SMSR*, vol. XXXVI, 1965, pp.38-40, who wishes to assimilate the adventures of Mintha to a deity-*dema* whose death and passion prepare the way for the appearance of an edible plant.

2 Cf. Oppian, *Hal.*, III, 486-98.

3 *Schol. vet. in Nic. Alex.* 375, ed. Keil, p.97, 42-4 and Strabo, VIII, 3, 14 (*kēpaia minthē*).

4 Oppian, *Hal.*, III, 491-6.

5 *Etym. Gud.*, 395, 1 ff. *O. F.* 44 Kern.

6 Cf. Photius, *s.v. Mintha* and Strabo, VIII, 3, 14.

7 *Infra*, pp.000-00.

8 Bois, III, pp.182-3. Cf. J. Murr, *Die Pflanzenwelt in der griechischen Mythologie*, Innsbruck 1890 (reprinted, Groningen 1969), p.244, who points out that the mint mentioned in Theophrastus and in Dioscorides is probably *Mentha piperita L. Contra*, A. C. Andrews, 'The Mints of the Greeks and Romans and their condimentary Uses', *Osiris*, 13, 1958, pp.127-49.

9 Mint, like Pennyroyal (*blékhōn, Mentha pulegium*) is used to flavour cyceon (cf. A. Delatte, 'Le Cycéon, breuvage rituel des mystères d'Eleusis', *Bull. Acad. royale de Belg., Classe des Lettres et des Sciences morales et politiques*, 5th series, vol. XL, 1954, pp.725-6). It is also a condiment which appears to be indispensable for the consumption of beans (cf. the remarks of Kalleris studied by G. Daux, *BCH*, 1957, pp.1-5), which is not to contradict the Graeco-Latin proverb: 'No flavouring with lentils (*phakê*)'. (Varro, F. 89 OEhler [1844], pp.228-9).

10 Diosc., *M. M.*, III, 34, 1.

11 Diosc., *M. M.*, III, 34, 2; Pliny, *H. N.*, XX, 147.

12 [Hipp.] *On Regimen*, II, 54, 4.

13 [Hipp.] *On the sacred disease*, 2. Cf. Sext. Emp., *Pyrrh. Hyp.*, III, 224.

14 [Arist.] *Problem.*, XX, 2, 923 a 9-13. Cf. *Paroemiographi graeci*, II, p.530-1, 2, ed. Leutsch-Schneidewin.

15 Cf. Theoph., *De caus. plant.*, II, 16, 2 and Plut., *Quaest. cony.*, VIII, 9, 3, p.732 D.

16 *Schol. Aristoph. Plut.*, 313 (where the verb *minthoûn* means to 'defile with excrement').

17 *Schol. Aristoph. Gren.* 1075; Hes., *s. v. míntha*, ed. K. Latte.

18 Cf. P. Kretschmer, *Mythische Namen*, 14. 'Die Nymphe und lat. mentual', *Glotta*, XII, 1923, pp.105-6.

19 *kēpaía minthē*, ap. Strabo, VIII, 3, 14.

20 *poíē d'outidanē*, ap. Oppian, *Hal.*, III, 496.

21 *kaláminthos, ágrion hēdúosmon*, ap. *Etym. Gud.*, p.395, 1 ff.

22 Aristoph., *Ecclesiazusae*, 648.

23 *Schol. in Aristoph. loc. cit.*; Aelian, *N. A.*, IX, 26.

24 Cf. Pliny, *H. N.*, XIX, 159 and Colum., XI, 3, 37 (cited by J. André, in his commentary to Pliny, Book XIX, pp.158-9).

25 Bois, III, pp.182-3 (on peppermint which is a hybrid produced by crossing *M. viridis L* and *M. aquatica L.*)

26 *O. F.* 44 Kern.

27 As opposed to oil and wine (*hugroí karpoí*), cereals represent 'dry

fruits' (*xēroì karpoî*); Eur., *Bacch.*, 274 ff.; Xen., *Oeconom.*, V, 19; *Tablettes du Temple de Zeus à Locres,* no. 15, 1. 11, ed. A. de Franciscis (*Klearchos,* 25-28, 1965, pp.21 and 25).

28 Ovid, *Metam.*, X, 431-71.

29 H. Le Bonniec, *Le Culte de Ceres à Rome,* Paris 1958, pp.400-23.

30 *Id., op. cit.,* pp.404-12.

31 *Id., op. cit.,* pp.417 ff.

32 *Id., op. cit.,* pp.420-3.

33 Servius Danielis, *in Virg. Aen.*, IV, 58: 'Romae cum Cereri sacra fiunt, observatur ne quis patrem aut filiam nominet, quod fructus matrimonii per liberos constet.' As H. Le Bonniec notes, (*op. cit.*, p.421), the explanation given by Servius Danielis — who refers to 'the procreative power of man' — only takes account of one of the terms in this twofold taboo. To account for the second term we must refer to the relations between Ceres-Demeter and her daughter as these are presented in myth (cf. H. Le Bonniec, *op. cit.*, p. 422).

34 H. Le Bonniec, *op. cit.*, p.422.

35 Cf. M.P. Nilsson, *Griechische Feste von religiöser Bedeutung,* Stuttgard 1906, pp.313-25; L. R. Farnell, *The Cults of the Greek States, III*, Oxford 1907, pp.75-112; E. Fehrle, 'Die kultische Keuschheit in Altertum', *RGVV*, VI, 1910, pp.137-54; L. Deubner, *Attische Feste,* Berlin 1932, pp.50-60; P. Arbesmann, *s. v. Thesmophoria,* P.-E. (1937), c. 15-28.

36 Cf. Isaeus, III, 80; VIII, 19-20 ed. P. Roussel, together with the remarks of L. Beauchet, *Histoire du droit privé de la republique athénienne,* I, Paris 1897, p.152.

37 Aristoph., *Thesmoph.*, 294; Isaeus, VI, 50.

38 Isaeus, VI, 50.

39 Lysias, I, 19, ed. L. Gernet and M. Bizos.

40 The *castus Cereris* is first and foremost a nine-day period of chastity, cf. H. Le Bonniec, *op. cit.*, pp.406-12.

41 *Sch. in Luc. Dial. Meretr.*, II, 1, pp.275, 23-276, 28 Rabe. Cf. E. Des Places, *La Religion grecque,* Paris 1969, pp.99-100. The entire corpus of rules concernin chastity during the Thesmophoria has been collected by E. Fehrle, *op. cit.*, p.138 ff.

42 Cf. H. Leclerq, *Précis de Phytothérapie,*[3] Paris 1935, p.186, for which reference we are indebted to F. Daumas, 'Sous le signe du gattilier en fleur', *REG*, 1961, p.63, n. 4.

43 E. Fehrle, *op. cit.*, p.140 ff.

44 Cf. *Etym. Magn., s. v. agnos,* and *s. v. móskhoisi lúgoisin,* together with the remarks of E. Fehrle, *op. cit.*, p.152.

45 Aelian, *N. A.*, IX, 26; Diosc., *M. M.* I, 134; Galienus, XI, 807 K.; *Schol. in Nic. Ther. 71,* ed. Keil, p.10, 19-22; Eust.,

In Od. X, 453, p.1639, 1-5. Having pointed out that Greek women use this plant during the Thesmophoria, for the purposes of their ritual chastity, Pliny (*H. N.*, XXIV, 59) remarks that its leaves not only have the property of reducing the ardour of love but are also most effective 'in combatting the poison of Tarentulas whose bite is believed to excite the genital organs'. Cf. E. De Martino, *La Terre du remords*, Paris (French translation) 1966 p.218 ff.

46 Diosc., *M. M.*, I, 134.

47 H. Leclerq, *op. cit.*, p.186.

48 The reputation of the *agnus castus* was maintained during the Middle Ages when it was known as the *piper monachorum* or *eunuchorum*. Cf. E. Fehrle, *op. cit.*, p.153. But there were other plants also associated with the Thesmophoria which were believed to possess antiaphrodisiac powers, for example the *kónuza* (or *knúza*), the viscous or fragrant inula (cf. Pliny, *H. N.*, XXI, 58, ed. and comm. by J. André, p.115), and the *knéōron*, a type of laurel which has abortive powers and provokes stomach aches (Diosc., *M. M.*, IV, 170). Cf. the texts quoted by E. Fehrle, *op. cit.*, p.153.

49 Cf. *infra*, pp.114-15.

50 Apollodorus of Athens, F Gr Hist. 244 F 89. Cf. Callimachus, *Hymn to Apollo*, 110-11.

51 Plut., *Praec. conj.*, 144 D-E; Aelian, *N.A.*, V, 11; *Geoponica*, XV, 2, 19.

52 The second day is called *nēstéia*. Cf. P. R. Arbesmann, 'Das Fasten hei den Griechen und Romern', *RGVV*; XXI, 1929, pp.91-2.

53 Plut., *De Isid. et Osir.*, 378 E.

54 Cf. L. Gernet, *Anthropologie de la Grèce Antique*, Paris 1968, p.298, and n. 49.

55 *Homeric Hymn to Demeter*, 200-1. Cf. 49-50.

56 Aristoph., *Birds*, 1515 ff.

57 [Arist.] *Problemata*, XIII, 7, 908 b 11-19.

58 Philichorus, F Gr Hist 328 F 89. W. Burkett, 'Jason, Hypsipyle and new fire at Lemnos. A Study in myth and ritual', *Class. Quart.*, XX, 1970, p.11, has suggested that the garlic purchased for the Thesmophoria, as proved in IG, II[2], 1184, was kept for the same use as that, which we know about, for the Skirophoria (cf. L. Deubner, *op. cit.*, p.49). In his commentary on this fragment of Philichorus (F Gr Hist, vol. III, B [*Suppl*], I, p.372 [Text], II, p.375 [notes], F. Jacoby, while accepting the information regarding the ritual, is cautious about the explanation offered by the Atthidographer and suggests that we should see the

alleged disgust provoked by the smell of garlic as no more than a prejudice on the part of a cultivated Athenian of the late fourth century.

59 Cf. F. Lenormant, *s. v. Ceres, Daremberg-Saglio-Pottier*, D. A. [1887], c. 1042, and L. R. Farnell, *op. cit.*, III, p. 80 ff.

60 Cf. H. Jeanmaire, *Couroi et Courètes,* Lille 1939 p.305.

61 *Homeric Hymn to Demeter*, 101 ff.

62 Just as at Eleusis she becomes nurse to Demophon so, at Sicyona, she alone is successful in raising the son of Plemnaios, he local king, all of whose children had formerly given up the ghost on uttering their first cry (Paus., II, 5, 8.)

63 Cf. Oppian, *Hal.*, III, 486-97.

64 F Gr Hist 19 F 4. Cf. also *Schol. V in Aristoph. Plut.* 313.

65 D'Arcy W. Thompson, *A Glossary of Greek Birds*[2], Oxford 1936, [reprinted, Hildesheim, 1966], *s. v. iunx*, pp.124-8; P. Géroudet *Les Passereaux*, I[2], *Du coucou aux corvidés*, Neuchatel 1961, pp.79-82.

66 Arist., *H.A.*, II, 12, 504 a 11 ff. Cf. Pliny, *H. N.*, XI, 256.

67 In fact, the adjective *poíkilos* here seems to refer, not so much to the many colours of the plumage but rather to the ever-changing sheen associated with the mobility of the Wryneck. (cf. for the different meanings of *poíkilos*, cf. J.-P. Vernant and M. Detienne, 'La métis d'Antiloque', *REG*'. vol. LXXX, 1967, pp.77-78). The *Iunx torquilla* is 'a grey-brown bird, a little larger than a sparrow, but slimmer and more elongated. Its plumage, which is dark with delicate markings and stripes, is strikingly similar to that of certain Owls and of the Nightjar, and is often indistinguishable from bark and dead wood' (P. Géroudet, *op. cit.*, p.79).

68 Arist. *Part. Anim*, IV, 12, 695 a 23.

69 Cf. P. Géroudet, *op. cit.*, P.80: 'But the most peculiar feature of the Wryneck, whch has occasioned its name in all languages, is the mobility of its neck. As soon as it senses danger, or when it is disturbed sitting on its nest, for example, its reactions are alarming: the neck stretches out and twists slowly in a reptilian movement, the head feathers stand on end and the eyes half close; the bird puffs itself up and then exhales abrubtly, bunching up and stretching out in turn. It is enough to frighten away many an animal and even man himself'.

70 By shooting out its filiform tongue it feeds on insects, in particular ants: Dionysios, *Ixeutikon* I, 23, ed. A. Garzya.

71 Aelian, *N. A.*, VI, 19. According to Tzetzes, *Schol. in Lycophr.*, 310 ed. Scheer, II, p.126, 22-3, some preferred to liken the song of the iunx to the melodious sound of a cithare, others to that of a simple flute: *Schol. in Opp. Hal.*, I, 565.

72 Pind., *Pyth.,* IV, 214 ff.

73 *Id. ibid.,* 216; *mainád' órnin.*

74 A.S.F. Gow, 'Iunx, Rhombos, Turbo', *JHS,* 54, 1934, pp.1-13.

75 Fig. 6 in the above mentioned article shows the eminent English philologist himself solemnly manipulating a *iunx* before an audience of readers of the *J.H.S.* Evidence from several vase paintings used by Gos (figs. 2-4) confirms the difference between this type of instrument and another with which it is often confused: the rhombus, which is a small piece of wood one end of which is attached to a piece of string and which is twirled in such a way as to emit a gentle hum. It is most unlikely that a curious terra cotta wheel, decorated with eleven birds, should be identified, as Grace W. Nelson suggests, as a *iunx,* even a votive one (cf. Grace W. Nelson, 'A Greek votive Iunx-Wheel in Boston', *AJA,* vol. 44, 1940, pp.443-56). For another interpretation of this object dating from the geometric period, cf. J. de la Genière, 'Une roue à oiseaux du Cabinet des Medailles', *REA,* vol. LX, 1958, pp.27-35.

76 Callimachus, F. 685 Pfeiffer. Cf. *Schol. in Lycophr.* 310, ed. Scheer, II, p.129, 9-22; Souda, *s. v. Iunx,* vol. II, p.677, 20ff; 678, 5-6, ed. A. Adler.

77 [Lucian], Epigram., 29, 3, ed. Jacobitz, vol. III, p.465.

78 Theocritus, II, ed. comm. A.S.F. Gow (who returns to the problem of the *iunx* in vol. II, Cambridge 1952, p.41).

79 Souda and Hes., *s. v. iunx.* In Dionysios, *Ixeutikon,* I, 23, ed. A. Garzya, the gait of the *Iunx torquilla* is compared to the walk of the effeminate youths taking part in the procession of Rhea.

80 Callimachus, F.685 Pfeiffer; The first version is that of Callimachus according to *Schol. Theocr.* II, 17; the second is vouched for by *Schol. Pind. Nem.* IV, 156 a and Photius, Souda, *s. v. iunx.*

81 Callimachus, F. 685 Pfeiffer; *Schol. Pind. Nem.,* IV, 156 a; *Schol. Lycophr.* 310, ed. Scheer, II, p.126, 21-2.

82 Photius, Souda, *s. v. Iunx.*

83 Cf. G. Nicole, *Meidias ou le style fleuri dans la céramique attique,* Geneva 1907, p.69 ff (pl. III, 2).

84 Aelian, *N. A.,* IX, 13.

85 *Id. ibid.,* XV, 19.

86 *Id. ibid.,* V, 40. Cf. Theophr., *Caus. Plant.,* VI, 5, I: [Arist.,] *Problem.,* XIII, 4, 908 a 35 ff; *Paroemiographi graeci,* II, p.711, 8 ff; Philes, *De anim. propriet.,* 866-86 (the effect of the panther is compared to the *iunges* of the sorcerors, the very ones mentioned by Psellus in several passages analysed by S. Eitrem, 'Les roues magiques', *Symbolae Osloenses,* XXII, 1942, pp.78-9).

87 *hypó tinos íuggos tês euōdías:* Aelian, *N. A.,* V, 40; *Paroem.gr.*

II, 711, 14-15. It is by means of the all-powerful balm of *Peithō* that Dejaneira hopes to lure Heracles, 'full of amorous desire' back to her (Sophocles, *Trachiniae*, 661 ff), but this *phármakon* later turns out to be a virulent and deadly poison.

88 Cf. Waser, *s. v. Ixion, R.-E.* (1919), c. 1373-1384; Weizsacker, *s. v. Ixion, Roscher* (1890-4), c.766-772.

89 Aeschylus, *Ixion,* F. 314 ed. H. J. Mette.

90 Pind., *Pyth.,* II, 32: *emphúlion haîma; Schol. Apoll. Rhod.,* III, 62: *emphúlion ándra.*

91 Aeschylus, *ibid:* Pind., *ibid.*

92 Pind., *Pyth.,* II, 42.

93 Pind., *Pyth.,* II, 24.

94 As will be shown by a book by D. Saintillan, on the concept of *charis,* that is soon to appear.

95 Cf. M. Detienne, *Les Maitres de Vérité dans la Grèce archaique,* Paris 1967, p.64 ff.

96 Aesch., *Supplices,* 1040-1041.

97 Hes., *Theog.,* 206.

98 Hes., Theog., 205. Cf. *Il.,* XIV, 216.

99 *Iliad,* XIV, 160 ff.

100 Cf. M. I. Finley, 'Marriage, Sale and Gift in the Homeric World,, *Rev. intern. des droits de l'Antiquité,* 3rd series, II, 1955, pp.167-94.

101 Aeschylus, F. 314 C ed. H. J. Mette.

102 On the subject of lovers who 'pursue in boys and women merely the mirrored image of Beauty', Plutarch, in the *Dialogue on Love* (*Amatorius,* 766A) writes: 'Probably this is the meaning of Ixion's constant whirling (*illigos*) and irregular course, for the object of his desire and pursuit was an illusion in the clouds, as if it were an empty shadow. It is like the eagerness of children to catch the rainbow in their hands, attracted by its mere appearance'.

103 Cf. the evidence of the illustrations analysed by L. Séchan, *Etudes sur la tragédie grecque,* Paris 1926, (reprinted 1967), pp.389-95.

104 A. B. Cook, *Zeus,* III, 2 (1940), pp.1025-65.

105 F. Salviat, *Les théogamies attiques, Zeus Teleios et l'Agamemnon d'Eschyle,* BCH, 1964, pp.647-54.

106 Arist. *Politics,* VII, 14, 7, 1335 a 36 ff. Cf. L. Gernet, *Anthropologie de la Grèce ancienne,* Paris 1968, p.40 ff.

107 This Hera *Teleía* is addressed by the chorus of women celebrating the Thesmophoria (Aristoph., *Thesmoph.,* 973-6).

108 Cf. F. Salviat, *art. cit.,* pp.652-4, on the Zeus *Téleios* of the *Agammemnon* (969-74).

109 Diodorus, V, 73.

110 Zeus and Hera are the *Prytaneis* of marriage, to adopt the expression of the *Schol. in Aristophanes, Thesmoph.,* 973.
111 The excellent analysis of G. Dumézil, *Le Crime des Lemniennes,* Paris 1924, has recently been made more precise on several points by W. Burkert, 'Jason, Hypsipyle and new fire at Lemnos. A Study in Myth and Ritual', *Classical Quarterly,* XX, 1970, pp.1-16.
112 Asclepiades of Tragilos, F Gr Hist 12 F 14; Myrsilos of Methymna, F Gr Hist 477 F 1 a); Hygienus, *Fab.,* XV, 1; *Paroem. gr.,* vol. II, p.503, 23 ff.
113 *Thusiásin omobórois íkelai:* Apoll. Rh., *Argon.,* I, 636.
114 Apoll. Rh., *Argon.,* I, 640 ff.
115 *Id. ibid.,* 846.
116 Pind., *Pyth.,* IV, 252 ff. Cf. Apoll. Rh., II, 30 ff; III, 120 ff; IV, 423 ff. and the remarks of L. Gernet, *Anthropologie de la Grèce ancienne,* Paris 1968, p.42, 119 and 203.
117 Apoll. Rh., *Argon.,* I, 859-60.
118 *Id., ibid.,* 850-3.
119 *Id, ibid.,* 858-60: *kapnôi kniséenti* and *thueéssi* (cf. for this last word, J. Casabona, *op. cit.,* pp.109-15.
120 Aeschylus, *Hypsipyle,* F. 40, ed. H. J. Mette.
121 J.-P. Vernant, *Introduction* to the volume entitled *Problèmes de la guerre en Grèce ancienne,* Paris 1968, p.15.
122 Eust, in *Il. I,* 592, p.158, 15-16.
123 *Schol. Eur. Hec.,* 887, ed. Dindorf, I, p.437, 18 ff. In this version the foul smell also emanates from the mouth.
124 Dio Chrys., *Or.,* 33, 50.
125 [Arist.] *Problem.,* XIII, 8, p.908 b 20-3.
126 Cf. *supra,* p.80, n.57.
127 Myrsilos of Methymna, *F Gr Hist* 477 Fl.
128 Written in the margin of a manuscript of Antigonus, *Hist. Mir.,* 118 F Gr Hist 477 F 1 b). cf. the critical work of F. Jacoby (p.437, 1.27).
129 Bois, III, p.194; J. André, *L'Alimentation et la cuisine à Rome,* Paris 1961, pp.205-6. The Greeks do not appear to have used this plant in their cooking: A.-C. Andrews, 'The use of Rue as a Spice by the Greeks and Romans', *Class. Journ.,* XLIII, 1948, pp.371-3.
130 It is also a plant which imparts a foul smell even to certain perfumes, [Arist.], *Problemata,* XX, 33, 926 b 16-19), and which is also believed to be a *baskanías phármakon* [*id.*], *ibid.,* XX, 34, 926 b 20-32).
131 Oribasius, II, p.674.
132 [Hipp.], *Nat. fem.,* 12; Plut., *Sympos.,* III, 1, 3, 647 B.
133 Diosc., *M. M.,* III, 45; Plut., *Sympos.,* III, 3, 647 B. (rue, *péganon,* hardens, *pégnusi,* and through its heat dries up human

sperm); Rufus, p.82; *Schol. vet. in Nic. Alex.* 410, ed. Abel (Budapest 1891), p.81, 15 ff; Oribasius V, p.632; VI, p.496. Cf. other sources of evidence ap. G. Wolff, *Porphyrii. De Philosophia ex oraculis haurienda,* Berlin 1856, pp.195-6.

134 *Schol. vet. in Nic. Alex.* 410. Rue, like *agnus castus* (*ágnos*) and Rocket (*eúzomon*), is one of the plants taken by priests so as to remain in a state of chastity (*hagneías khárin: Cyranides,* I, in *Lapidaires grecs,* ed. de Mély and Ruelle, vol. II, Paris 1898, p.16, 1. 20-1).

135 Myrsilos of Methymna, *F Gr Hist* 477 F 1 a) and b). To the same extent as mothers and daughters are united in the Thesmophoria, so are mothers and sons disunited in the Lemnian ritual.

136 Ibid. (a). *kat 'eniautòn hēméran tiná*; (b). *kaì málista en taútais taîs hēmérais.*

137 Cf. W. Burkert, *art. cit.,* p.10.

138 Philostratos, *Heroicos,* 19, ed. C. L. Kayser, II, 1871, p.207.

139 The text of the manuscript is corrupt: *kaì kath'héna toû étous.* The passage, which has often been emended after Boissonade and Westermann, to *kath'hékaston étos* was improved by the suggestions of A. Wilhelm, *Die Pyrphorie der Lemnier, Anz. Wien,* 1939, p.41-6, who proposed to read the text of the manuscripts as it stood, dividing the words as follows: *kath'henátou étous,* 'every nine years'. The suggestion was adopted by M. Delcourt, *Hephaistos ou la légende du magicien,* Paris 1957, pp.173-80. But W. Burkert (*art. cit.,* pp.2-3) has recently put forward a number of reasons for discarding A. Wilhelm's correction, and proposes a reading as follows: *kai [ròn] kath'héna toû étous,* preserving the reference to the annual extinction of the fires and the parallelism of this rite and the separation of the sexes.

140 Cf. C. Lévi-Strauss, *Le cru et le cuit,* Paris 1964, pp.299-302; *Du miel aux cendres,* Paris 1966, p.356 ff.

141 Sophocles, *Philoctetes,* 295-6.

142 *Homeric Hymn to Hermes,* 108-11.

143 Cf. Plutarch, *Numa,* IX, 10-12, together with the remarks of R. Flacelière, *REG,* 1948, pp.417-20, and also the data collected by M. Delcourt, *Pyrrhos et Pyrrha,* Paris 1965, pp.106-7.

144 Plut., *Numa,* IX, 12, in the edition translated by M. Delcourt.

145 *Id. ibid.,* IX, 13-14.

146 On the evidence of an indication in the *Philoctetes* (800-81: *anakaloúmenon,* used to describe the fire, might be an allusion to the ritual of the new fire at Lemnos itself), W. Burkert, *art. cit.,* pp.5-6, suggests that, in a more ancient form of the festival, the fire was lit by blacksmiths (whose importance on Lemnos is

indisputable) using large bronze mirrors (p.6, n. 1).

147 There is technological evidence for this, ap. Theophrastus, *De igne*, 73. Cf. J. Morgan, 'De ignis eliciendi modis', *Harvard Studies of Classical Philology*, I, 1890, pp.50-64.

148 Plut., *Numa*, IX, 11. This is probably how Plutarch's expression should be understood: 'Not virgins, *parthénoi,* but women abstaining from all marital relations, *gunaîkes dè pepauménai gámōn.*'

NOTES TO CHAPTER FIVE

1 Aristoph. *Lysistrata*, 387-98. On the role of Demostratos and the meaning of Aristophanes' account as compared to those of Plutarch and Thucydides, cf. N. Weill, 'Adôniazousai ou les femmes sur le toit', *Bull. Corres. Hellen., vol. XC*, 1966, pp.684-7.

2 Cf. *supra.*

3 Plut., *Nicias*, XIII, 7; *Alcibiades*, XVIII, 4.

4 Thucydides, VI, 30. The problem of the date of the Adonia has provoked many discussions. These have been assessed in W. Atallah's study entitled *Adonis* (pp.229-58) and the discussion was carried further in the same year by N. Weill's work of major importance (*art. cit.* pp.664-98). Each of the three seasons, autumn, spring and summer has been favoured in its turn by modern scholars as the date for the celebration of the festival. The theory of an autumn date is based on evidence as vague and debateable as the geographical information given in Lucian's *Dea Syria*, 8, or the timing of the Adonia of Alexandria as deduced from a Fayoum papyrus of G. Glotz (cf. G. Glotz 'Les fêtes d'Adonis sous Ptolémée II', *REG*, 1920, pp.169-222). The second hypothesis — that it took place in spring — is based principally on the arbitrary calendar (cf. the criticisms of N. Weill, *art. cit.*, p.683 and n.5) reconstructed on the evidence of one of Alciphron's letters (IV, 14) by F. R. Walton, 'The date of the Adonia at Athens', *The Harvard Theological Review*, 1938, pp.65-72. Walton attempted to amalgamate the festival of Eros with that of Adonis. However, the bulk of explicit testimonies — the more important of which we shall be examining — supported by the various arguments put forward by N. Weill (*art. cit.*, pp.675-98) must lead to the conclusion that the Adonia are a summer festival and even a mid-summer one. The hypothesis of a double festival proposed by W. Attallah (*op. cit.* pp.255-8) is not necessary.

5 Plato, *Phaedrus*, 276 B.

6 Theophrastus, *H. Pl.*, VI, 7, 3: 'The *habrótonon* (santolina or white cedar, *Santolina chamaecyparissus L*) actually grows more

readily from seed than from a root or a piece torn off, though it grows even from seed with difficulty. However, it can be propagated *in summer (toû thérous) in pots like the gardens of Adonis.* It is very sensitive to cold and generally delicate *even when the sun shines very brightly (hélios sphódra lámpei)'.* Cf. Pliny, *H. N.,* XXI, 60, in the edition with commentary by J. André (1969, pp.117-18).

7 W. K. Pritchett and B. L. Van der Waerden, 'Thucydidean Time-Reckoning and Euctemon's Seasonal Calendar', *BCH,* 1961, pp.17-52, whose conclusions have been used by N. Weill, *(art. cit.,* pp.688-90) to decide the date of the Adonia.

8 N. Weill, *art. cit.,* p.690. But the evidence of Ammianus Marcellinus (XIX, 1, 11; XXII, 9, 15) and that of J. Lydus (*De mensibus,* IV, 64) both of which are cited, along with Thucydides, by N. Weill, are worthless for dating the ritual precisely. When J. Lydus associates Adonis' death with the wheat harvest in mid-summer, his argument is the same as that of modern scholars who see in the story of Adonis an image of vegetation dying in the autumn.

9 Cf. Geminus, *Elementa astronomiae,* ed. K. Manitius (1896), p.212, 1.3. As F. Cumont has pointed out (*Adonies et canicule, Syria,* 1935, pp.49-50, n. 2, Meton's mistake proves that he had taken over this date from observers operating at a lower latitude, in Egypt.

10 Gundel, *s. v. Sirius, R.-E.* (1927), c.340.

11 F. Cumont, *Les Syriens en Espagne et les Adonies à Séville, Syria,* 1927, pp.330-41. Cf. *Id.,* 'Adonis at Sirius', *Mélanges G. Glotz,* I, Paris 1932, pp.257-64; *Adonies et canicule, Syria,* 1935, pp.46-50.

12 Theophrastus, *H. Pl.,* IX, 1, 6.

13 R. de Vaux, 'Sur quelques rapports entre Adonis et Osiris', *Rev. biblique,* 1933, p.34; N. Weill, *art. cit.,* p.696; W. Atallah, *op. cit.,* p.323: 'Plus que les fruits mûrs, Adonis aurait representé la poussée de la végétation printanière qui meurt sous les ardeurs du soleil estival' (Adonis appears to have represented not ripe fruits but rather the growth of spring vegetation which dies under the onslaught of the summer sun); and a little further on, on the same page: 'Nous verrons donc dans les Jardins d'Adonis une transposition en été de la poussée du printemps pour associer dans un diptyque saisissant la vie et la mort pleurée de ce bel amant d'Aphrodite' (We should thus see the Gardens of Adonis as a transposition to summer of the growth of spring, giving a striking illustration in two parts of the life and lamented death of this handsome lover of Aphrodite).

14 J. G. Frazer, *Adonis, Attis, Osiris. Studies in the history of*

Oriental religion, pp.197; 199-216; F. Cumont, *Les Religions orientales dans le paganisme romain*[4], Paris 1929, p.101; 'Adonis et Sirius', *Mélanges G. Glotz*, I, Paris 1932, pp.263-4; L. Deubner, *Attische Feste*, Berlin 1932, p.221 ('Sie stellen einen sympathetischen Zauber dar, der in der Zeit, wo die Erde erschöpft ist [D. thinks that the festival took place in the autumn], daren Fruchtbarkeit für das kommende Jahr sichern soll'); H. Metzger, *Les représentations dans la céramique attique du IVe siècle*, Paris 1951, p.99 n. 1.

15 M. P. Nilsson, 'La mythologie' in *l'Histoire générale des Religions (Grèce-Rome)*, Paris, A. Quillet, 1944, p.231. But perhaps this sentence as it stands, should be considered the responsibility of the translator who had the task of putting the author's Swedish text into French.

16 Such evidence taken from ancient authors has been most clearly presented by R. Rochette, 'Mémoire sur les Jardins d'Adonis', *Revue Archéologique*, 1851, pp.97-123.

17 *Paroem. gr.*, I, p.19, 6 ff. Leutsch and Schneidewin; *Suda, s. v. Akarpóteros Adõnidos kêpon*. Cf. *Paroem, gr.*, II, p.140, 20-1, L.-S.

18 Suda, *s. v. Adõnidos kêpoi*; Pausanias Attic., *Lexic.*, 27, ed. H. Erbse, p.154, 1. 23-5.

19 *Paroem. gr.*, I, p.183, 3-8 L.-S. The author of this remark was careful to point out that those responsible for these gardens could belong to either sex (*phuteúontes è phuteúousai*).

20 *Paroem. gr.*, II, p.3, 10-13. Cf. II, p.93, 13; *Schol. in Plat. Phaedr.*, 276 B.

21 Eust., *In Od.* XI, 590, p.1701, 45 ff.

22 J. G. Frazer, *op. cit.*, p.197.

23 The whole of the first part of R. Rochette's 'Mémoire sur les Jardins d'Adonis' is devoted to refuting the thesis of his 'erudite colleague, Mr. Durcau de Lamalle', who wanted to see the gardening of Adonis as a kind of forced cultivation, implying the use of 'hot houses'.

24 Plato, *Phaedrus*, 276 B. Cf. J. Derrida, 'La pharmacie de Platon'. *Tel Quel*, 1968, p.75 ff.

25 On agriculture as a form of *paideía* cf. *supra*, p.12. The *paidiá* of the Adonia is referred to in Menander's *Woman of Samos* (1.41).

26 Cf. Stob., *Ecl. Eth.*, II, 6, 4, ed. Wachsmuch, II, p.37, 10-13.

27 Simplicius, *In Arist. De Caelo* 269 a 9 ff. (*Comment. gr. in Aristot.*, vol. VII, 1894, p.25, 34-6).

28 Similarly, the sorceress Iunx is changed sometimes into a wryneck bird and sometimes into a block of stone.

29 Plut., *De sera numinis vindicta*, 17, 560 B-C.

30 Arist., *Physics*, V. 230 a 31 230 b 2.

31 In the tables of Euktemon the Heliacal rising of the Dog is accompanied by the onset of a stifling heat (*pnîgos*): Geminus, *Elementa astronomiae,* ed. K. Manitius, p.212, 1. 17.

32 Simplicius, *In Arist. Phys.* 230 a 18 (*Comment. gr. in Aristot*)., X, 1895, p.911, 13-15.

33 Epictetus, *Discourses,* IV, 8, 39-43.

34 Theoph. *De causis plantarum*, I, 12 2: *katà kairón. Cf. eis tò prosêkhon* in Plato, *Phaedrus*, 276 b.

35 Cf. the distinction drawn by Xenophon, *Hellenica*, III, 2, 10, between *gê spórimos* and *gê pephuteuménē*.

36 All these terms are taken from the paroemiographers mentioned above, p.102. One of these *óstraka* is depicted on the aryballisc lekythus in the Karlsruhe Museum (Metzger, *op. cit.*, no.41, p.92 and pl. VII/2): the receptacle containing the gardens of Adonis can be seen to be 'the upper part of a broken and upturned amphora' (Atallah, *op. cit.*, p.179, who raises reasonable objections to the interpretation defended by Metzger, *op. cit.*, pp.89-92 and pl. V/4).

37 Julian, *Symposion*, 329 D.

38 In Greece, as in Rome (cf. Pliny, *H. N.*, XIX, 57), gardening is a matter for the women as is the gathering of fruit. Women no more work on the land than they guard the herds, except among the barbarians (among the Thracians, cf. Plato, *Laws*, 805 E) or in exceptional conditions (among the Athamanae in the valley of the Pindus, the women work the land while the men pasture the herds).

39 Cf. Aristoph. *Lysistrata*, 389; *Schol. in Arist. Lys.* 389; Menander, *The Woman of Samos*, 45, ed. R. Kasser; Suda, *s. v. Adôneioi kêpoi*. The pictorial evidence consists of the vases mentioned by H. Metzger, *Les représentations dans la céramique attique du IVe siècle*, Paris 1951, pp.92-4, no. 41-6. As N. Weill points out, *art. cit.*, p.671, the criterion for recognising depictions of the Adonia is the ladder used by the women to reach the roof-tops.

40 Philichorus, *F Gr Hist* 828 F 61 (cf. L. Deubner, *Attische Feste*, p.67). According to the *Schol. in Soph. Oed. Col.*, 1600, the sacrifice offered up on the sixth of Thargelion is in hommage to Demeter *Eúkhloos*, 'on account of the *kêpoi* turning green'. (Cf. F. Jacoby, *F Gr Hist*, III B. *Suppl.* I, 1954, p.335 and II, 1954, p.240).

41 *Paroem. gr.*, I, p.19, 9-10; Julian, *Sympos.*, 329 D.

42 *Schol. in Theocr.* XV, 112; Hes., *s. v. Adônidos kêpoi*; Suda, *s.v. Anônidos Kêpoi*; Pausanias Attic., *Lexic.*, 27, ed. H. Erbse, p.154, 1. 23-5.

43 Bois, I, pp.245-6. On its use in Roman cookery, cf. J. André,

L'Alimentation et la cuisine à Rome, Paris 1961, p.203. Epicharmus, however, F. 159-61 Kaibel (cited by Athanaeus, II, 70 f-71) numbers fennel among the vegetables, alongside lettuces, radishes and several others.

44 Oribasius, II, p.661. Cf. Olck, *s. v. Fenchel, R.-E.* (1909), c.2172-77.

45 Pliny, *H. N.*, XX, 257; Diosc., *M. M.*, III, 71.

46 Pliny, XX, 254; Diosc., *M. M.*, III, 70, 2.

47 Theoph., *H. Pl.*, I, 11, 2; VII, 3, 2; Pliny, *H. N.*, XIX, 119.

48 Galienus, VI, p.641.

49 Fennel, together with cinnamon and spikenard, is one of the aromatic plants that the Phoenix uses to build the nest which is to serve as its funeral pyre in order to be reborn every 500 years: Apollonius in J. Lydus, *De mensibus*, IV, 11, ed. Wünsch, p.76, 12. Cf. J Hubaux and M. Leroy, *Le Mythe du Phénix*, Liège-Paris 1939, p.243, who suggest that this author is really Apollonius of Tyanus.

50 *Maraínesthai* or *maraínein*, to wilt, to dry up, is part of the technical terminology of the Gardens of Adonis; Julian, *Sympos.*, 329D; Stob., *Ecl. Eth.*, II, 6, 4; Plut., *Nicias*, XIII, 7 (this describes the anxiety felt because the festival of the Adonia coincided with the departure of the Athenian fleet for Sicily. It is a description in which the use of this word reveals, as N. Weill points out, *art. cit.*, pp.690-1, 'an implicit comparison between the Gardens of Adonis in full flower but soon to wither and the splendid fleet destined to a similar fate.). Other words convey the same image: *apoxēraínein*, Epictetus, IV, 8, 39-43; *aposbennúnai*, Simplicius, *in Arist. De Caelo*, 269 a 9 *Comment. gr. in Aristot.*, VII, 1894, p.25, 36.

51 *eis krēnas (Paroem. gr.*, I, p.19, 6 ff.); *katà thalássēs (Eust.,* p.1701, 45).

52 Cf. the criticisms already made of the Frazerian interpretation by R. de Vaux, *art. cit.*, p.35 and W. Atallah, *op. cit.*, p.227.

53 Oribasius, II, 638.

54 On the grounds of the similarity between two vase paintings, both showing a woman standing by a ladder and holding a bowl containing grapes ('Adōniazousai ou les femmes sur le toit', *BCH,* vol. XC, 1966, pp.664-98), N. Weill has, quite recently, suggested that we should see the offering of grapes as another episode in the ritual of the Adonia. It is an unusual episode and we may well doubt, together with H. Metzger (*Bulletin archéologique, REG,* vol. LXXXI, 1968, no.185, pp.155-6) whether, despite the presence of a ladder, this is really a phase in the festival of Adonis given that, according to all ancient Greek accounts, the essential ritual of the Adonia consisted in gardening carried out on

the rooftops, with the significance we have already discussed. However, if this evidence is to be taken to refer to a part of the ritual, we believe that account should be taken of the opposition made in Plato's *Laws*, between two types of grapes: one which is gathered as early as the beginning of July and eaten, and the other which must not be cut until the time for the wine harvest and the rising of Arcturus. This then is an opposition between two types of fruit, one of which cannot be stored and is connected with *paidia* (844 d 6). The other, which is to be preserved, is to be turned into wine, the drink which, together with cereals and meat, forms the basis of the human diet.

55 *Supra*, p.100.

56 *Schol. in Arist. Eq. 729* and *Plut. 1054*. The parallelism is also emphasised by the role of the *eiresiōnē* and the *passpermia*, one at the beginning and the other at the end of the period. Cf. the information provided by J.-P. Vernant, 'Ambiguité et renversement, Sur la structure énigmatique d'OEdipe-Roi', *Mélanges C. Lévi-Strauss* Paris-The Hague 1970, p.1269, n.46, who basis it upon remarks made by L. Deubner, *Attische Feste*, pp.198-201; 224-6, and especially by H. Jeanmaire, *Couroi et Courètes* Lille 1939, pp.312-3; 347 ff (the period of Theseus' initiation, in Athenian myth, lasts from *Mounichion* — the month immediately preceding *Thargélion* — to *Pyanopsion*). The problems raised by Theophrastus' account of the procession in honour of the Sun and the Seasons are discussed by W. Pötscher, *Theophrastos. Perì Eusebeías*, Leiden 1964, pp.101; 132-4.

57 C. W. Pötscher, *op. cit.*, p.133.

58 Philichorus, *F Gr Hist* 328 F 173.

59 Menander, *Dyskolos*, 456 ff. and 519.

60 *IG*, XII, 7, 515 ff. Cf. the sacrifices of boiled meats offered up to Ceres of the Latins: H Le Bonniec, *op. cit.*, pp.463-6.

61 F. Sokolowski, *Lois sacrées d'Asie Mineure*, Paris 1955, no. 50, 1. 34.

62 G. Ricci, 'Una hydria ionica da Caere', *Annuario della Scuola archeologica di Atene*, vol. XXIV-XXVI, 1946-8, pp.47-57, pl. IV (1-2-3). However, the grilling on the spit is shown more often in the scenes of sacrifice depicted on vase paintings (cf. H. Metzger, *Recherches sur l'imagerie athénienne*, Paris 1965, pp.107-18).

63 Euripides, *Cyclops*, 243-7; 356 ff. (*hepthà kaì optá*). Both types of cooking are used for Thyestes' meal and also for Lycaon's sacrifice. The former is prepared by Atreus 'who employs the spit as well as the cooking pot' (Seneca, *Thyestes*, 1060-5, cf. also 765). As for Lycaon, 'he softens some of the palpitating limbs of the victim in boiling water whilst roasting the rest over the fire'

(Ovid, *Metam.* I, 228-9. Cf. G. Piccaluga, *Lykaon. Un tema mitico,* Rome 1968, p.44).

64 Cf. J. Schmidt, *s. v. Omophagia, R.-E.* (1939) c. 380-2. Once Dionysus became a part of the city and required a place in the official system of religious practices, the eating of raw meat only survived in attenuated forms illustrated, for example, by the gesture — made originally by the priestess 'in the name of the city' — of placing in the sacred basket a mouthful of raw meat (*ōmophágion emballeîn,* in F. Sokolowski, *Lois sacréesd'Asie Mineure,* Paris 1955, no. 48, 1.2. We are adopting the interpretation suggested by A.-J. Festugière in *Classica Mediaevalia,* 1956, pp.31-4).

65 *O. F.* 35 Kern.

66 [Arist.], *Problemata,* III, 43, ed. Bussemaker, vol. IV, p.331, 15 ff. Cf. S. Reinach, 'Une allusion à Zagreus dans un problème d'Aristote', referred to in *Cultes, Mythes et Religions,* vol. V, Paris 1923, pp.61-71, and C. Lévi-Strauss *L'Origine des manières de table,* Paris 1968, p.398 ff.

67 Sosibius ap Athanaeus, XIV, 648 B. There is further evidence in L. Ziehen, *s. v. Panspermia, R.-E.* (1949), c.680-3.

68 The ordering of the year's seasons brings about a harmonious combination of the hot and cold, and the dry and the wet, which makes for prosperity and good health (*euetēria te kaì hugíeia*): Plato, *Symposium,* 188 a.

69 Different ancient writers have different views on the respective merits of what is roasted and what is boiled. Sometimes the roasted meats are held to be more raw and dry than those that have been boiled and sometimes the reverse obtains (Athanaeus, XIV, 656 A-B; [Arist.], *Problemata,* V, 34, 884 a 36 ff; III, 43, ed. Bussemaker, vol. IV, p.331, 15. *Contra,* Arist., *Meteor.,* IV, 3, 380 b 12 ff.). The most subtle analysis is to be found in Aristotle's *Meteor.,* IV, 3, 381 a 27 ff. where what is boiled and what is roasted are described as two forms of equilibrium — the one being the reverse of the other — between the dry and the wet: food that is grilled is dryer on the outside than on the inside; food that is boiled is wetter on the outer parts than in the inner ones.

70 Arist., *Meteor.,* IV, 3, 380 a 12 ff.

71 Cf. *supra* p.9.

72 A kind of meningitis: *Etym. Magn., s. v. astrobolēthênai* ...; Paul Aeg., I, 13, p.13, 5, Heiberg; Pliny, *H. N.,* XXX, 135; XXII, 59; XXXII, 183. Cf. Gundel, *s. v. Sirius, R.-E.* (1927), c.343.

73 Theoph., *H. Pl.,* IV, 14, 2; *Caus. Plant.,* V, 9, 7; Aratos, *Phainomena,* 331; *Schol. Arat.* 332, p.408, 14 Maass; Pliny,

H. N., XVII, 222 (together with the notes by J. André, pp.177 and 179 of his commentary). Cf. Gundel, *art. cit.*, c.343.

74 Theoph., *H. Pl.*, VI, 14, 2.

75 H. Metzger, *op. cit.*, p.93, no.43-6 (pl. VII); W. Atallah, *op. cit.*, pp.185-8, figs. 44-8.

76 H. Metzger, *op. cit.*, no. 46; W. Atallah, *op. cit.*, p.187, fig. 47.

77 H. Metzger, *op. cit.*, pp.96-8. This author has elsewhere shown the importance of incense-burners and of sacrifices of frankincnese in scenes depicting festivals and cults of Aphrodite: 'Lébès gamikos à figures rouges du Musée National d'Athènes', *Bull, Corr. hell.*, 1942-3, p.233; 241-2.

78 This objection against Furtwängler's thesis was expressed by F. Hauser, 'Adōniazusai', *Jahreshefte des Oesterreichischen archäologischen Institutes*, XII, 1909, p.97. Elsewhere, he saw the *thumiatḗrion*, in which the myrrh is burned, as a perfect illustration of the myth of Adonis, the son of Myrrha who was changed into a Myrrh tree.

79 H. Metzger, *op. cit.*, pp.97-8, has distinguished between the two most carefully.

80 The traditional formula uttered by the father when giving away his daughter in marriage is extremely clear on this point: I give you this daughter with a view to a labour productive of legitimate children (Menander, *Perikeiroménē*, 436; F. 682 Körte). Cf. J.-P. Vernant, *Mythe et Pensée chez les Grecs. Etudes de Psychologie historique*, Paris 1965, pp.113-15, and A. R. W. Harrison, *The Law of Athens*, Oxford, 1968, p.18.

81 Pollux, I, 246 (cf. Aristoph., *Ecclesiazusae*, 221). The grilling of barley preceded the use of the pestle and the invention of milling. In Greece, the *phrúgetron* was used for preparing 'polenta' (J. André, *L'Alimentation et la cuisine à Rome*, Paris 1961, pp.57-8, and P. Herfst, *Le Travail de la femme dans la Grèce ancienne*, Diss., Utrecht 1922, pp.28-32.

82 Pollux, III, 37-8. Cf. E. Pernice, 'Griechisches und Römisches Privatleben', in Gerke and Norden, *Einleitung in die Altertumswissenschaft*, II[3], 1922, p.56.

83 *Paroem. gr.*, I, 82, 10 ff.; II, 429, 8 ff.; Suda, ed. Adler, vol. V, p.491, 20 ff.; Hesychius, ed. Latte, vol. II, p.248; Eust., p.1726, 18 ff.

84 Cf. also Suda, *s. v. Bíon alēlesménon* (d) and Eust., p.1859, 47-8, who no doubt go back to Theophrastus, as was suggested by A. Delatte, 'Le Cycéon, breuvage rituel des mystères d'Eleusis', *Bull. Acad. Belg., Cl. Lettres, Sc. mor. et polit.*, 5th series, vol. XL, Brussels 1954, pp.692-3.

85 [Hipp.], *On regimen*. IV, 90, 3. 'Tree without fruits': the expression

is very appropriate for mint, originally a large tree laden with fruits but now struck by *akarpiē*. Cf. *supra*, pp.73 and 75.

86 Cf. Plut., *Lycurgus*, XV, 4.

87 Epictetus, *Discourses*, IV, 8, 36.

88 Cf. R. B. Onians, *The Origins of European Thought*[2], Cambridge 1954, p.174 ff.

89 Pollux, III, 38. Cf. J. Harrison, *Prolegomena to the study of Greek Religion*,[3] 1922 (reprinted, New York 1955), pp. 620-1, and F. Salviat, *BCH*, 1964, pp.650-4.

90 Plato, *Laws*, VIII, 841D. *Áthuta*, meaning in its proper sense 'not consecrated by sacrifice' is no doubt a reference to the religious ceremonies for consecrating marriage, as seems to be suggested by a ruling in *Laws*, VI, 784 a, which makes certain carefully chosen women responsible for supervising young married couples and 'for reporting to one another any case they may have noticed where any man or woman of the procreative age is devoting his attention to other things instead of to what is ordained for them at the marriage sacrifices and ceremonies (*hupò tôn en toîs gámois thusiôn te kaì hierôn genoménōn*). And also at 841 D Plato opposes women who are 'brought into the house, whether purchased or otherwise acquired by a man' to those who enter a household with the approval of the gods and through the ritual of marriage.

91 *Laws*, 838 E 5 ff.

92 Aesch., *Ag.,* 966-70; *Choeph.*, 204; 236; 503; Soph., *Electra*, 764-5: Orestes is the seed and root of the house of the Atreidae. Cf. J.-P. Vernant, *Mytheet Pensée chez les Grecs,* Paris 1965, p.109, n. 43.

93 In the *Theaetetus*, Plato writes that the midwife is not only competent to gather the fruits of the marriage but also the best qualified to make the unions that will have the most perfect fruits. A similar skill is necessary to gather the fruits of the earth and discern in which soil a particular seed should be sown or particular plants planted. But, for the sake of the argument, Socrates adds a third skill to these two, and it is the most important, in his opinion: it is the skill of testing (*basanizeín*) the newborn child to find out whether it is a deceitful sham or the product of good stock, a true scion (*gónimón te kaì alēthés*). Cf. J.-P. Vernant, *op. cit.*, p.136.

94 Aeschylus, F. 171 a) and b) ed. H. J. Mette, Cf. H. Bolkestein, 'The Exposure of children at Athens and the enchutristriai', *Classical Philology*, vol. XVII, 1922, pp.222-39, and L.-R. F. Germain, 'Aspects du droit d'exposition en Grèce', *Rev. histor. de droit français et etranger*, 1969, pp.177-97.

95 Simplicius, *In Arist. Phys.* 255a 20 ff. (*Comment. gr. in Arist.*,

vol. X, 1895, p.1212, 18 ff.)

96 According to Aristotle, *Phys.*, V, 230 b.

97 Oribasius, III, p.165. Cf. III, pp.110-11. We have already noticed a similar characteristic where mint is concerned; while exciting sexual desire, it thwarts it in its child-producing function (*supra,* p.74).

98 *Id.,* III, pp.107-9.

99 Arist., *Gen. Anim.*, II, 7, 746 b 29. Cf. 765 b 2.

100 As Plato says, *Laws,* 839 A: *lútta erōtikè kaì manía,*

101 Hesiod, *Works,* 582-4.

102 *Id., ibid.*, 585-96. Cf. the edition and commentary by P. Mazon (Paris 1914) pp.128-31. 'Moisten your lungs with wine', says Alcaeus, F.347 Lobel and Page (in *Poetarum lesbiorum fragmenta*, Oxford 1955, p.270). This advice is echoed by a medical precept which goes back at least to the fifth century (cf. Eupolis, F.147, Kock, I, 297) and which a Pythian oracle expresses as follows: 'During the twenty days preceding the canicular period and the twenty days following it, keep to the shade of your room, taking Dionysus as your doctor' (cited by Athanaeus, I, 22 E). Other medical reasons are put forward by *Schol. in Hippocr. et Galen.*, II, 387, 5 Dietz. Cf. Gundel, *s. v. Sirius, R.-E.* (1927), c.343.

103 Hes., *op. cit.*, 586-7. 'Moisten your lungs with wine but beware of lovable Aphrodite' (Suda, *s. v. tégge,* ed. Alder, vol. IV, p.514, 18).

104 *Il.*, XXIV, 30; Hdt., IV, 154; *Anth. Pal.*, V, 301, 10. In his commentary on line 25 of Book XXIV of the *Iliad*, Aristonicos notes that *makhlosúnē* 'usually denotes shamelessness, when speaking of a woman' (cf. A. Severyns, *Le Cycle épique dans l'Ecole d'Aristarque*, Liège-Paris 1928 p.263). Hera punishes the daughters of Proetus for their mockery, with *makhlosúnē*: they are condemned to wander in the wild, indecently clad or even completely naked (cf. F. Vian, 'Mélampous et les Proitides', *REA*, 1965, p.27).

105 This is the epithet used by Alcaeus, F. 347, 4, Lobel and Page.

106 *Ibid.*

107 *Probl.*, IV, 25, 879 a 26 ff. Cf. IV, 28, 880a 12 ff. This interpretation is repeated in the *Schol. vet. in Hes. Oper.*, 582-7 ed. Pertusi.

108 J.-P. Vernant, 'Le mythe hésiodique des races, Sur un essai de mise au point', *Rev. Philol.*, 1966, p.256, and note 1 (where there is a comparison between *Works* 586-7 and 705).

109 Hes., *Works*, 704-5: *eúei áter daloîo kaì ōmôi gḗrai dôken.* The same image of a 'premature old age' appears in the *Odyssey*, XV, 357.

110 Hes., *Theogony*, 570; *antì puròs.*

111 There is no more indomitable fire: Aristoph., *Lysistrate*, 1014-15. According to Plutarch, the woman in the verses of Archilochus 'carries water in one hand but in the other she hides fire' (Archilochus, F.190 Tarditi 86 D. and 225 L.B.)

112 The equivalence between woman and fire, which is evident in the text of Hesiod himself, was emphasised by a whole series of writers of whom Euripides, F.429 N[2]. and Palladas, *Anthol. Palat.*, IX, 165; 167 are examples. 'The woman is the anger of Zeus. She was given to us to make up for the fire, as a fatal gift and as a counter-gift to fire. For a woman burns up her man through the worries she brings him, she consumes him (*maraínei*) and brings him a premature old age' (*Anthol. Palatin.* IX, 165). We should like to thank J.-P. Vernant for having brought to our notice these texts which confirm his interpretation of lines 704-5 of *Works*.

113 *ánandros: supra* p.122.

114 Plut., *Erōtikós*, 756 c.

115 Cf. Plato, *Laws*, 838 B 4.

116 As are Persephone and Aphrodite themselves, in the excessive, passionate love that they feel for Adonis: 'hunc (Adonem) Venus *vehementissime* dilexit' Servius, *In Verg. Aen.*, V, 72, ed. Harvardiana, III [1965], p.493, 1-20).

NOTES TO CONCLUSION

1 'Heraclès héros pythagoricien', *Revue d l'Histoire des Religions.* 1960, pp.32-4.

2 Cf. the information given in a summary form in a paper on the social structure of Pythagoreanism, given at the *Vth Convegno di Studi sulla Magna Grecia*, and published in *Filosofia e Scienze in Magna Grecia*, Naples 1966 (1969), pp.149-56.

3 *Laws*, 781 a-b.

4 Iambl., *V. P.*, 48, ed. Deubner, p.27, 1-3; 84, p.49, 4-6; 84, p.48, 21-2; 187, p.104, 10-11.

5 Théodoret, *Graecor. affect. curatio*, XII, 7, 3, ed. Raeder, p.317, 19-21. Cf. Diogenes Laertius, VIII, 43, ed. A. Delatte p.139, 8-10 (with many parallel passages) and *The Pythagorean Texts of the hellenistic period*, ed. H. Thesleff, Abo 1965, pp.193-201.

6 Iambl., V.P. 132, ed. Deubner, p.74, 26-75, I; 195, p.107, 13-15 (*apékhesthai tês athútou kaì nóthēs pròs tàs pallakídas sunousias*).

7 Aristoxenes, F. 39 Whrli.

8 Diodorus, X, 9, 4.

9 Diogeses Laertius, VIII, 9, ed. A. Delatte, p.110, 5-9; *aphrodísia*

kheimônos poiéesthai, mē théreos (Cf. Diodorus, X, 9, 3).

10 Lycon or Iccos(?) ap. Athenaeus, II, 69 E. Cf. *The Pythagorean Texts*, ed. H. Thesleff, Abo 1965, pp.109-10.

11 Pliny, *H.N.*, XIX, 127.

12 Cf. W. Atallah, *Adonis dans la littérature et l'art grec*, Paris 1966, pp.16-17,; for an idea of the poverty of evidence for the Near-East, see *Wörterbuch der Mythologie* by H. W. Haussig, vol. I. *Götter und Mythen in Vorderen Orient*, Stuttgart, pp.234-5 (W. Röllig), and also Th. Jacobsen, *Toward the Image of Tammuz and other Essays on Mesapotamian History and Culture*, ed. by William L.Monan Cambridge, Mass. 1970, 73-103.

13 J.-P. Vernant drew my attention to this point, and my remarks are directly inspired by his seminars on the problems of marriage in Greece.

14 In his description of Argos (II, 20, 6) Pausanias mentions the existence of a house, an establishment (*oíkēma*) where the women of Argos used to go to mourn Adonis. Is it possible that the city might in this way have been attempting to control the behaviour of the women?

15 Cf. P. Vidal-Naquet, 'Athènes au IVe siècle: fin d'une démocratie ou crise de la cité?' *Annales E.S.C.*, 1963, pp.348-9.

16 W. Atallah, *op. cit.*, pp. 98-105.

Index

Abaris, 47
ádipsa, 47, 48
Adonia, 3, 4, 64-66, 78, 79-81, 98,
99-101, 103, 104, 106, 108-109, 110,
113, 114, 116, 118, 120, 126, 129-130
ágnos, Cf. *agnus castus*, 79, 82, 94
ákarpos, Cf. sterility
alábstron, 69, 154 n.11
álima, 47, 48
amusement, Cf. *paidiá*
aóros, 102, 107, 117
aphrodísia, 62
Aphrodite, 2, 3, 37, 62, 64-66, 68,
69-70, 72, 73, 80-82, 84, 85, 88, 91,
92, 94, 101, 102, 109, 115, 117, 119,
120, 177 n.116
Hēdonḗ, 62
Apollo *Genétōr*, 40, 41, 46-47, 147 n.64
aposbennúnai, Cf. dessication
apoxēraínein, Cf. dessication
Arabia, 5-36
Arcturus, 14, 15
Argonauts, 91-92, 95
aroma, 39-40, 45, 49, 58, 92
asphodel, 46-49
atelḗs, 117 Cf. immaturity
áthuta, 119, 175 n.90

balsam tree, 9
barley, 107, 109-110
Basileía, 39
baskets, 105, 107
bats, 15, 17-19, 35, 36
bean, 49-52, 56-59
bees, 79-80, 81
birds, 15-16, 17-19, 21-22
from the heights, 19-20, 23, 27-28 Cf.
eagle, Phoenix, vulture
blood, 41, 50-51
boiling, 14, 143 n.23, 111-113

Bouphonia, 54-55
Bouzyges, 152 n.117
bread, 117-118

calamint, 74-75, 94
Canicular period, Dog Days, 9, 14, 100-
101, 106-107, 109, 113, 120-122, 125-
126, 127
cannibalism, 112
cassia, 5, 9-10, 15-20, 135 n.15
Centaurs, 87
cereals, 14, 15, 45, 46, 47, 55, 59, 73, 75,
77, 103-104, 108, 127
Ceres, 76-87
Ceylon, 16
charis, 69, 87-89, 92, 104, 107
chastity, 79, 166 n.134
cinnamon, 5, 7, 9, 15-20, 28, 29, 35
cinnamon, Cf. cassia
cold, 11, 13, 18, 68, 120, 121
commensality, 45, 49, 58, 126
concoction, 10-14, 60, 113
concubine, 73, 76, 78, 82, 129
continence, 77, 79, 82, 93-94
cooked, 12-13
cooking, 12-13, 44, Cf. concoction
cooking pots, 105, 107, 119
corn, wheat, 107, 108-110
corruption, 10, 13, 24-25, 28-29, 34-35,
50, 58, 68, 96
courtisan, 65-66, 82, 121, 124, 129
Croton, 76, 77, 123
cultivated life (*bíos hēmeros*), 117-118
cultivation of plants (*paideía*), 12, 104
Cyclops, 112

dates, 15
daughter, 37, 64, 73, 76-77, 80, 81-83,
89
Delos, 96-97

wild plants, 12-13, 46, 48, 49
winter, 125
woman (women), 81, 82-83, 89, 91,
    94-96, 98, 105, 116, 121-122, 123-124
working ox, 37-58
worm, 33-35

wryneck, Cf. *iunx*, 83-85, 89

Zeus, 39, 45, 85, 87-88, 89, 90,
    Polieus, 106-107
    Teleius, 171